AWS Certified Cloud Practitioner CLF-C02 Cert Guide

Companion Website and Pearson Test Prep Access Code

Access interactive study tools on this book's companion website, including practice test software, review exercises, Key Term flash card application, a study planner, and more!

To access the companion website, simply follow these steps:

1. Go to **pearsonitcertification.com**.

2. Enter the **print book ISBN**: 9780138285999.

3. Answer the security question to validate your purchase.

4. Go to your account page.

5. Click on the **Registered Products** tab.

6. Under the book listing, click on the **Access Bonus Content** link.

When you register your book, your Pearson Test Prep practice test access code will automatically be populated with the book listing under the Registered Products tab. You will need this code to access the practice test that comes with this book. You can redeem the code at **PearsonTestPrep.com**. Simply choose Pearson IT Certification as your product group and log into the site with the same credentials you used to register your book. Click the **Activate New Product** button and enter the access code. More detailed instructions on how to redeem your access code for both the online and desktop versions can be found on the companion website.

If you have any issues accessing the companion website or obtaining your Pearson Test Prep practice test access code, you can contact our support team by going to **pearsonitp .echelp.org**.

AWS Certified Cloud
Practitioner CLF-C02
Cert Guide

Companion Website and Pearson Test Prep Access Code

AWS Certified Cloud Practitioner CLF-C02 Cert Guide

Anthony Sequeira, CCIE No. 15626

Pearson

Hoboken, New Jersey

AWS Certified Cloud Practitioner CLF-C02 Cert Guide

ISBN-13: 978-0-13-828599-9
ISBN-10: 0-13-828599-3

Library of Congress Cataloging-in-Publication Data: 2024906720

1 2024

GM K12, Early Career and Professional Learning
Soo Kang

Director, ITP Product Management
Brett Bartow

Executive Editor
Nancy Davis

Managing Editor
Sandra Schroeder

Development Editor
Christopher Cleveland

Senior Project Editor
Mandie Frank

Copy Editor
Kitty Wilson

Technical Editor
John Stuppi

Editorial Assistant
Cindy Teeters

Designer
Chuti Prasertsith

Composition
codeMantra

Indexer
Timothy Wright

Proofreader
Jennifer Hinchliffe

Trademarks

Warning and Disclaimer

This book is designed to provide information about the AWS Certified Cloud Practitioner CLF-C02 exam. Every effort has been made to make this book as complete and accurate as possible, but no warranty or fitness is implied. The information provided is on an "as is" basis. The author and the publisher shall have neither liability nor responsibility to any person or entity with respect to any loss or damages arising from the information contained in this book or from the use of the supplemental online content or programs accompanying it.

Special Sales

For information about buying this title in bulk quantities, or for special sales opportunities (which may include electronic versions; custom cover designs; and content particular to your business, training goals, marketing focus, or branding interests), please contact our corporate sales department at corpsales@pearsoned.com or (800) 382-3419.

For government sales inquiries, please contact governmentsales@pearsoned.com.

For questions about sales outside the U.S., please contact intlcs@pearson.com.

Contents at a Glance

Table of Contents

About the Author

Anthony Sequeira, CCIE No. 15626, is a seasoned trainer and author regarding various levels and tracks of Cisco, Microsoft, and AWS certifications. Anthony formally began his career in the information technology industry in 1994 with IBM in Tampa, Florida. He quickly formed his own computer consultancy, Computer Solutions, and then discovered his true passion—teaching and writing about information technologies.

Anthony joined Mastering Computers in 1996 and lectured to massive audiences around the world about the latest in computer technologies. Mastering Computers became the revolutionary online training company KnowledgeNet, and Anthony trained there for many years.

Anthony is currently a full-time instructor with ACI Learning. ACI Learning is a leader in audit, cybersecurity, and IT professional training.

Dedication

This book is dedicated to my dear friend Pierre Smith, who has provided many decades of advice, banter, and, of course, laughs. Pierre will most likely never certify in AWS, but he certainly could if he wanted to—in record time.

Acknowledgments

This update to the text was made possible by Nancy Davis of Pearson. Nancy, thank you so much for this opportunity!

Thank you, John Stuppi, for the intense technical review. Your work helped this text tremendously.

Finally, I would also like to express my gratitude to Chris Cleveland, development editor of this book and of the previous edition. I was so incredibly lucky to work with him again on this text. Like John, he helped make this book several cuts above the rest.

About the Technical Reviewer

John Stuppi, CCIE No. 11154, is an Engineering Program Manager in the Security & Trust Organization (S&TO) at Cisco, where he works with Cisco customers to investigate suspected compromises in their network environment as well as to protect their networks against existing and emerging cybersecurity threats, risks, and vulnerabilities. Current projects include working with newly acquired entities to integrate them into Cisco's PSIRT Vulnerability Management processes and advising some of Cisco's most strategic customers on vulnerability management and risk assessment.

John has presented multiple times on various network security topics at Cisco Live, Black Hat, and other customer-facing cyber security conferences. John is also the co-author of the *Official Certification Guide for CCNA Security 210-260*, published by Cisco Press. Additionally, John has contributed to the Cisco Security Portal through the publication of white papers, Security Blog posts, and Cyber Risk Report articles. Prior to joining Cisco, John worked as a network engineer for JPMorgan and then as a network security engineer at Time, Inc., with both positions based in New York City. John is also a CISSP (#25525) and holds AWS Cloud Practitioner and Information Systems Security (INFOSEC) professional certifications. In addition, John has a BSEE from Lehigh University and an MBA from Rutgers University. John splits his time between Eatontown, New Jersey, and Clemson, South Carolina, with his wife, son, and daughter.

We Want to Hear from You!

As the reader of this book, *you* are our most important critic and commentator. We value your opinion and want to know what we're doing right, what we could do better, what areas you'd like to see us publish in, and any other words of wisdom you're willing to pass our way.

We welcome your comments. You can email or write to let us know what you did or didn't like about this book—as well as what we can do to make our books better.

Please note that we cannot help you with technical problems related to the topic of this book.

When you write, please be sure to include this book's title and author as well as your name and email address. We will carefully review your comments and share them with the author and editors who worked on the book.

Email: community@informit.com

Reader Services

Register your copy of *AWS Certified Cloud Practitioner CLF-C02 Cert Guide* for convenient access to downloads, updates, and corrections as they become available. To start the registration process, go to www.pearsonitcertification.com/register and log in or create an account*. Enter the product ISBN 9780138285999 and click Submit. When the process is complete, you will find any available bonus content under Registered Products.

*Be sure to check the box that you would like to hear from us to receive exclusive discounts on future editions of this product.

Introduction

The AWS Certified Cloud Practitioner exam tests candidates' overall understanding of the AWS Cloud and many of its critical services. This certification also serves to validate candidates' knowledge with an industry-recognized credential. This exam covers four domains:

- Cloud Concepts

- Security and Compliance

- Cloud Technology and Services

- Billing, Pricing, and Support

Obtaining the AWS Certified Cloud Practitioner certification is a recommended path to achieving further specialty certifications or can be a start toward associate certifications in various disciplines, such as solutions architect, SysOps administrator, and developer.

The Goals of the AWS Certified Cloud Practitioner Program

After a candidate studies this text carefully, they should be more than ready for their certification exam. The exam validates a candidate's ability to do the following:

- Explain the value of the AWS Cloud.

- Understand and explain the AWS shared responsibility model.

- Understand security best practices.

- Understand AWS Cloud costs, economics, and billing practices.

- Describe and position the core AWS services, including compute, network, database, and storage services.

- Identify AWS services for common use cases.

Ideal Candidates

While this text provides you with the information required to pass this exam, Amazon considers ideal candidates to be those who possess the following:

- Six months of exposure to AWS Cloud design, implementation, and/or operations

- AWS knowledge in the following areas:

  - AWS Cloud concepts

  - Security and compliance in the AWS Cloud

- Core AWS services

- Economics of the AWS Cloud

The Exam Objectives (Domains)

The AWS Certified Cloud Practitioner CLF-C02 exam is broken down into four major domains. The contents of this book cover each of the domains and the subtopics included in them, as illustrated in the following descriptions.

The following table lists those domains and the percentage of the exam dedicated to each of them:

Domain	Percentage of Representation in Exam
1: Cloud Concepts	24%
2: Security and Compliance	30%
3: Cloud Technology and Services	34%
4: Billing, Pricing, and Support	12%
	Total 100%

Domain 1: Cloud Concepts

Chapters 1 through 6 of this book cover Domain 1: Cloud Concepts. This domain covers critical topics such as the services and categories of services provided by AWS. It also covers important information on how AWS can save your IT team large sums of money. It comprises 24% of the exam and includes the following topics:

- Task Statement 1.1: Define the benefits of the AWS Cloud.

- Task Statement 1.2: Identify design principles of the AWS Cloud.

- Task Statement 1.3: Understand the benefits of and strategies for migration to the AWS Cloud.

- Task Statement 1.4: Understand concepts of cloud economics.

Domain 2: Security and Compliance

Chapters 7 through 10 cover Domain 2: Security and Compliance. This domain covers security in general with AWS, and it also provides details on the implementation of strong security with AWS services such as IAM and a wide variety of management tools. This domain makes up 30% of the exam and includes the following topics:

- Task Statement 2.1: Understand the AWS shared responsibility model.

- Task Statement 2.2: Understand AWS Cloud security, governance, and compliance concepts.

- Task Statement 2.3: Identify AWS access management capabilities.

- Task Statement 2.4: Identify components and resources for security.

Domain 3: Cloud Technology and Services

Chapters 11 through 18 cover Domain 3: Cloud Technology and Services. This domain digs into the "nuts and bolts" of AWS, such as the global infrastructure and core services of AWS. It encompasses 34% of the exam and includes the following topics:

- Task Statement 3.1: Define methods of deploying and operating in the AWS Cloud.

- Task Statement 3.2: Define the AWS global infrastructure.

- Task Statement 3.3: Identify AWS compute services.

- Task Statement 3.4: Identify AWS database services.

- Task Statement 3.5: Identify AWS network services.

- Task Statement 3.6: Identify AWS storage services.

- Task Statement 3.7: Identify AWS artificial intelligence and machine learning (AI/ML) services and analytics services.

- Task Statement 3.8: Identify services from other in-scope AWS service categories.

Domain 4: Billing, Pricing, and Support

Chapters 19 through 21 cover Domain 4: Billing, Pricing, and Support. In these chapters, you'll learn about the tools and techniques for controlling costs inside AWS as well as the resources that are available to assist you. This domain accounts for 12% of the exam and includes the following topics:

- Task Statement 4.1: Compare AWS pricing models.

- Task Statement 4.2: Understand resources for billing, budget, and cost management.

- Task Statement 4.3: Identify AWS technical resources and AWS Support options.

Steps to Becoming an AWS Certified Cloud Practitioner

To become an AWS Certified Cloud Practitioner, a test candidate should meet certain prerequisites and follow specific procedures. Once they deem themselves ready, a test candidate can sign up for the exam.

Signing Up for the Exam

The steps required to sign up for the AWS Certified Cloud Practitioner exam are as follows:

Step 1.   To schedule your exam, first create an AWS Certification account at https://www.aws.training/certification

Step 2.   Complete the Examination Agreement, attesting to the truth of your assertions regarding professional experience and legally committing to adhering to the testing policies.

Step 3.   Submit the examination fee.

Facts About the Exam

The exam is a computer-based test. The exam consists of multiple-choice questions only. You must bring a government-issued identification card. No other forms of ID will be accepted.

TIP   Refer to the AWS Certification site at https://aws.amazon.com/certification/ for more information regarding the AWS Certified Cloud Practitioner and other AWS certifications.

How to Use This Book

This book maps directly to the topic areas of the exam and uses a number of features to help you understand the topics and prepare for the exam.

Objectives and Methods

This book uses several key methodologies to help you discover the exam topics on which you need more review, to help you fully understand and remember those details, and to help you prove to yourself that you have retained knowledge of those topics. This book does not try to help you pass the exam only by memorization; it seeks to help you truly learn and understand the topics. This book is designed to help you pass the AWS Certified Cloud Practitioner exam by using the following methods:

- Helping you discover which exam topics you have not yet become proficient in

- Providing explanations and information to fill in your knowledge gaps

- Supplying exercises that enhance your ability to recall and deduce the answers to test questions

- Providing practice exercises on the topics and the testing process via test questions on the companion website

Book Features

To help you customize your study time using this book, the core chapters have several features that help you make the best use of your time:

- **Foundation Topics**: These are the core sections of each chapter. They explain the concepts for the topics in that chapter.

- **Exam Preparation Tasks**: After the "Foundation Topics" section of each chapter, the "Exam Preparation Tasks" section lists a series of study activities that you should do at the end of the chapter:

  - **Review All Key Topics**: The Key Topic icon appears next to the most important items in the "Foundation Topics" section of the chapter. The "Review All Key Topics" activity lists the key topics from the chapter, along with the page number for each one. Although the contents of the entire chapter could be on the exam, you should definitely know the information listed in each key topic, so you should review these.

  - **Define Key Terms**: Although the Cloud Practitioner exam may be unlikely to ask a question such as "Define this term," the exam does require that you learn and know a lot of AWS-related terminology. This section lists the most important terms from the chapter, asking you to write a short definition and compare your answer to the Glossary at the end of the book.

  - **Q&A Questions**: Confirm that you understand the content you just covered by answering these questions and reading the answer explanations.

- **Web-based practice exam**: The companion website includes the Pearson Cert Practice Test engine, which allows you to take practice exams. Use it to prepare with a sample exam and to pinpoint topics where you need more study.

How to Access the Companion Website

Register this book to get access to the Pearson IT Certification test engine and other study materials, as well as additional bonus content. Check this site regularly for new and updated postings written by the author that provide further insight into the more troublesome topics on the exam. Be sure to check the box indicating that you would like to hear from us to receive updates and exclusive discounts on future editions of this product or related products.

To access this companion website, follow these steps:

Step 1. Go to **www.pearsonitcertification.com/register** and log in or create a new account.

Step 2. Enter the ISBN: **9780138285999**.

Step 3. Answer the challenge question as proof of purchase.

Step 4. Click the **Access Bonus Content** link in the Registered Products section of your account page to be taken to the page where your downloadable content is available.

Please note that many of our companion content files can be very large, especially image and video files.

If you are unable to locate the files for this title by following the steps above, please visit www.pearsonITcertification.com/contact and select the Site Problems/ Comments option. Our customer service representatives will assist you.

Pearson Test Prep Practice Test Software

As noted previously, this book comes complete with the Pearson Test Prep practice test software, containing two full exams. These practice tests are available to you either online or as an offline Windows application. To access the practice exams that were developed with this book, please see the instructions below.

How to Access the Pearson Test Prep (PTP) App

You have two options for installing and using the Pearson Test Prep application: a web app and a desktop app. To use the Pearson Test Prep application, start by finding the registration code that comes with the book. You can find the code in these ways:

- You can get your access code by registering the print ISBN (9780138285999) on pearsonitcertification.com/register. Make sure to use the print book ISBN regardless of whether you purchased an eBook or the print book. After you register the book, your access code will be populated on your account page under the Registered Products tab. Instructions for how to redeem the code are available on the book's companion website by clicking the Access Bonus Content link.

■ If you purchase the Premium Edition eBook and Practice Test directly from the Pearson IT Certification website, the code will be populated on your account page after purchase. Just log in at pearsonitcertification.com, click Account to see details of your account, and click the Digital Purchases tab.

NOTE   After you register your book, your code can always be found in your account on the Registered Products tab.

Once you have the access code, to find instructions about both the Pearson Test Prep web app and the desktop app, follow these steps:

Step 1.   Open this book's companion website, as shown earlier in this Introduction, under the heading, "How to Access the Companion Website."

Step 2.   Click the **Practice Test Software** button.

Step 3.   Follow the instructions listed there for both installing the desktop app and using the web app.

Note that if you want to use the web app only at this point, just navigate to pearsontestprep.com, log in using the same credentials used to register your book or purchase the Premium Edition, and register this book's practice tests using the registration code you just found. The process should take only a couple of minutes.

Customizing Your Exams

Once you are in the exam settings screen, you can choose to take exams in one of three modes:

■ **Study mode**: Allows you to fully customize your exam and review answers as you are taking the exam. This is typically the mode you use first to assess your knowledge and identify information gaps.

■ **Practice Exam mode**: Locks certain customization options, as it is presenting a realistic exam experience. Use this mode when you are preparing to test your exam readiness.

■ **Flash Card mode**: Strips out the answers and presents you with only the question stem. This mode is great for late-stage preparation when you really want to challenge yourself to provide answers without the benefit of seeing multiple-choice options. This mode does not provide the detailed score reports that the other two modes do, so you should not use it if you are trying to identify knowledge gaps.

In addition to these three modes, you will be able to select the source of your questions. You can choose to take exams that cover all of the chapters, or you can narrow your selection to just a single chapter or the chapters that make up a specific part in the book. All chapters are selected by default. If you want to narrow your focus to individual chapters, simply deselect all the chapters and then select only those on which you wish to focus in the Objectives area.

You can also select the exam banks on which to focus. Each exam bank comes complete with a full exam of questions that cover topics in every chapter. The two exams printed in the book are available to you, as are two additional exams of unique questions. You can have the test engine serve up exams from all four banks or just from one individual bank by selecting the desired banks in the exam bank area.

There are several other customizations you can make to your exam from the exam settings screen, such as the time of the exam, the number of questions served up, whether to randomize questions and answers, whether to show the number of correct answers for multiple-answer questions, and whether to serve up only specific types of questions. You can also create custom test banks by selecting only questions that you have marked or questions for which you have added notes.

Updating Your Exams

If you are using the online version of the Pearson Test Prep software, you should always have access to the latest version of the software as well as the exam data. If you are using the Windows desktop version, every time you launch the software while connected to the Internet, it checks if there are any updates to your exam data and automatically downloads any changes that were made since the last time you used the software.

Sometimes, due to many factors, the exam data may not fully download when you activate your exam. If you find that figures or exhibits are missing, you may need to manually update your exams. To update a particular exam you have already activated and downloaded, simply click the **Tools** tab and click the **Update Products** button. Again, this is only an issue with the desktop Windows application.

If you wish to check for updates to the Pearson Test Prep exam engine software, Windows desktop version, simply click the **Tools** tab and click the **Update Application** button. This ensures that you are running the latest version of the software engine.

Credits

Figures 1.1-1.8, 2.1-2.5, 3.1, 4.1-4.4, 5.1, 6.1-6.7, 7.2, 8.2, 8.3, 9.1-9.5, 10.1-10.3, 11.1, 11.2, 12.1-12.3, 13.1-13.4, 14.1-14.3, 15.1, 15.2, 16.1-16.4, 17.1-17.3, 18.1-18.4, 19.1-19.3, 20.1-20.3, 21.1-21.5-Amazon Web Services, Inc

Figures 6.8 & 11.3-Microsoft Corporation

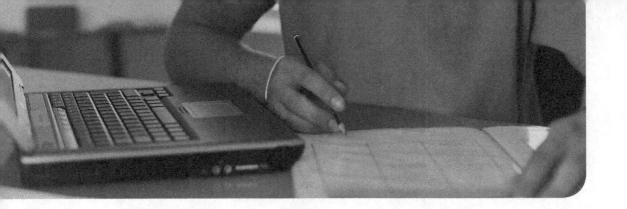

This chapter covers the following subjects:

- **Introduction to the Cloud:** You might have heard of cloud technologies before. This is, of course, a bit of a joke since cloud is one of the hottest topics in information technology—and, not surprisingly, one of the most significant areas of demand in tech employment. This section of the chapter introduces you to cloud technologies and details why they are so important and exciting.

- **Introduction to the AWS Cloud:** This section of the chapter provides an overview of crucial service categories and the services themselves. While these services are covered in greater detail later in this text, this early look is critical for you to start building your AWS understanding and vocabulary.

CHAPTER 1

The AWS Cloud Defined

In this critical chapter, we talk about the various characteristics of technology that would qualify a solution as "cloud." This chapter also examines the specifics of Amazon Web Services (AWS) that help to make it the most popular (by user base) public cloud offering.

"Do I Know This Already?" Quiz

The "Do I Know This Already?" quiz allows you to assess whether you should read the entire chapter. Table 1-1 lists the major headings in this chapter and the "Do I Know This Already?" quiz questions covering the material in those sections so you can assess your knowledge of these specific areas. The answers to the "Do I Know This Already?" quiz questions appear in Appendix A, "Answers to the 'Do I Know This Already?' Quizzes and Q&A Sections."

Table 1-1 "Do I Know This Already?" Foundation Topics Section-to-Question Mapping

Foundation Topics Section	Questions
Introduction to the Cloud	1–3
Introduction to the AWS Cloud	4–6

CAUTION   The goal of self-assessment is to gauge your mastery of the topics in this chapter. If you do not know the answer to a question or are only partially sure of the answer, you should mark that question as wrong for purposes of the self-assessment. Giving yourself credit for an answer you correctly guess skews your self-assessment results and might provide you with a false sense of security.

1. Which of the following is not a common cloud characteristic, as defined by NIST?

    a. On-demand self-service

    b. Measured service

    c. Broad network access

    d. Dedicated hardware

2. What is the term commonly used for the cloud's capability to scale outward and inward automatically based on demand?

    a. Agility

    b. Reliability

    c. Elasticity

    d. Fault tolerance

3. What is the very popular "as a service" model that permits a cloud provider to make applications available anywhere there is an Internet connection?

    a. IaaS

    b. SaaS

    c. PaaS

    d. GaaS

4. What service in AWS allows you to easily create and manage virtual machines (VMs)?

    a. S3

    b. EC2

    c. Route 53

    d. ELB

5. What is the object-based storage solution available in AWS?

    a. S3

    b. EC2

    c. VPC

    d. IAM

6. Where are your own private subnets located in AWS?

    a. IAM

    b. EC2

    c. Lambda

    d. VPC

Foundation Topics

Introduction to the Cloud

To help us define the "cloud," we turn to the National Institute for Standards and Technology (NIST). You can find NIST's very beneficial site at https://www.nist.gov. According to NIST, cloud computing is "a model for enabling ubiquitous, convenient, on-demand network access to a shared pool of configurable computing resources (e.g., networks, servers, storage, applications, and services) that can be rapidly provisioned and released with minimal management effort or service provider interaction."

This statement certainly says a lot, and we really need to break it down. Fortunately, NIST helps us with this as well. Here are the five essential cloud characteristics that truly define the technology:

- **On-demand self-service:** This characteristic means that a customer of cloud technologies can provision and manage resources without the intervention of cloud-hosting administrative personnel. For example, you might deem that you need a new web server to advertise a particular product or service. You can completely provision, configure, and deploy this web server without contacting anyone responsible for hosting the cloud solution. It can be as easy as filling out a few fields and clicking a few buttons in an easy-to-use graphical user interface (GUI).

- **Broad network access:** Your cloud resources should be available over the network and accessed through standard mechanisms. These standard access approaches (such as HTTPS) promote the use of cloud by thin or thick client platforms (for example, mobile phones, tablets, laptops, and workstations).

- **Resource pooling:** The provider's compute and other resources are pooled to serve multiple clients using a multitenant model. This model allows multiple customers to securely use the same physical hardware of the provider. At any time, the cloud provider can use different physical and virtual resources that are dynamically assigned and reassigned according to consumer demand. You should note that this approach provides a sense of location independence in that the customer generally has no control over or knowledge about the exact location of the provided resources. The customer is typically able to specify location at a higher level of abstraction (such as country, state, or geographical zone) when required. Examples of resources that are typically pooled include storage, processing, memory, and network bandwidth.

- **Rapid *elasticity*:** Resources can be elastically provisioned and released—in some cases automatically—to scale rapidly outward and inward in accordance with demand from customers. To the consumer, the capabilities available for provisioning often appear to be unlimited and can be appropriated in any quantity at any time.

- **Measured service:** Cloud systems automatically control and optimize resource use by leveraging a metering capability. This is done by the provider at some level of abstraction appropriate to the type of service. For example, the metering might be based on storage, processing, bandwidth, or active user accounts. Resource usage can be monitored, controlled, and reported, providing transparency for both the provider and consumer of the utilized service. This is where the cloud services your IT department pays for are often compared to a utility bill. As with the electric bill, you can be billed monthly, for just the services you used.

Another excellent way to make sense of the many cloud technologies today is to break them down by the "as a service" category they fall under. The concept of "as a service" means that customers "subscribe" to IT resources as needed. The "as a service" technologies we see today include the following:

- ***Software as a Service (SaaS)*:** This is currently the most popular cloud service model. Here the customers access a provider's applications running on a cloud infrastructure. The applications are accessible from various client devices through either a thin client interface, such as a web browser, or a program's interface. Note that in this model, the customer does not manage or control the underlying cloud infrastructure, apart from limited user-specific application configuration settings. This is often revolutionary for IT departments as it means they can provide high-performance and high-value applications to their employees without having to maintain or worry about the underlying infrastructure that allows the applications to run. Gmail is a prime example of a SaaS application in use today.

- ***Platform as a Service (PaaS)*:** This "as a service" model provides a cloud infrastructure to the customer that enables the development and deployment of consumer-created or acquired applications developed for the cloud. The provider ensures that the required programming languages, libraries, services, and tools are available for the customer. Typically, this is done on a pay-per-use or charge-per-use basis. Notice that the customer does not manage or control the underlying cloud infrastructure, including the network, servers, operating systems, and storage, but has control over the deployed applications and possibly configuration settings for the application-hosting environment. The AWS competitor of Microsoft Azure started as a simple PaaS offering, but then quickly followed in the footsteps of AWS to offer more "as a service" models.

- **Infrastructure as a Service (IaaS):** This cloud service model allows the customer to provision processing, storage, networks, and other fundamental computing resources. The customer is then able to deploy and run arbitrary software, which can include operating systems and applications. The customer does not manage or control the underlying physical infrastructure but has control over operating systems, storage, and deployed applications. The customer might also have limited control of select networking components such as host firewalls. Notice that this level of control is much greater than is found with PaaS and SaaS models.

How are cloud technologies commonly deployed? These deployment models are all in use today:

- **Private cloud:** With this model, the cloud infrastructure is provisioned for exclusive use by a single organization comprising multiple consumers, which might be business units. It might be owned, managed, and operated by the organization, a third party, or some combination of both, and it might exist on or off premises. The key is that this cloud is not for use by multiple organizations.

- **Community cloud:** With this model, the cloud infrastructure is provisioned for exclusive use by a specific community of consumers from organizations that have shared concerns (for example, an overall mission or shared security requirements). It might be owned, managed, and operated by one or more of the organizations in the community, a third party, or some combination of both. It might exist on or off premises. A classic example of this deployment model is cloud.gov, which is a conglomeration of various cloud tools and technologies for the US government that are provided by a wide variety of vendors.

- **Public cloud:** With this model, the cloud infrastructure is provisioned for open use by the general public. It might be owned, managed, and operated by a business, an academic institution, a government organization, or some combination of the three. It exists on the premises of the cloud provider, and these premises are typically located all over the globe to facilitate reduced latency from any location. This is the model presented by AWS and its main competitors, Microsoft Azure and the Google Cloud Platform (GCP).

- **Hybrid cloud:** With this model, the cloud infrastructure is a composition of two or more distinct cloud infrastructures (private, community, or public) that remain unique entities but are bound together by standardized or proprietary technology that enables data and application portability. This is a widespread deployment model today. For example, an organization might build a private cloud for operational financial transactions while relying on a public cloud model for encrypted archiving of legacy transactions that must be maintained for compliance reasons.

Introduction to the AWS Cloud

It is time to examine (at a high level) just some of the service categories in the AWS Cloud and some of the services and tools in each. This section provides this vital introduction for you. Remember that we will be covering these services in some detail later in the book.

Compute Service

AWS offers many different options for your acquisition and execution of compute resources. Just some of the options available today include:

- *Elastic Compute Cloud* (EC2): EC2 is a web service that provides secure and resizable compute resources (virtual machines) in the AWS Cloud. The EC2 service allows you to provision and configure capacity with minimal effort. It provides you with easy control of your computing resources. EC2 reduces the time required to obtain and boot new virtual machines (EC2 instances) to minutes or even seconds. This efficiency allows you to scale capacity vertically (up and down, making your server resources bigger or smaller, respectively) and horizontally (out and in, adding more capacity in the form of more instances) as your computing requirements change. We refer to this remarkable quality as *elasticity*, and we cover it in greater detail in Chapter 2, "Some Benefits of the AWS Cloud." Figure 1-1 shows virtual machines in the AWS EC2 dashboard.

- *Lambda*: AWS Lambda is a prime example of a new revolution in cloud computing called *serverless compute*. Lambda lets you run code without the burden of provisioning or managing servers. The code you run against Lambda can be for various aspects of an application or service. For example, perhaps you want to automatically resize images that are uploaded to your website. With the help of Lambda, you can use a script to handle the resizing and run this script against the Lambda pool of resources in the cloud. When you use Lambda, you upload your code, and Lambda does everything required to run and scale your code with high availability and fault tolerance. Again, you are not required to provision or configure any server infrastructure yourself. Figure 1-2 shows the Lambda GUI in AWS.

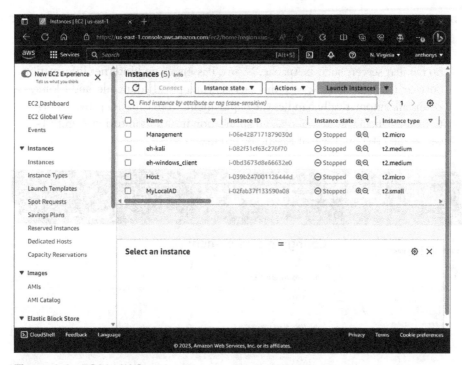

Figure 1-1   EC2 in AWS

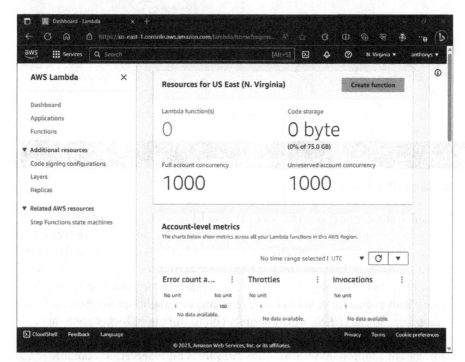

Figure 1-2   AWS Lambda

■ *Elastic Beanstalk*: AWS Elastic Beanstalk is an easy-to-use service for deploying and scaling web applications and services developed with popular languages such as Java, PHP, and Python, to name a few. These web applications are run on familiar servers such as Apache, Nginx, Passenger, and Internet Information Services (IIS). Amazingly, with this service, you upload your code, and Elastic Beanstalk automatically handles the deployment, from capacity provisioning to load balancing, auto-scaling, and application health monitoring. Figure 1-3 shows the GUI interface of Elastic Beanstalk.

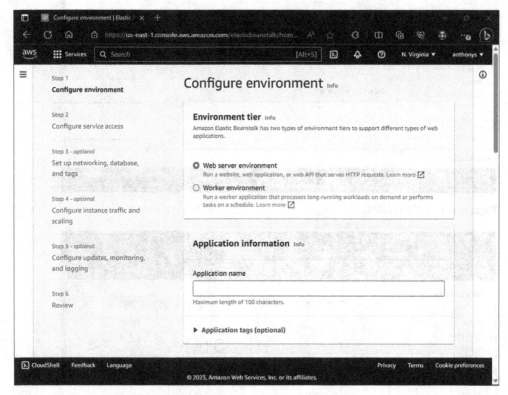

Figure 1-3   Elastic Beanstalk in AWS

■ *Elastic Container Service* (*ECS*): Amazon's ECS is a highly scalable, high-performance container management service that supports Docker containers. ECS permits you to efficiently run applications on a managed cluster of EC2 instances. It eliminates the need for you to install, operate, and scale your own cluster management infrastructure. If your organization is already using Kubernetes for container management, you might opt for *Amazon Elastic Kubernetes Service* (*EKS*), which permits you to run your Docker containers at massive scale (if needed) and provides a vast array of orchestration options for you. In addition, AWS also offers *Fargate*. This is serverless compute (think Lambda) but for containers. That's right: You can run containers without worrying about the management of the underlying clusters or Kubernetes.

Storage Services

The demands placed on storage for digital information today are higher than ever before—and getting bigger all the time. It is no wonder that AWS offers many services in this regard. The list that follows highlights just some of the important services we will discuss further in this text:

- **Simple Storage Service (S3):** AWS S3 is object storage with a simple web service interface for storing and retrieving any amount of data from anywhere on the web. It is designed to deliver 99.999999999% durability. This means that the amount of time per year you are not going to be able to access your data should be only 315 microseconds! You can use S3 for a vast number of purposes, such as primary storage for cloud-native applications or a bulk repository (or "data lake") for analytics. It is so flexible and so easy to work with that there are far too many potential uses to list. Figure 1-4 shows the AWS S3 dashboard in the web-based GUI.

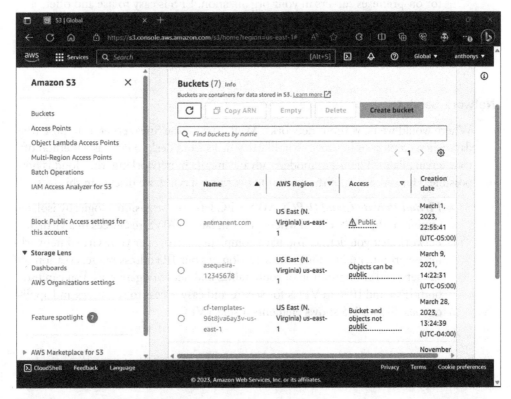

Figure 1-4   The AWS S3 Service

- *Elastic Block Store (EBS):* EBS provides persistent block storage volumes for use with EC2 instances in the AWS Cloud. Each Amazon EBS volume is automatically replicated within its Availability Zone to protect you from component failure, offering high availability and durability. EBS volumes offer the consistent and low-latency performance needed to run workloads. With Amazon EBS, you can scale your usage up or down within minutes—all while paying a low price for only what you provision.

- *Glacier:* Amazon Glacier is part of the AWS S3 storage service. It is a secure, durable, and extremely low-cost storage service for data archiving and long-term backup. With Glacier, you can reliably store large or small amounts of data for as little as $0.0036 per gigabyte per month. Glacier provides different price options for access to archives, depending on whether you need access immediately or in several days. It is important to carefully plan when purchasing Glacier archive services because the speed at which you can recover data is directly related to your choice of pricing option.

- *Elastic File System (EFS):* AWS EFS provides simple, scalable file storage for use with AWS EC2 instances in the AWS Cloud. You can even use this service for on-premises servers in your organization. EFS is easy to use and offers a simple interface that allows you to create and configure file systems quickly and easily. EFS fully integrates with the Network File System (NFS) storage protocol that is popular with Linux systems.

Network Services

Where would we be without networks? Well, back to the Sneakernet, I suppose (the days when employees in offices would carry disks from desk to desk as a method of transferring data). Thanks to modern advancements in networking, the cloud is now possible. Here are some of the critical networking services we discuss in this text:

- *Virtual Private Cloud (VPC):* AWS VPC lets you provision a logically isolated section of the AWS Cloud where you can launch AWS resources in a virtual network that you define. You have complete control over your virtual networking environment, including the selection of your IP address range, creation of subnets, and configuration of route tables and network gateways. You can use both IPv4 and IPv6 in VPCs for secure and easy access to resources and applications. Figure 1-5 shows elements inside a VPC.

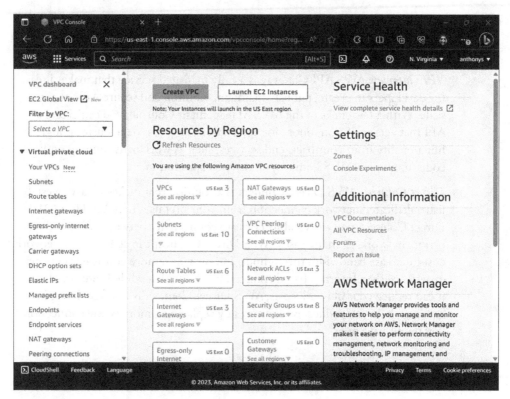

Figure 1-5   Components of an AWS VPC

- **Route 53**: AWS Route 53 is a highly available and scalable cloud Domain Name System (DNS) web service. Route 53 effectively directs user requests to infrastructure running in AWS—such as EC2 instances, Elastic Load Balancing load balancers, or S3 buckets—and can also be used to route users to infrastructure outside of AWS. You can use Route 53 to configure DNS health checks to route traffic to healthy endpoints or to monitor the health of an application and its endpoints independently. Of course, AWS also acts as a domain registrar, so it handles the details when you need to establish and host a new domain name. In fact, you can even host a website in an AWS S3 bucket for as little as pennies per month. Having a website hosted from a simple S3 bucket is yet another example of serverless compute capabilities in the AWS Cloud.

- **CloudFront**: AWS CloudFront is a global content delivery network (CDN) service. It accelerates delivery of your websites, APIs, video content, or other web assets. The service automatically routes requests for your content to the nearest edge location, so it delivers content with the best possible performance.

If you are hosting websites in S3 buckets as described earlier, you can secure them (using HTTPS) and make them globally available for low-latency access, thanks to CloudFront.

- *API Gateway*: AWS API Gateway is a fully managed service that makes it easy for developers to create, publish, maintain, monitor, and secure APIs at any scale. With a few clicks in the AWS Management Console, you can create an API that acts as a "front door" for applications to access data, business logic, or functionality from your back-end services, such as workloads running on EC2, code running on AWS Lambda, or any web application.

- *Direct Connect*: AWS Direct Connect is a solution that makes it easy to establish a dedicated network connection from your premises to AWS. Using AWS Direct Connect, you can establish private connectivity between AWS and your private network. In many cases, AWS Direct Connect can reduce your network costs, increase bandwidth throughput, and provide a more consistent network experience than Internet-based connections. Note that while I indicate that it can reduce your network costs, AWS Direct Connect is not free. It might, however, help you reduce expenditures by replacing a more costly connection you might have now.

Database Services

There are many different approaches to databases these days, as our data needs have grown more varied and complex. AWS does a great job of keeping up with the advancements in a variety of services:

- *Relational Database Service* (RDS): AWS RDS makes it easy to set up, operate, and scale a relational database in the cloud. RDS allows you to choose from many database engines, including Db2, Aurora, PostgreSQL, MySQL, MariaDB, Oracle, and Microsoft SQL Server. Figure 1-6 shows the RDS service GUI.

- *DynamoDB*: Amazon DynamoDB is a fast and flexible NoSQL database service for all applications that need consistent, single-digit millisecond latency at any scale. It is a great fit for mobile, web, gaming, ad tech, Internet of Things (IoT), and many other applications. The popular language learning app Duolingo took part in an AWS case study about just how much the company relied on the powerful DynamoDB service of AWS.

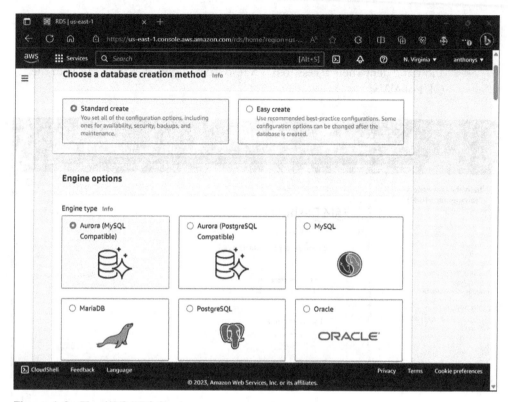

Figure 1-6 The AWS RDS Service

- *ElastiCache*: ElastiCache is a web service that makes it easy to deploy, operate, and scale an in-memory cache in the cloud. The service improves the performance of web applications by allowing you to retrieve information from fast, managed, in-memory caches instead of relying entirely on slower disk-based databases. Interestingly, ElastiCache is not an AWS proprietary solution; it runs the standardized Redis or Memcached solutions.

- *Redshift*: Redshift is a fast, fully managed, petabyte-scale data warehouse that makes it simple and cost-effective to analyze all your data using your existing business intelligence tools. Many believe the name Redshift was selected to tease the rival database company Oracle, whose corporate color scheme is red.

Security Services

If you do it correctly, you can be more secure with the cloud than with any approach you could take by yourself in your own data center. Here are the major technologies in the security area that you should be aware of:

■ *Identity and Access Management (IAM):* AWS IAM enables you to securely control access to AWS services and resources for your users. Using IAM, you can create and manage AWS users and groups, and you can use permissions to allow and deny their access to AWS resources. Figure 1-7 shows IAM in the GUI of AWS.

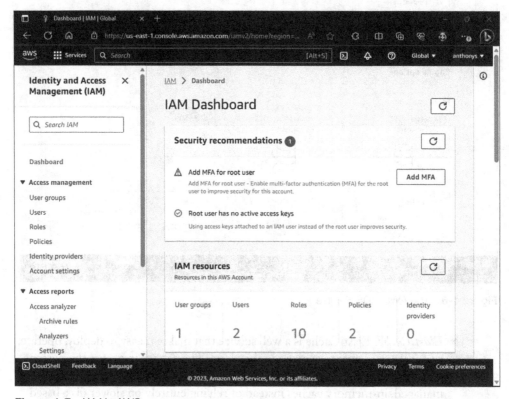

Figure 1-7   IAM in AWS

■ *Security groups:* AWS security groups, which are associated with EC2 instances (specifically their virtual network interface cards [VNICs]), provide security at the protocol and port access levels. Each security group contains a set of rules that filter traffic coming into and going out of an EC2 instance. Think of a security group as a simple virtual firewall that protects your virtual machine. If there is no rule that explicitly permits a particular data packet, it will be dropped. Security groups also can be applied to many other services within VPC, including ELB, RDS, Redshift, and ElastiCache.

- *Network ACLs*: Network access control lists (NACLs) are used to control traffic moving between your AWS VPC subnets. They function like traditional ACLs and are made up of permit and deny entries for various addresses and ports.

NOTE Do not confuse network ACLs with security groups. Remember that security groups are assigned to EC2 instances using VNICs, while network ACLs exist between subnets that are typically populated with VMs and other virtual network infrastructure components.

Automation and Application Support

Many tools enable the deployment of applications and automation in AWS. Here are some of the major ones:

- *CodeDeploy*: AWS CodeDeploy is a fully managed deployment service that automates software deployments to a variety of compute services, such as EC2, Lambda, and your on-premises servers. CodeDeploy makes it easier for you to rapidly release new features, helps you avoid downtime during application deployment, and handles the complexity of updating your applications.

- *CloudFormation*: AWS CloudFormation gives you an easy way to provision and configure related AWS resources based on a template. The tool even offers a designer that permits you to build architectures in templated code from your "sketches" using the design tool.

- *OpsWorks*: AWS OpsWorks is a configuration management service that uses automation platforms such as Chef or Puppet that treat server configurations as code. OpsWorks uses Chef or Puppet to automate how servers are configured, deployed, and managed across EC2 instances or on-premises compute environments.

Management Tools

Here are just some of the tools available to help you manage all the important stuff in the AWS Cloud:

- *Service Catalog*: AWS Service Catalog allows organizations to create and manage catalogs of IT services that are approved for use on AWS. These IT services can include everything from virtual machine images, servers, software,

and databases to complete multitier application architectures. AWS Service
Catalog allows you to centrally manage commonly deployed IT services. It
helps you achieve consistent governance and meet your compliance requirements while enabling users to quickly deploy only the approved IT services
they need.

- **Systems Manager:** AWS Systems Manager gives you visibility into and control
  of your infrastructure on AWS. Systems Manager provides a unified user interface so you can view operational data from multiple AWS services and allows
  you to automate operational tasks across your AWS resources. With Systems Manager, you can group resources (EC2 instances, S3 buckets, or RDS
  instances) by application, view operational data for monitoring and troubleshooting, and take action on your groups of resources.

- **Trusted Advisor:** AWS Trusted Advisor is an online resource to help you
  reduce cost, increase performance, and improve security by optimizing your
  AWS environment. Trusted Advisor provides real-time guidance to help you
  provision your resources following AWS best practices. This tool is free for
  several categories of recommendations. You can upgrade your plan to get even
  more detailed guidance from Trusted Advisor.

Monitoring

Do you need to accurately track the performance and status of your resources and
services? There are tools for this in AWS:

- **CloudWatch:** Amazon CloudWatch is a monitoring service for AWS Cloud
  resources and the applications you run on AWS. CloudWatch can collect and
  track metrics, collect and monitor log files, set alarms, and automatically react
  to changes in your AWS resources. Figure 1-8 shows the CloudWatch service
  in AWS.

- **CloudTrail:** AWS CloudTrail is a web service that records AWS API calls for
  your account and delivers log files to you. Features include detailed reports
  of recorded information, which can include the identity of the API caller, the
  time of the API call, the source IP address of the API caller, the request parameters, and the response elements returned by the AWS service.

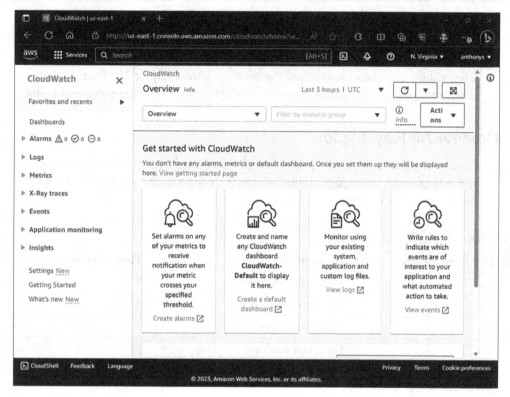

Figure 1-8 CloudWatch in AWS

Exam Preparation Tasks

As mentioned in the section "How to Use This Book" in the Introduction, you have a few choices for exam preparation: the exercises here, Chapter 22, "Final Preparation," and the exam simulation questions in the Pearson Test Prep Software Online.

Review All Key Topics

Review the most important topics in this chapter, noted with the Key Topics icon in the outer margin of the page. Table 1-2 lists these key topics and the page number on which each is found.

Table 1-2 Key Topics for Chapter 1

Key Topic Element	Description	Page Number
List	Cloud characteristics	5
List	"As a service" models	6
List	Deployment models	7
List	Computer services	8

Define Key Terms

Define the following key terms from this chapter and check your answers in the Glossary:

elasticity, software as a service (SaaS), platform as a service (PaaS), infrastructure as a service (IaaS), private cloud, community cloud, public cloud, hybrid cloud, Elastic Compute Cloud (EC2), Lambda, Elastic Beanstalk, Elastic Container Service (ECS), Elastic Kubernetes Service (EKS), Fargate, Simple Storage Service (S3), Elastic Block Store (EBS), Glacier, Elastic File System (EFS), Virtual Private Cloud (VPC), Route 53, CloudFront, API Gateway, Direct Connect, Relational Database Service (RDS), DynamoDB, ElastiCache, Redshift, Identity and Access Management (IAM), security groups, network ACLs, CodeDeploy, CloudFormation, OpsWorks, Service Catalog, Systems Manager, Trusted Advisor, CloudWatch, CloudTrail

Q&A

The answers to these questions appear in Appendix A. For more practice with exam format questions, use the Pearson Test Prep Software Online.

1. Name at least three cloud characteristics, as defined by NIST.
2. Name the four cloud deployment models.

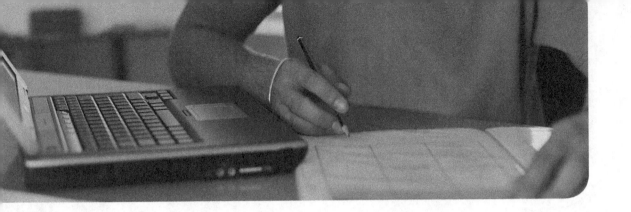

This chapter covers the following subjects:

- **Economic Benefits:** This section covers the biggest potential economic advantages of moving to the AWS Cloud. You need to follow design best practices and consistently monitor operations in order to realize cost savings.

- **The Benefits of the Global Infrastructure:** This part of the chapter focuses on the incredible advantages presented by Amazon's massive global infrastructure. Here you will learn about key principles of AWS, including Regions and Availability Zones (AZs). Knowledge of these global architecture components will assist you with the configuration options and design goals you need to understand in AWS.

- **High Availability, Elasticity, and Agility:** This part of the chapter focuses on the specific advantages of AWS that are made possible by high availability (HA), elasticity, and agility. If you are not quite sure what these terms mean in terms of AWS, have no fear: This section also defines these principles for you.

CHAPTER 2

Some Benefits of the AWS Cloud

Why are cloud engineers in such high demand? In fact, why is the cloud so popular today to begin with? This chapter ensures that you understand the many advantages of adopting cloud technology. Many of these advantages are also possible with Amazon's cloud competitors (such as Microsoft Azure and Google Cloud Platform), but here we focus on the AWS Cloud.

"Do I Know This Already?" Quiz

The "Do I Know This Already?" quiz allows you to assess whether you should read the entire chapter. Table 2-1 lists the major headings in this chapter and the "Do I Know This Already?" quiz questions covering the material in those sections so you can assess your knowledge of these specific areas. The answers to the "Do I Know This Already?" quiz questions appear in Appendix A, "Answers to the 'Do I Know This Already?' Quizzes and Q&A Sections."

Table 2-1 "Do I Know This Already?" Foundation Topics Section-to-Question Mapping

Foundation Topics Section	Questions
Economic Benefits	1–2
The Benefits of the Global Infrastructure	3–4
High Availability, Elasticity, and Agility	5–6

CAUTION The goal of self-assessment is to gauge your mastery of the topics in this chapter. If you do not know the answer to a question or are only partially sure of the answer, you should mark that question as wrong for purposes of the self-assessment. Giving yourself credit for an answer you correctly guess skews your self-assessment results and might provide you with a false sense of security.

1. In a cloud economic model, what can often replace CapEx?

    a. FIFO

    b. GARP

    c. ROI

    d. OpEx

2. What cost model can you take advantage of when you are using the AWS Cloud?

    a. Pay as you terminate

    b. Pay as you go

    c. Pay as you can

    d. Pay as you will

3. What major global infrastructure component exists in AWS Regions?

    a. Offline stores

    b. Availability Zones

    c. Hotspots

    d. Clusters

4. What AWS global infrastructure components power the AWS CloudFront caching service?

    a. Regions

    b. Availability Zones

    c. Edge Locations

    d. Host Spots

5. What AWS service monitors applications and automatically adjusts capacity to maintain steady, predictable performance at the lowest possible cost?

    a. AWS Elastic Load Balancing

    b. AWS Auto Scaling

    c. AWS CloudFormation

    d. AWS Clustering

6. Which of the following is not a form of ELB in AWS?

    a. Application Load Balancer

    b. Gateway Load Balancer

    c. Network Load Balancer

    d. Virtual Load Balancer

Foundation Topics

Economic Benefits

It is not a big surprise that various public cloud vendors (led by AWS) are experiencing more success than ever before. The list of advantages continues to grow. In this section of the chapter, we are going to present just some of the economic advantages available with the use of AWS services.

One of the fundamental economic advantages for AWS that leads to many of the others is the economic concept of economies of scale. According to the Oxford dictionary, *economies of scale* is "a proportionate saving in costs gained by an increased level of production." This definition describes AWS accurately. Amazon has been able to consistently grow the infrastructure and increase production as it gains more and more subscribers of all sizes. Thanks to AWS, subscribers get more efficient and pass the savings on to customers. This fundamental concept leads to many more specific advantages, including the following:

- *CapEx* **are replaced by** *OpEx*: Using public cloud technologies enables start-ups and existing organizations to provide new features and services with a minimum of capital expenditures (CapEx). Instead, public cloud expenses revolve around monthly operating expenses (OpEx). For most organizations, OpEx represent significant advantages compared to CapEx investments.

- **Lack of contractual commitments:** Many public cloud vendors charge on an hourly (if not less) basis. For most services, there is no long-term commitment to an organization. You can roll out new projects or initiatives and, if needed, roll back with no contractual long-term commitments. This lack of contractual commitment helps increase the agility of IT operations and reduces the financial risk associated with innovative technologies.

- **Reduction of required negotiations:** New account establishment with public cloud vendors is simple, and prices for the major public cloud vendors are decreasing. These factors reduce the need for cost negotiations that existed early in the world of service provider interactions.

- **Reduced procurement delays:** Additional resources can be set up with most cloud implementations within seconds.

- **"Pay as you go" model:** If more resources are needed to support a growing cloud presence, you can get those resources on demand and pay for them only when needed. Conversely, if fewer resources are required, you can run less and pay for only what you need. Figure 2-1 shows an example of a cost dashboard in AWS. Notice how each service is incurring a cost on a monthly basis, and the costs are broken down, as on a modern utility bill.

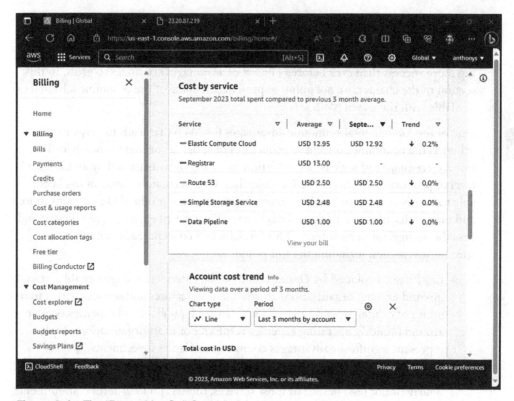

Figure 2-1   The "Pay as You Go" Cost Model

The Benefits of the Global Infrastructure

Perhaps at the very core of AWS is what makes it all possible: the ***AWS global infrastructure*** (also termed the global architecture). This is what makes the incredible elasticity, scalability, and reliability possible across a vast number of IT services. The AWS global infrastructure is made up of many components, including these:

- ***Regions***: Regions are physical locations in geographically dispersed parts of the world. For example, there are US West Regions and US East Regions, and there are Regions in Europe and Asia. Inside each Region are multiple Availability Zones (AZs). The AZs house the data centers that actually contain the physical network resources and massive amounts of data. Figure 2-2 shows the Regions available in North America at this writing.

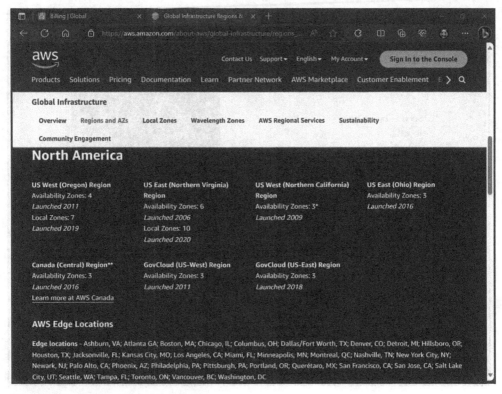

Figure 2-2   Regions in North America

Figure 2-3 demonstrates how easy it is to drop a menu at the top of the management console in order to select a new Region of the world for the initialization of localized resources for that Region.

- *Availability Zones (AZs):* An AZ is made up of one or more data centers. These data centers feature redundancy at every level, from network connections to physical devices. The data centers are also physically distant from one another in order to help mitigate the effects of localized disasters. They feature incredible high availability (HA) and fault tolerance (FT).

- *Edge Locations:* Edge Locations power the AWS CloudFront service. Edge Locations are strategically distributed data centers located in various cities and regions around the world. Their primary purpose is to cache and deliver content and services to end users with low latency and high availability through AWS CloudFront.

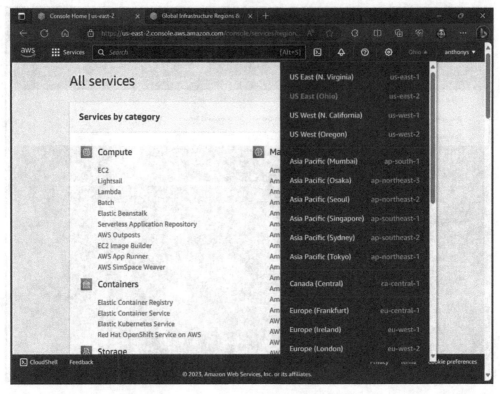

Figure 2-3   Selecting a Region in AWS

The AWS global infrastructure brings advantages to security and compliance. Thanks to the AWS global infrastructure, you maintain control of where your resources are stored geographically, and this makes it easier for you to comply with regional governance responsibilities. AWS permits you to achieve the strictest security requirements, and you can rest easy, knowing that AWS uses the most cutting-edge security-heavy data centers in the world.

High Availability, Elasticity, and Agility

There are some other reasons that many users are flocking to the AWS Cloud today. Mainly, they want to take advantage of the high availability, elasticity, and increased agility provided by the AWS Cloud. Many AWS customers might lack the technical expertise or the budget to make these desirable qualities a reality in their own on-premise facilities. Let's break down each of these concepts and how AWS addresses them.

High Availability (HA)

High availability (HA) involves designing an AWS solution in a way that keeps systems and services operational and accessible for long, extended periods of time. High availability is commonly presented as a percentage of uptime. Most companies today are looking for 99.9% to 99.999% uptime. Incredibly, various services of AWS offer well beyond 99.999% uptime.

Like many other advantages of AWS, superior HA is not automatic. AWS recommends several guidelines to help ensure high availability:

- Design systems to have no single point of failure.

- Correctly deploy and then test system availability.

- Prepare procedures to respond to, mitigate, and recover from failures.

Elasticity

Thanks to features in public cloud vendors like AWS, you can quickly scale the cloud-based infrastructure up and down as well as out and in, as needed. This advantage is often termed *elasticity*. AWS Auto Scaling allows for the dynamic creation and destruction of resources based on actual client demand. Such scaling can occur with little or no administrator interaction. When discussing scaling the resources of a service, we are talking about scaling those resources horizontally (out and in, with elasticity); the service made up of those resources is being scaled up and down (vertically, with the single service getting bigger or smaller). A single service scales up and down as well as out and in, depending on the context.

AWS provides easy-to-use tools that foster overall cloud benefits such as elasticity. There are two tools in particular you should be aware of:

- *Auto Scaling*: Auto Scaling monitors your applications and automatically adjusts capacity to maintain steady, predictable performance at the lowest possible cost. Thanks to this powerful tool, you can enable application scaling for multiple resources across multiple services in minutes. The service provides a simple, powerful user interface that lets you build scaling plans for resources like AWS EC2 instances.

- *Elastic Load Balancing (ELB)*: ELB automatically distributes incoming application traffic across multiple targets, such as EC2 instances, containers, and IP addresses. It can handle the varying load of your application traffic in a single Availability Zone or across multiple Availability Zones. Elastic Load Balancing offers four types of load balancers that all feature the high availability, automatic scaling, and robust security necessary to make your solutions fault tolerant: Application Load Balancer, Network Load Balancer, Gateway Load Balancer, and Classic Load Balancer. Figure 2-4 shows the ELB options in AWS.

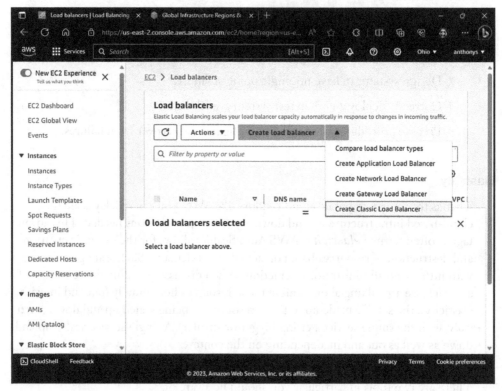

Figure 2-4   Elastic Load Balancing in AWS

Agility

Thanks to the pay-as-you-go model of AWS, engineers can really focus on innovation and new business solutions instead of worrying about infrastructure and other resource shortfalls.

Before the broad adoption of AWS solutions, engineers would waste time and money overprovisioning resources in an attempt to provide reliability and performance, even under peak load conditions. AWS allows cloud engineers to "spin up" new resources in seconds and view these resources as temporary and disposable. In fact, it is not uncommon for AWS customers to deploy massive amounts of infrastructure for a very short period of time in order to test new technologies without paying massive up-front costs.

At an AWS re:Invent conference, I heard about a large university that needed to conduct some artificial intelligence testing. The university turned to AWS for help and spun up millions of CPUs across hundreds of thousands of EC2 virtual machines. The university required this horsepower only over the course of a weekend. All the resources were "terminated" (that's the AWS term for deleting an EC2 VM) once the testing was complete. Amazon did not tell us what the bill was for this weekend of work, but the cost of all those resources if purchased as CapEx would have been massive, and the university would have been stuck with those unneeded resources when the testing was complete.

Amazon Web Services enables an organization to be flexible with the provisioning of resources because there are far fewer constraints. Efficiency is also achieved because the duration to provision new resources is remarkably small.

One of the most significant advantages companies see in moving to AWS is the ability to increase their *agility*. There are three main aspects of AWS that accomplish this:

- **Speed:** The AWS global infrastructure spans the entire globe. This global reach ensures that you can place resources geographically close to those that need to consume them. This reduces latency and fosters excellent performance. As described earlier, massive amounts of resources can be provisioned within seconds in the AWS Cloud.

- **Experimentation:** With AWS, you can implement your IT operations as code. In addition to allowing you to run with administrative ease and without errors, AWS fosters the ease of experimentation and testing. Templates are available with services like AWS CloudFormation that permit you to instantly create complex networks and IT resources for testing and experimenting. Remember that once you are done experimenting, you can dispose of the resources and are no longer charged for their use. Figure 2-5 shows an example of CloudFormation.

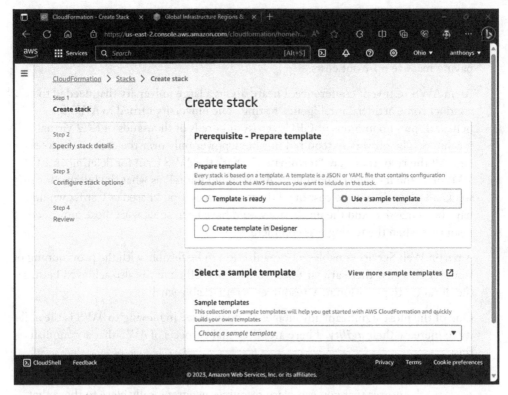

Figure 2-5   CloudFormation in AWS

- **Culture of innovation:** These enablers of agility previously listed also help foster a culture of innovation in your enterprise. In fact, an increasing number of companies participate in AWS functions because of this. It is no longer merely about saving costs for them. They love the ability to experiment with new technologies at very low risk to their organization. New innovations are very possible thanks to AWS.

Exam Preparation Tasks

As mentioned in the section "How to Use This Book" in the Introduction, you have a few choices for exam preparation: the exercises here, Chapter 22, "Final Preparation," and the exam simulation questions in the Pearson Test Prep Software Online.

Review All Key Topics

Review the most important topics in this chapter, noted with the Key Topics icon in the outer margin of the page. Table 2-2 lists these key topics and the page number on which each is found.

Table 2-2   Key Topics for Chapter 2

Key Topic Element	Description	Page Number
List	Economic advantages	25
List	AWS global infrastructure major components	26
List	Elasticity tools	29

Define Key Terms

Define the following key terms from this chapter and check your answers in the Glossary:

economies of scale, CapEx, OpEx, AWS global infrastructure, Region, Availability Zone (AZ), high availability, elasticity, Auto Scaling, Elastic Load Balancing (ELB), agility, edge locations

Q&A

The answers to these questions appear in Appendix A. For more practice with exam format questions, use the Pearson Test Prep Software Online.

1. Describe the concept of elasticity as it applies to the AWS Cloud.

2. Provide a definition for the following AWS global infrastructure components: Regions, Availability Zones, and Edge Locations.

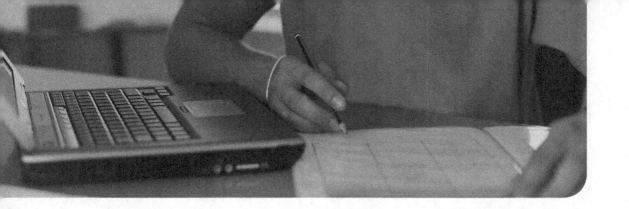

This chapter covers the following subjects:

- **The AWS Well-Architected Framework:** AWS provides detailed guidance on how to architect a brilliant design on the AWS Cloud. Learning the principles of this framework can help you deliver AWS solutions like a pro. To simplify things, AWS breaks down the massive number of recommendations in its framework into six categories called pillars. We will cover all of them in this chapter.

- **Operational Excellence:** Once you get good at following the recommendations of the operational excellence pillar, you will be able to development and run workloads on AWS very effectively. You will be able to view valuable insights into how they are performing, and you will be able to consistently support these solutions and keep improving them. This is important because if your AWS solutions are not well received operationally, no one is going to be very happy with the cloud.

- **Security:** Security is an important pillar of the Well-Architected Framework that tends to be foremost on the minds of those who move enterprise workloads to the cloud. There is certain to be at least one member of any IT department who thinks a move to the cloud is a terrible idea due to security. While you certainly surrender some levels of control with a cloud move, as you will learn in this section, you can easily design solutions with security in mind. In fact, you should be able to enhance security with a cloud move if you do it right.

- **Reliability:** In this section, you'll learn about design best practices that help ensure your cloud solutions work as you intended. This is especially important where things might fail. Fortunately, one of the major advantages of cloud solutions is that it is typically possible to increase the availability and reliability of solutions without major investments in time or money.

- **Performance Efficiency:** In this section, you will learn the design best practices that will help you engineer solutions that perform efficiently. This will make your customers and your accountants happy. "Right sizing" cloud resources makes for efficient operations and helps drive down costs. A big part of this pillar also has to do with being able to carefully and consistently monitor your cloud workloads to ensure that they remain efficient, especially with changing demand.

- **Cost Optimization:** While you can often save costs over traditional solutions when you use the cloud, cost savings are not automatic. This section teaches you all about the design goals you can use to help ensure that you are being as efficient as possible and saving plenty of money.

- **Sustainability:** What about the environmental impacts of creating the next big thing in the cloud? If you are the type who worries about such things, you are going to love the sustainability pillar. In this section, we look at what AWS has to say when it comes to designing solutions that will minimize the impact on the environment.

CHAPTER 3

Design Principles of the AWS Cloud

As you can probably already tell, this chapter is an important one. In it, you will be learning about the tools and tricks of the trade from those who know them best—the brilliant engineers from AWS who have been impressing the brightest IT minds all around the world. Get ready to get excited as you take your AWS Cloud expertise to the next level in this chapter.

"Do I Know This Already?" Quiz

The "Do I Know This Already?" quiz allows you to assess whether you should read the entire chapter. Table 3-1 lists the major headings in this chapter and the "Do I Know This Already?" quiz questions covering the material in those sections so you can assess your knowledge of these specific areas. The answers to the "Do I Know This Already?" quiz questions appear in Appendix A, "Answers to the 'Do I Know This Already?' Quizzes and Q&A Sections."

Table 3-1 "Do I Know This Already?" Foundation Topics Section-to-Question Mapping

Foundation Topics Section	Questions
The AWS Well-Architected Framework	1
Operational Excellence	2–3
Security	4–5
Reliability	6–7
Performance Efficiency	8–9
Cost Optimization	10–11
Sustainability	12–13

CAUTION The goal of self-assessment is to gauge your mastery of the topics in this chapter. If you do not know the answer to a question or are only partially sure of the answer, you should mark that question as wrong for purposes of the self-assessment. Giving yourself credit for an answer you correctly guess skews your self-assessment results and might provide you with a false sense of security.

1. Which of the following is not a pillar of the AWS Well-Architected Framework?

   a. Simplicity

   b. Performance efficiency

   c. Security

   d. Reliability

2. Which of the following is a design goal of the operational excellence pillar?

   a. Automate failure recovery as much as possible

   b. Keep people away from data

   c. Perform operations as code

   d. Take resources global in minutes

3. According to the operational excellence pillar, what types of changes should you be making to your AWS solutions?

   a. Rare, large, and atomic

   b. Rare, small, and independent

   c. Frequent, large, and idempotent

   d. Frequent, small, and reversible

4. Which of the following is a design goal of the security pillar in the AWS Well-Architected Framework?

   a. Automatically scale horizontally when needed

   b. Assure full traceability in all operations

   c. Target serverless computing as much as possible

   d. Experiment freely and often

5. Where does AWS suggest that you implement security, according to the Well-Architected Framework?

   a. In all layers of the architecture

   b. In any customer-facing interfaces

   c. In any service-facing interfaces

   d. At the lowest layer of the architecture

6. Which of the following is a valid recommendation from the reliability pillar of the Well-Architected Framework?

    a. Manage changes through automation

    b. Refine your operational procedures frequently to improve them

    c. Target serverless computing as much as possible

    d. Use strong identity practices in your architecture

7. Which pillar of the AWS Well-Architected Framework stresses that it should be possible to mitigate disruptions with relative ease?

    a. Sustainability

    b. Operational excellence

    c. Reliability

    d. Security

8. Which of the following is a design goal of the performance efficiency pillar of the Well-Architected Framework?

    a. Secure information at rest as well as in transit

    b. Make frequent small and reversible changes to the architecture

    c. Adopt a consumption model

    d. Democratize advanced technologies

9. What does it mean to achieve mechanical sympathy?

    a. You have helped your organization use technologies in ways that had been thought impossible.

    b. You have matched business goals to the appropriate technologies.

    c. You have built your architectures using an IaC approach.

    d. You have been cognizant of the environmental impact of your technologies.

10. Which of the following design objectives is a part of the cost optimization pillar of the AWS Well-Architected Framework?

    a. Maximize utilization

    b. Use managed services

    c. Adopt a consumption model

    d. Target serverless computing as much as possible

11. Tagging and labeling cloud resources can be considered part of what discipline?

   a. Cloud Security Framework

   b. Cloud Adoption Framework

   c. Cloud Sustainability

   d. Cloud Financial Management

12. Which of the following is a design goal from the sustainability pillar of the AWS Well-Architected Framework?

   a. Anticipate and adopt new and more efficient technology solutions

   b. Perform operations as code

   c. Take resources global in minutes

   d. Ensure there is full traceability in all operations

13. Which pillar of the AWS Well-Architected Framework seeks to use the cloud to meet current needs without sacrificing the needs of future generations?

   a. Operational excellence

   b. Sustainability

   c. Reliability

   d. Cost optimization

Foundation Topics

The AWS Well-Architected Framework

You might think that really smart engineers sat down to pen the *AWS Well-Architected Framework* based on their experience with cloud design. That is only partially true. To provide you with a document as critical as the Well-Architected Framework, engineers and architects also analyzed actual implementations of successful designs by some of their largest and most successful customers (with their permission, of course). All of this research gave rise to the framework that we cover here.

The goals of the Well-Architected Framework are pretty lofty. They include designing for security, performance, resiliency, efficiency, and more. The framework also provides valuable opportunities to evaluate a proposed design against the tried-and-true principles contained in the document. This makes it an even more valuable tool.

AWS had many goals when it created this framework. These are the most important of them:

- Build and deploy solutions faster than ever before
- Reduce and mitigate the risks associated with a move to the cloud
- Make informed decisions about how to implement solutions in the cloud
- Learn the most powerful best-practice approaches to using AWS services and tools

 To help organize the framework and make it more valuable, AWS focused the framework around six pillars:

- Operational excellence
- Security
- Reliability
- Performance efficiency
- Cost optimization
- Sustainability

Before we examine each of these pillars in detail, let's examine the general design recommendations contained in the framework. They are as follows:

- **Stop guessing your capacity needs:** Thanks to the AWS Cloud, you can leverage autoscaling capabilities and rapid elasticity. While you might be "pre-trained" to guess at some large capacity number for your solution from traditional IT development, you should remember that it is no longer always necessary to do so in the cloud. You can save money by using just the resources that you need based on actual demand.

- **Test systems at production scale:** With the practically limitless AWS resources at your fingertips, you should have an easier time stress testing your solutions by employing large amounts of AWS resources for a short testing period. This is often difficult if not impossible in traditional environments.

- **Automate with architectural experimentation in mind:** AWS embraces automation at every turn in its services and resources. As a result, you can easily test changes to your solutions and quickly roll back if there are issues.

- **Consider evolutionary architectures:** AWS stresses making consistent changes to architectures in order to keep up with changing conditions and even new technologies. Doing this in a traditional IT environment is difficult.

- **Drive architectures using data:** AWS makes it easy to monitor your solutions in great detail. Based on your monitoring data, you can make meaningful and efficient improvements to your design over time.

- **Improve through game days:** Do you wonder if your AWS solution can withstand a major failure or massively spiked workload? These types of events can be easily simulated in the cloud. Such "game-day" simulations are often very difficult to pull off in traditional IT environments.

In the sections of this chapter that follow, we are going to examine the design principles for each of the six pillars of the Well-Architected Framework. If you would also like to see the specific best practices that AWS recommends for each pillar, you can consult the official online documentation for the framework right from the AWS Documentation. We will not cover the many best practices in this text as the Cloud Practitioner level of AWS certification does not require this knowledge.

NOTE Do not confuse the AWS Well-Architected Framework with the AWS Well-Architected Tool. The AWS Well-Architected Tool is a service provided by AWS that helps customers assess their workloads and applications for architectural best practices. It allows users to perform self-assessments or work with AWS solutions architects to review their workloads against the six pillars of the Well-Architected Framework. So, whereas the framework is critical documentation you should know, the tool helps you achieve these documented best practices.

Figure 3-1 shows the AWS Well-Architected Tool in the AWS Management Console.

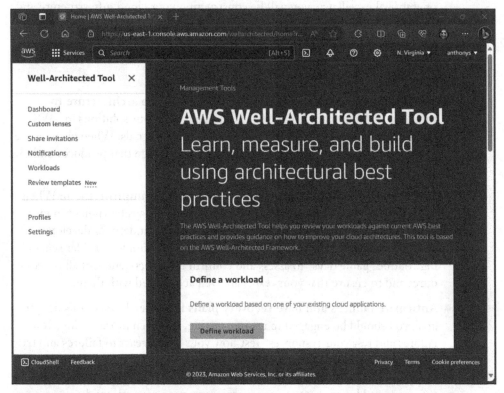

Figure 3-1   The AWS Well-Architected Tool

Operational Excellence

The overall objective of the *operational excellence* pillar is to make sure you run and monitor systems to ensure that they are providing value for the business goals of the organization. This pillar focuses on operational best practices for running and monitoring systems and continuously improving processes and procedures.

NOTE   While many of us in technology find the cloud incredibly "cool," we should never use technology just because it is very clever and exciting. Instead, we should use technology because it assists our organization in achieving the most important business objectives.

This pillar consists of the following important design principles:

- **Perform operations as code:** When you are really humming along with operational excellence, you will be constructing your cloud infrastructure and services as code. The fancy acronym for this that is very popular now is *IaC*, which is short for *infrastructure as code*. Why the obsession with doing everything as code? Because it helps eliminate human errors and ensures consistency in your operations.

- **Make frequent small and reversible changes to the architecture to improve it:** A big part of this pillar is ensuring that your solutions in AWS continue to evolve to help you achieve your business goals. When changes are small and reversible, it is very easy to roll back a change that produces undesirable results for you or your customers.

- **Refine your operational procedures frequently to improve them:** When implementing operational procedures, you should always be vigilant in identifying chances for improvements. As your workload undergoes development, ensure that your procedures evolve accordingly. You should consider scheduling routine "game days" to assess and confirm the effectiveness of all procedures and to ensure that your teams are well acquainted with them.

- **Anticipate failures and have recovery plans in place:** To meet this design goal, you should be engaged in testing, testing, and even more testing. Test failures and test your responses. Test how your teams react to failures and try and make the unknown variables known facts moving forward. It is much easier to operate in the face of adversity if you have thoroughly tested your failure responses and know that your recovery procedures are rock solid.

- **Learn from any operational failures in your architecture:** You should promote the evolution of your AWS solutions by extracting insights from every operational event and—perhaps even more importantly—every failure. Of course, once you gain this knowledge, it is important to disseminate it to all teams and throughout the entire organization.

Security

The job of the *security* pillar is to help protect your assets, your systems, and your information associated with AWS. This pillar should also assist you with risk assessments and your mitigation practices.

This pillar consists of the following important design principles:

- **Use strong identity practices in your architecture:** Fortunately, AWS provides tools to make this easy. For example, with AWS Identity and Access

Management (IAM), you can create multiple accounts for users and administrators, which helps ensure that there is a least privilege practice in place. Users can select the account that provides just the permissions they need. Of course, IAM also centralizes the user accounts that need to interact with AWS, and centralization of accounts is another strong identity practice.

- **Ensure full traceability in all operations:** It is important to continuously monitor, alert, and audit actions and modifications in your environment as they occur. AWS provides excellent tools to accomplish this. For example, you can use AWS CloudWatch and AWS CloudTrail together to monitor, alert, and audit seamlessly. As part of this design principle, you should incorporate log and metric collection into your systems to enable automated investigations and responses.

- **Implement security in absolutely all layers of your architecture:** To achieve this design principle, you should examine your AWS solution layer by layer and component by component from a security perspective. You should use tools at each layer to help secure that layer and its resources. This is what we like to call a "defense in depth" solution in IT.

- **Make a concerted effort to automate as many security best practices as possible:** Don't forget security when you are focusing on automation in your AWS solutions. Automation reduces human errors and helps your security scale in a big way.

- **Secure information at rest, in transit, and in use:** In addition to following a defense-in-depth approach, you should mentally divide your AWS data and resources into three categories—data at rest, data in transit, and data in use—and apply the appropriate security controls to each category. The AWS Cloud has a number of tools integrated right into the platform. You can also lean on third-party solutions from AWS partners and customers in the AWS Marketplace.

- **As much as possible, keep people away from data:** You can use the technologies of AWS to prevent people from directly interacting with data. I know this sounds really harsh, but it eliminates all kinds of security concerns and also addresses accuracy and operational excellence concerns.

- **Prepare as much as possible for the inevitable security events in your architecture and cloud:** Are you and your teams ready for a major security incident in the cloud? How can you be sure? You should establish incident management policies and procedures that are in line with your organization's needs. Conduct incident response drills and leverage automation tools to expedite detection, investigation, and recovery processes.

Reliability

The *reliability* pillar consists of many important design principles that all focus on ensuring that your design can easily recover from service failures. It also ensures that your architecture can grow resources as needed on demand. Reliability in the cloud also means that disruptions can be mitigated with relative ease. Sound great? It is. A major factor in the popularity of the public cloud is the ability to dramatically increase your IT reliability without massive expenditures that might be required in your traditional IT environment.

Here are the design goals around this pillar:

- **Automate failure recovery as much as possible:** If automation should be used with security controls, it makes sense that you should carefully monitor for issues with our AWS solutions and automate appropriate responses. Think about AWS Auto Scaling as an example. If your AWS solution is in danger of running low on resources, AWS can automatically add more. Once things settle back down to normal, AWS Auto Scaling can reduce the resources consumed. In this specific example, you even get the added benefit of cost optimization, which is one of the upcoming pillars.

- **Test recovery:** We tend to practice and work with our backups and their strategies, but unfortunately, we do not tend to test and work with our restore procedures. If your organization falls into this trap, you might have chaos when it comes time to restore things. The AWS Cloud allows you to fully test recovery scenarios for all types of failure scenarios. In fact, if you followed the previous design principle of automation for failure recovery, then what you are really testing here is the automation you set up.

- **Automatically scale horizontally when needed:** With AWS, you can scale vertically or horizontally. For example, with an EC2 virtual machine type of solution, you could scale vertically by adding more resources to a single EC2 VM. AWS does not want you to use this approach if you can avoid it. Rather, AWS wants you to scale horizontally. This means adding more small, efficient VMs to handle the increase in demand. Of course, you need to distribute client requests across these different VMs. Once you have all that set up, you experience the benefit of having no single point of failure, which increases reliability even more.

- **Stop guessing at capacity for IT resources:** This design principle is so important that it appeared in the list of general recommendations earlier in this chapter. Notice that this design principle is referring to a problem that often occurs in traditional IT environments: Engineers are often forced to guess at the capacity that solutions need, and at some point, their guess is not accurate. Starvation of resources begins to occur, and there is a mad scramble, typically accompanied by a big jump in spending to fix the issues. In the cloud, with tools like Auto Scaling at your disposal, you do not need to guess at capacity at all. You know you have the massive power and quantity of AWS resources at your disposal, as well as the benefit of their economies of scale. (Remember that we covered economies of scale with AWS in Chapter 2, "Some Benefits of the AWS Cloud.")

- **Manage changes through automation:** Yes, it's automation again. Earlier we established that changes should be small and reversible. To this list we now add the excellent characteristic of automated. Let's say you know you are going to need additional AWS user accounts that have monitor privileges for EC2 and Lambda running in your solution. You should create a script that automates the creation of these accounts. This is easy to do, thanks to the AWS command-line interface (CLI).

Performance Efficiency

The *performance efficiency* pillar is concerned with the most efficient use of AWS resources possible. The efficiency should be maintained as demand changes and technology evolves.

Here are the design goals around this pillar:

- **Democratize advanced technologies (that is, make them available to the masses):** Budgeting for massive amounts of storage and compute horsepower should not stop your company from taking advantage of artificial intelligence (AI) and other advanced technologies. AWS wants you to leverage its economies of scale to avail yourself of cutting-edge technologies like AI, business analytics, big data, the Internet of Things (IoT) and more.

- **Take resources global in minutes:** You might not be able to achieve this design principle without the help of the massive AWS global infrastructure. Thanks to AWS, it is simple to make a solution globally available in seconds. You can even take advantage of global content delivery networks (CDNs) such as CloudFront. Customers will be impressed by the level of latency (little or none) they experience when they are accessing your solutions, no matter where they are located on the planet.

- **Target serverless computing as much as possible:** Why worry about your own virtual machines or containers when you need compute resources in AWS? Take advantage of serverless options and let AWS do all the work for you. Remember that AWS provides many options for serverless compute, from hosting a website out of an S3 bucket to having massive compute resources waiting for you in the cloud-based pool of resources called AWS Lambda.

- **Experiment freely and often:** Thanks to the convenience of resources on demand and many automation tools, it is easy for you to experiment with new topologies and technologies in the AWS Cloud. Once again, this would be nearly impossible (and expensive) in a traditional IT infrastructure. Sadly, for most IT organizations, just keeping up with day-to-day needs is all the staff can focus on; there simply aren't the resources available for experimentation.

- **Maintain *mechanical sympathy* (that is, match business goals to the appropriate technologies):** As you are quickly learning, AWS has a service or tool for just about anything you can think of related to IT. Part of your job as a cloud practitioner (and beyond) is to be able to match these technologies to the specific business needs and goals of your organization. Thankfully, the solutions are all there for you to learn and explore. Once again, traditional IT environments tend to lack most of what you truly need.

Cost Optimization

The goal of the ***cost optimization*** pillar is quite simple: to save money and stop wasting investments in technology.

The design goals are also straightforward:

- ***Implement Cloud Financial Management (CFM):*** CFM refers to the set of practices, tools, and strategies that organizations use to manage their finances and control costs in the context of cloud computing. Aspects of a solid CFM approach include tasks such as cost management and allocation, budgeting and forecasting, cost optimization, right-sizing, and tagging and labeling cloud resources.

- **Adopt a consumption model (which emphasizes the OpEx approach to IT):** With your move to AWS, you can start paying for only the resources that you need, including temporary resources. For example, if you need a staging or test environment while you are improving one of your solutions, you can spin it up, do your testing, and then shut it off or even shut it off and delete it.

- **Measure the efficiency of your architecture closely:** AWS makes this simple with many cost-related tools we will be covering in this text. It is very easy to make changes and then monitor the financial implications of those changes. You typically have much greater visibility into the cost of your solutions with the AWS Cloud than you would have in a traditional environment.

- **Stop spending money needlessly to try to solve IT problems:** AWS inherently makes this design goal possible. You no longer have to worry about buying new server racks, new cabling, new storage arrays, and so on when it comes to the latest advanced technologies.

- **Closely analyze the expenditures in your AWS implementation:** Here is another design goal that AWS makes simple, thanks to the numerous tools available for tracking costs. You can even use tagging and labeling of your AWS resources so that it is easy to attribute your costs to specific solutions, departments, or teams. Your internal accountants should love this new ability.

Sustainability

AWS would like to be kinder to the environment, and as a result, the *sustainability* pillar was added to the AWS Well-Architected Framework during the re:Invent 2021 conference. The goal of this pillar is a lofty one: to try to help customers minimize the environmental impacts of running cloud workloads. For the development of this pillar, AWS looked to the United Nations World Commission on Environment and Development, whose definition of sustainability encourages development that "meets the needs of the present without compromising the ability of future generations to meet their own needs."

The major design principles for this newer pillar of the architecture are as follows:

- **Understand your impact:** AWS allows you to quantify the influence of your cloud workload and forecast its future ramifications. This evaluation should encompass all sources of impact, encompassing impacts arising from customer product utilization and the ultimate product phase-out and retirement. You can analyze the resources and emissions needed per unit of work and compare them against the overall impact of your cloud workloads. This information can serve as the foundation for establishing key performance indicators (KPIs), assessing strategies to enhance productivity while minimizing impact, and projecting the impact of proposed alterations over time.

- **Establish sustainability goals:** It is important to define enduring sustainability objectives for each cloud workload, such as the reduction of compute and storage resources needed per transaction. You should also create return on investment (ROI) models to assess the sustainability enhancements for current workloads and provide workload owners with the necessary resources to invest in achieving these sustainability goals.

- **Maximize utilization:** This principle might seem counterintuitive, but AWS is saying that you should not overprovision your resources. Sadly, overprovisioning is very common in traditional IT environments, where capacity is often handled by allocating and provisioning many more resources than are actually required. With AWS, you can right-size the resources you need to consume.

- **Anticipate and adopt new, more efficient hardware and software offerings:** Here is another design principle where AWS helps you by default. AWS is constantly making newer and more efficient technologies available to you and using them itself.

- **Use managed services:** When you call upon the massively popular managed services of AWS (for example, S3 storage), you are taking advantage of the efficient maximization of resources principle. AWS has appropriated truly massive amounts of resources and helps you use them efficiently. This is much better for the environment than for each AWS customer across the globe to try to create their own resources.

- **Reduce the downstream impact of your cloud workloads:** To help achieve this design principle, you can take several steps. First, reduce the amount of energy or resources required to use your services. Next, reduce the need for customers to upgrade their devices to use your services. Finally, test solutions with customers to understand the actual impact from using your services.

Exam Preparation Tasks

As mentioned in the section "How to Use This Book" in the Introduction, you have a few choices for exam preparation: the exercises here, Chapter 22, "Final Preparation," and the exam simulation questions in the Pearson Test Prep Software Online.

Review All Key Topics

Review the most important topics in this chapter, noted with the Key Topics icon in the outer margin of the page. Table 3-2 lists these key topics and the page number on which each is found.

Table 3-2 Key Topics for Chapter 3

Key Topic Element	Description	Page Number
List	The pillars of the AWS Well-Architected Framework	41
List	The operational excellence pillar design principles	44
List	The security pillar design principles	44
List	The reliability pillar design principles	46
List	The performance efficiency pillar design principles	47
List	The cost optimization pillar design principles	48
List	The sustainability pillar design principles	49

Define Key Terms

Define the following key terms from this chapter and check your answers in the Glossary:

AWS Well-Architected Framework, operational excellence, infrastructure as code (IaC), security, reliability, performance efficiency, mechanical sympathy, cost optimization, Cloud Financial Management (CFM), sustainability

Q&A

The answers to these questions appear in Appendix A. For more practice with exam format questions, use the Pearson Test Prep Software Online.

1. Name at least three design principles of the operational excellence pillar of the AWS Well-Architected Framework.

2. Name at least three design principles of the security pillar of the AWS Well-Architected Framework.

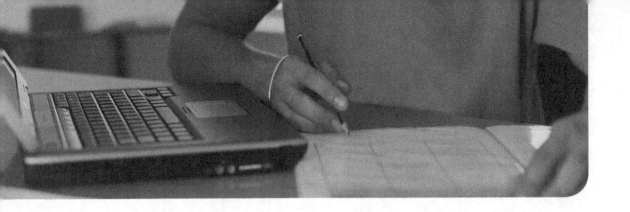

This chapter covers the following subjects:

- **The AWS Cloud Adoption Framework:** Moving to the cloud from your traditional on-premises environments can be a daunting task. To make it easier, AWS has created the Cloud Adoption Framework to provide detailed guidance. This section of the chapter walks you through this excellent guide for migration to the AWS Cloud.

- **Resources for Migration Support:** This section of the chapter describes specific resources that are available in AWS that can aid in migration to the cloud.

CHAPTER 4

Strategies for Migration to the AWS Cloud

Just like any other large information technology (IT) undertaking, a cloud migration to AWS should be well planned and thoughtfully executed. AWS provides great guidance in the form of a powerful framework for cloud migration as well as tools and resources to directly assist with this important transformation. If you are looking for knowledge of these tools, this chapter is for you.

"Do I Know This Already?" Quiz

The "Do I Know This Already?" quiz allows you to assess whether you should read the entire chapter. Table 4-1 lists the major headings in this chapter and the "Do I Know This Already?" quiz questions covering the material in those sections so you can assess your knowledge of these specific areas. The answers to the "Do I Know This Already?" quiz questions appear in Appendix A, "Answers to the 'Do I Know This Already?' Quizzes and Q&A Sections."

Table 4-1 "Do I Know This Already?" Foundation Topics Section-to-Question Mapping

Foundation Topics Section	Questions
The AWS Cloud Adoption Framework	1–3
Resources for Migration Support	4–5

CAUTION The goal of self-assessment is to gauge your mastery of the topics in this chapter. If you do not know the answer to a question or are only partially sure of the answer, you should mark that question as wrong for purposes of the self-assessment. Giving yourself credit for an answer you correctly guess skews your self-assessment results and might provide you with a false sense of security.

1. A move to the AWS Cloud might enable your company to provide brand-new services to its customers. What area of the cloud value chain describes such advantages?

   a. Process transformation

   b. Organizational transformation

    c. Technological transformation

    d. Product transformation

2. What AWS CAF perspective would have the greatest focus on risk?

    a. Business

    b. Governance

    c. People

    d. Platform

3. If your organization wants to improve its use of technologies such as autoscaling and unlimited storage capabilities, what CAF perspective is it most concerned with?

    a. People

    b. Business

    c. Platform

    d. Operations

4. Your organization wants to migrate and convert an on-premises MongoDB database to a DocumentDB database in AWS. What service can assist with this?

    a. EFS

    b. SQS

    c. DMS

    d. EC2

5. What AWS technology should you consider if you have petabytes worth of on-premises data that you would like to efficiently move to the cloud?

    a. S3

    b. Snowball

    c. CAF

    d. RDS

Foundation Topics

The AWS Cloud Adoption Framework

As AWS continues to grow in scale and scope, more and more organizations realize that they should make a move to cloud technologies to stay competitive and perhaps even to expand and improve their business offerings. To help these organizations make the move to the AWS Cloud successfully, AWS offers the *Cloud Adoption Framework (CAF)*. Using this framework provides many advantages, including the following:

- Reducing the business risk after a cloud migration

- Improved environmental, social, and governance (ESG) performance

- Increased revenue

- Increased operational efficiency

How can such remarkable advantages be achieved? AWS identifies what it calls a cloud transformation value chain in the CAF. This value chain describes the power of transforming technology, processes, organizations, and products:

- **Technological transformation:** This is an appropriate starting point and probably represents exactly what you think about when you envision a cloud migration. Thanks to the cutting-edge nature of AWS technologies, you have the ability to modernize (maybe even revolutionize) your use of technology in the cloud compared to what you can achieve on premises.

- **Process transformation:** This area highlights the digitalization, automation, and enhancement of your business operations. Maybe thanks to the AWS migration, your company will start leveraging big data and data analytics after struggling mightily to try to achieve this using its own technologies. Many organizations report that a successful AWS migration enables them to enhance operational efficiency, reduce operating costs, and elevate both employee and customer experiences.

- **Organizational transformation:** A successful migration to the AWS Cloud may permit a company to improve its operations due to the freedom and flexibility the public AWS Cloud provides even the smallest of businesses.

■ **Product transformation:** Migrating to the AWS Cloud can be very exciting for companies that believe their products or services are stale. When you leverage the power of AWS to create new products or services, you may be able to gain new customers or generate new revenue streams that you can use to improve your overall business performance.

Foundational Capabilities

Based on what you have now read about the cloud transformation value chain, you are likely excited to make improvements in your own organization. But how do you accomplish this? AWS identifies foundational capabilities that make a successful migration a reality. It organizes these capabilities into six areas called perspectives (see Figure 4-1).

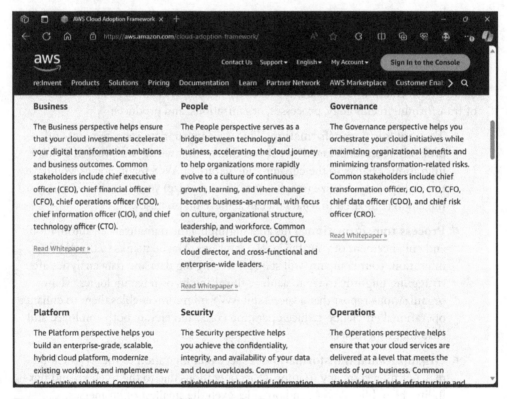

Figure 4-1   Perspectives in the Cloud Adoption Framework

Be sure you are familiar with these perspectives:

- **Business:** Is your migration to the cloud really improving your business processes and helping you achieve your business goals? Typical stakeholders for this foundational capability in your organization include key C-suite personnel, like the chief executive officer (CEO), chief financial officer (CFO), chief operations officer (COO), chief information officer (CIO), and chief technology officer (CTO).

- **People:** What are technology and business processes without the people who make it all happen? It is important to ensure that there is a culture of innovation and learning among the people in your organization. Key stakeholders in this area include the CIO, COO, CTO, cloud director, and cross-functional and enterprise-wide leaders.

- **Governance:** What about the risks of moving to the cloud from a rules and policies perspective? The governance foundational capability is all about minimizing the potential risks to your governance initiatives. Typical stakeholders in this area include the chief transformation officer, CIO, CTO, CFO, chief data officer (CDO), and chief risk officer (CRO).

- **Platform:** What about the really cool stuff of the AWS Cloud—things like autoscaling and high-performance compute and artificial intelligence (AI)? These are part of the platform foundational capability. Traditional on-premises facilities often lack the budgets and the expertise to make these types of platform enhancements a reality. Typical stakeholders in this area include the CTO, technology leaders, architects, and engineers.

- **Security:** Many people in your organization might be concerned about a loss of security with a cloud migration. Just as we are obsessed with the CIA (confidentiality, integrity, and availability) triad in our own networks, we work hard to make this a reality in the AWS Cloud. Common stakeholders include the chief information security officer (CISO), chief compliance officer (CCO), internal audit leaders, and security architects and engineers.

- **Operations:** It is important to ensure that business needs are met by the services and functionality of the AWS Cloud. You do not want to adopt AWS Cloud technologies just because it is the current trend; you want to really address business needs with the technology. Common stakeholders in this area include the infrastructure and operations leaders, site reliability engineers, and information technology service managers.

Cloud Transformation Journey

Migrating to the cloud can be a very complex set of tasks for an organization, and so the AWS Cloud Adoption Framework provides us with another valuable tool. It suggests a cloud transformation journey that consists of four phases, as shown in Figure 4-2.

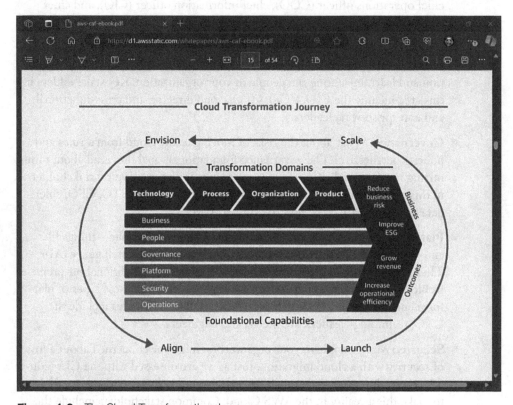

Figure 4-2 The Cloud Transformation Journey

These phases are as follows:

- **Envision phase:** In this initial phase of cloud adoption, you work on demonstrating how the cloud will help your business achieve its key business outcomes. This is all about making sure that the new technologies that are adopted will really make a difference. In this phase, AWS recommends that you get together with the key stakeholders in the organization to work with them so that the benefits you all envision can become reality.

- **Align phase:** In this phase, you carefully examine the six foundational capabilities and their perspectives and take an honest look at your organization for gaps and cross-organizational dependencies that may make your migration to the cloud tricky. If you lean into this phase, you will be able to create strategies to make sure you are ready to take full advantage of the many strengths AWS has to offer.

- **Launch phase:** This phase is all about pilots. No, we are not talking about aviation here; we are talking about tests and demonstrations of AWS technologies in the context of a business and its needs. In this launch phase, you should be learning as much as possible from the pilots so that when you are ready to actually migrate, it will be as if you have already performed many of the steps and learned from many of the potential pitfalls.

- **Scale phase:** The launch phase involves building a test and learning from pilots of your migration. This is fine and is certainly valuable, but in the scale phase, it is time to expand those pilots (which tend to be very small in scale) to full production workloads in the cloud. It is no surprise, therefore, that this is the last phase of initial migrations.

Keep in mind that these phases are very much a revolving cycle. For example, your organization might decide to start taking on new products or services (like AI), and the cycle will start over again for these new business areas.

Resources for Migration Support

AWS provides tools that help when you are actually ready to start migrating data and solutions into AWS. This section covers just a few of the many that are available.

Database Migration Service

One of the many areas where AWS shines is in managed database services. For example, with AWS Relational Database Services (RDS), customers can rely on AWS to do the hard work of managing underlying servers for the hosting of massive customer databases. Is it any surprise that AWS also offers a fully managed database migration and replication service? The AWS *Database Migration Service (DMS)* helps you move databases to the AWS Cloud while ensuring security and reliability. Figure 4-3 shows the AWS DMS.

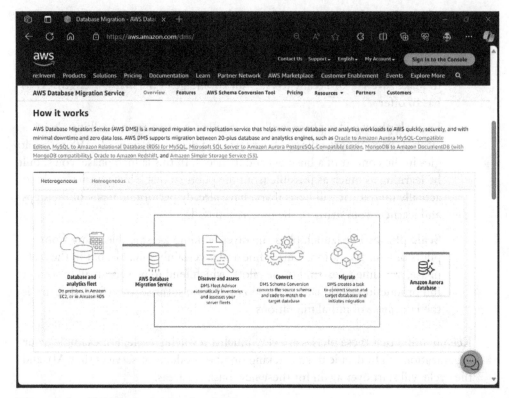

Figure 4-3 AWS Database Migration Service

In order to be appropriate for many different migrations, AWS DMS supports migration between more than 20 database and analytics engines. Here are just some examples:

- Oracle to Aurora MySQL-Compatible Edition

- MySQL to RDS for MySQL

- Microsoft SQL Server to Aurora PostgreSQL-Compatible Edition

- MongoDB to DocumentDB (with MongoDB compatibility)

- Oracle to Redshift and Simple Storage Service (S3)

Notice from these sample options that DMS gives customers the ability to perform both homogenous and heterogeneous migrations. This means you can move your database to the same type of database technology in the cloud, or you can use DMS to move the database and transform it into a new database technology. This permits AWS customers to take advantage of cloud benefits as well as the benefits of new database technologies.

Snowball

What if you have petabytes of miscellaneous data that you want to migrate to the AWS Cloud without having to worry about saturating your Internet connection and worrying about reliability during the transfer? Another area of strength for AWS is providing various types and reliability levels of cloud-based data storage. The answer for moving large amounts of data to the cloud is the AWS *Snowball* family, which features shipping container options in a variety of form factors for your data. Figure 4-4 shows an example of an AWS Snowball device.

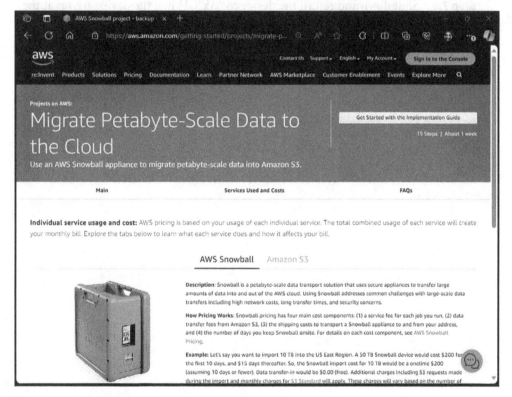

Figure 4-4   AWS Snowball

Using AWS Snowball typically consists of the following steps:

Step 1.   Use the AWS Snow Family console to select a preferred type of Snowball device.

Step 2.   Create a job with an S3 bucket.

Step 3.   Select the Simple Notification Service (SNS) for tracking. AWS then prepares and ships the device to you, and you receive it in approximately 4-6 days.

Step 4.   Once the device arrives, power it up and use AWS OpsHub to unlock it.

Step 5.   Connect the device to your LAN.

Step 6.   Use AWS OpsHub to manage the device, transfer data, or launch EC2 instances.

Step 7.   Shut down and return the device to AWS. When the device arrives at the AWS Region, any data stored in your on-board buckets is moved to your S3 bucket and verified. All data is then securely erased from the device, and the device is sanitized of any customer information.

Exam Preparation Tasks

As mentioned in the section "How to Use This Book" in the Introduction, you have a few choices for exam preparation: the exercises here, Chapter 22, "Final Preparation," and the exam simulation questions in the Pearson Test Prep Software Online.

Review All Key Topics

Review the most important topics in this chapter, noted with the Key Topics icon in the outer margin of the page. Table 4-2 lists these key topics and the page number on which each is found.

Table 4-2   Key Topics for Chapter 4

Key Topic Element	Description	Page Number
List	AWS CAF perspectives	57
List	Phases of the cloud transformation journey of the CAF	58
Overview	Database Migration Service (DMS)	59
Overview	Snowball	61

Define Key Terms

Define the following key terms from this chapter and check your answers in the Glossary:

Cloud Adoption Framework (CAF), Database Migration Service (DMS), Snowball

Q&A

The answers to these questions appear in Appendix A. For more practice with exam format questions, use the Pearson Test Prep Software Online.

1. Name at least three AWS CAF perspectives.

2. What AWS service provides assistance with migrating and transforming databases from on premises to the AWS Cloud?

This chapter covers the following subjects:

- **Cloud Economics:** This part of the chapter discusses the many potential economic benefits of the AWS Cloud, including fixed costs versus variable costs and the many licensing forms supported.

- **Other Benefits:** This section provides information about additional benefits brought by the AWS Cloud, including the benefits of automation and the benefits stemming from the use of managed AWS services.

CHAPTER 5

Concepts of Cloud Economics

AWS services bring many benefits that are economic in nature. While economic benefits are not the only benefits an organization can achieve through a cloud migration, they tend to be some of the most celebrated and discussed. One way AWS provides economic benefits is through automation and managed services that are not available in a traditional on-premises environment. This chapter ensures that you are familiar with all of these benefits so that you can make your AWS migration a great success to the largest number of stakeholders possible.

"Do I Know This Already?" Quiz

The "Do I Know This Already?" quiz allows you to assess whether you should read the entire chapter. Table 5-1 lists the major headings in this chapter and the "Do I Know This Already?" quiz questions covering the material in those sections so you can assess your knowledge of these specific areas. The answers to the "Do I Know This Already?" quiz questions appear in Appendix A, "Answers to the 'Do I Know This Already?' Quizzes and Q&A Sections."

Table 5-1 "Do I Know This Already?" Foundation Topics Section-to-Question Mapping

Foundation Topics Section	Questions
Cloud Economics	1–3
Other Benefits	4–5

CAUTION The goal of self-assessment is to gauge your mastery of the topics in this chapter. If you do not know the answer to a question or are only partially sure of the answer, you should mark that question as wrong for purposes of the self-assessment. Giving yourself credit for an answer you correctly guess skews your self-assessment results and might provide you with a false sense of security.

1. Which of the following is a disadvantage associated with the on-premises CapEx model often required in traditional on-premises IT operations?

   a. Limited flexibility in adjusting to changing business requirements

   b. Reduced up-front capital investments for hardware and software

   c. Faster response to dynamic market conditions

   d. Lower risk of technological obsolescence

2. What is a key advantage associated with the variable cost model in the AWS Cloud?

   a. Limited flexibility in adapting to changing workloads

   b. No financial stresses of large up-front capital expenditures

   c. Decreased elasticity in resource allocation

   d. Reduced cost transparency, making optimization challenging

3. What is a cost that is typical in on-premises IT environments but not often found with cloud technology like AWS?

   a. Compute costs

   b. Storage costs

   c. Physical security costs

   d. HA/DR costs

4. Which of the following is a benefit of using automation in the AWS Cloud?

   a. Increased complexity in deploying solutions

   b. Decreased reliability due to human errors

   c. Increased collaboration between development and operations teams through DevOps practices

   d. Slower deployment of solutions in the cloud

5. What is a key benefit of using managed services in the AWS Cloud?

   a. Increased routine maintenance tasks for teams

   b. Reduced high availability due to global architecture

   c. Fixed cost for the resources consumed

   d. Improved disaster recovery mechanisms, including automated backups

Foundation Topics

Cloud Economics

One of the biggest factors driving the move to public cloud technologies like AWS is economics. Organizations become aware of several major factors that make a cloud move almost inevitable. In this part of the chapter, we break them down to ensure that you fully understand them, even if finance is not your primary focus.

Fixed Costs Versus Variable Costs

When you are operating IT solutions in a typical on-premises environment, you face many costs that are fixed (instead of variable). We commonly refer to these fixed costs as capital expenses (*CapEx*). Operating with these fixed costs tends to come with more disadvantages than operating in the cloud with a model that tends to offer variable costs made up of operating expenses (*OpEx*). Here are just some disadvantages to consider with the on-premises CapEx model:

- **Large CapEx costs:** Fixed costs in on-premises environments tend to involve significant up-front capital investments for hardware, software, and infrastructure. These large up-front costs tend to put strain on organizations, especially smaller businesses and startup organizations. Dealing with CapEx costs typically involves guessing at required capacity, which adds even more stress to the process.

- **Limited flexibility:** On-premises fixed costs tend to offer limited flexibility in adapting to changing business requirements. Adjusting the capacity or upgrading hardware often involves additional investments and may take time, leading to delays in responding to dynamic market conditions.

- **Technological obsolescence:** In today's IT environment, technology is advancing faster than ever before. This can be another huge disadvantage to the CapEx model seen typically in on-premises environments. Your company risks making large, up-front investments in technology that might be at risk if the purchased technology becomes out of date with new approaches.

When you migrate to the public AWS Cloud, you switch to a cost model that is primarily based on variable costs. This presents many potential advantages, especially compared to dealing with the large, fixed-cost investments often required on premises. Here are the main advantages to keep in mind:

- **Increased flexibility:** The variable costs that are associated with pay-as-you-go pricing offer flexibility in adapting to changing workloads.

Organizations pay only for the resources they consume, making the cloud suitable for organizations whose resource needs frequently change.

- **Little to no up-front commitment:** Unlike with the CapEx model frequently experienced on premises, variable pay-as-you-go costs in the AWS Cloud eliminate the financial stresses of large, up-front capital expenditures. Figure 5-1 shows a sample pay-as-you-go cost report from AWS.

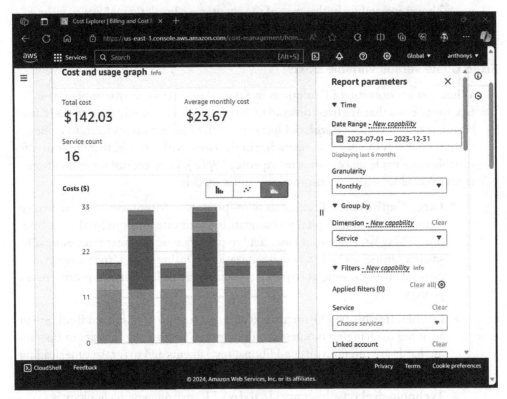

Figure 5-1 An AWS Cost Report

- **Increased elasticity:** Thanks to variable costs, organizations enjoy the ability to pay less as demand decreases and pay more only as resource demand increases. The cost model of AWS is often compared to a utility bill.

- **Increased cost transparency:** Another advantage to the variable cost model of AWS stems from the fact that organizations can see the direct correlation between their resource usage and the costs of these resources. This advantage permits companies to more easily optimize resource utilization and often helps companies identify opportunities for cost savings.

Costs Associated with On-Premises Environments

Even if you are not working in the finance department of your organization, you might be curious about the costs that your company typically faces when operating its IT infrastructure in an on-premises environment. Here are some costs associated with on-premises environments that might not be found in a public cloud like AWS:

- **Hardware costs:** Often the largest CapEx costs on premises are for the hardware that must be purchased to power IT. This includes components like servers, networking devices, and security devices.

- **Building/facilities costs:** Buildings are not typically free. Your organization most likely has lease or mortgage costs associated with the buildings and facilities that house your IT infrastructure.

- **Maintenance:** When you are operating on premises with your IT resources, you have to spend money on the ongoing maintenance of the hardware and software. It is not a matter of *if* something is going to fail but *when*.

- **Personnel:** Operating on premises requires people in addition to equipment. Your organization must be sure to spend the money required to have the right personnel in the right places for your on-premises data centers and remote locations.

- **Scalability:** Whereas you can easily grow infrastructures in the cloud (often in an automated fashion), you typically need to spend money to grow the infrastructure in an on-premises environment.

- **Power and energy costs:** While you can operate in the cloud under a pay-as-you-go model and have your IT costs operate like an electric bill, when you operate on premises, you need to worry about the *actual* electric bill. On-premises power costs can be substantial—especially during times of increased utilization.

- **Redundancy:** Once again, the cloud can make high levels of redundancy relatively inexpensive. This is not typically the case when operating on premises. In the on-premises model, you often need to purchase duplicate network and server systems in order to guarantee desired levels of redundancy.

- **Software licensing:** On-premises environments often require licenses for operating systems, virtualization software, and other applications. Licensing costs can add up, especially for larger deployments.

- **Physical security costs:** Ensuring the physical security of on-premises data centers involves additional costs for surveillance, access control systems, and other security measures. You don't have to worry about any of this when you are in a public cloud.

- **Insurance:** Your organization most likely requires insurance coverage for much of the IT infrastructure when you host it yourself on premises.

Other Benefits

As you know, there are plenty of benefits when you move to the AWS Cloud, and these benefits certainly impact the economic benefits that we have discussed so far. Let's now investigate the benefits of AWS automation and the benefits of using managed services inside of AWS. While these benefits may seem out of place in a chapter that is focused on economic benefits, both automation and managed service usage can have profound effects on cost savings for an organization. In fact, you will note that the very first benefits we list here for each are none other than cost savings.

Benefits of Automation

AWS makes automation simple for engineers. This is a design goal because automation in the AWS Cloud brings many benefits in terms of efficiency, scalability, and overall operational excellence. Here are some key advantages of automation in the AWS Cloud:

- **Cost savings:** When automation is used in the AWS Cloud, it can ensure that resources are used the most appropriately for the given demands. The use of Auto Scaling in EC2 provides a great example of cost savings due to automation. You provide the basic parameters desired for EC2 resources, and AWS ensures that the resources scale as needed. This can have a massive impact on costs, of course, especially when you remember that EC2 resource costs are based on EC2 runtimes.

- **Elasticity:** Thanks to automation (as just described for EC2 Auto Scaling), it is easy to scale resources as needed in the AWS Cloud.

- **Fast deployments:** With automation, you can create solutions in the cloud with remarkable speed. Consider the time and effort and costs that you would incur if you needed to build database servers from scratch and then run those servers in different parts of the world to accommodate local users. This might be a massive and complex deployment. With AWS Relational Database Services (RDS), you can have the required environment built and running in seconds.

- **Increased reliability:** The use of automation helps eliminate human errors and increases the consistency of deployments.

- **Increased security:** Automation assists in securing your solutions in the cloud. It also helps detect and respond to security issues. AWS also makes it possible to automate the deployment of security to begin with.

- **Lifecycle management:** Thanks to automation, you can more effectively implement the various phases of lifecycles for your various solutions. For example, in AWS S3, you can automate the transfer of storage between various storage classes, and you can even automate the archival and deletion processes.

- **DevOps practices:** Automation can foster your use of DevOps practices. By automating build, test, and deployment pipelines, development teams can deliver software more rapidly and reliably and foster collaboration between development and operations teams.

- **IT focus:** When you automate repetitive maintenance types of tasks, your IT teams can focus on new technologies and advancements of solutions and their efficiency.

Benefits of Managed Services

To varying degrees, you can call upon managed services when you develop solutions in the AWS Cloud. For example, you can use EC2 to help with the automation and deployment of your virtual machines, and you can go even further and use a serverless compute service like Lambda in order to perform even fewer tasks. There are many benefits of using managed services in AWS. Here are some important ones:

- **Cost savings:** Managed services often follow a pay-as-you-go model, allowing you to pay only for the resources you consume. This can result in cost savings compared to maintaining and managing equivalent services on premises or through traditional hosting.

- **Lower operational overhead:** Because managed services reduce the routine maintenance tasks your teams must perform, they can save time and money and allow you to focus on tasks that can improve operations.

- **High availability:** Using managed services typically means you experience great gains in availability for your solutions and your data. The AWS global architecture enables you to deploy resources all over the world in seconds. You can achieve levels of high availability you might never be able to afford or implement by using your own company resources.

- **Disaster recovery:** The use of managed services often provides an increase in disaster recovery mechanisms such as automated backups and offsite storage.

Exam Preparation Tasks

As mentioned in the section "How to Use This Book" in the Introduction, you have a few choices for exam preparation: the exercises here, Chapter 22, "Final Preparation," and the exam simulation questions in the Pearson Test Prep Software Online.

Review All Key Topics

Review the most important topics in this chapter, noted with the Key Topics icon in the outer margin of the page. Table 5-2 lists these key topics and the page number on which each is found.

Table 5-2 Key Topics for Chapter 5

Key Topic Element	Description	Page Number
List	Advantages of the variable cost model of AWS	67
List	The benefits of AWS automation	70
List	The benefits of AWS managed services	71

Define Key Terms

Define the following key terms from this chapter and check your answers in the Glossary:

CapEx, OpEx

Q&A

The answers to these questions appear in Appendix A. For more practice with exam format questions, use the Pearson Test Prep Software Online.

1. Name at least two advantages of the variable cost model with the AWS Cloud.

2. Name at least four costs typically found with on-premises IT operations.

3. Name at least four advantages provided through the use of automation with AWS.

This chapter covers the following subjects:

- **Creating Your Free Tier Account:** The Free Tier account level in AWS is an excellent way for you to get started with Amazon Web Services. In this section of the chapter, you get details about a Free Tier account and walk through the setup of such an account.

- **Building a Web Server with the Free Tier:** This section of the chapter walks you through the steps required to build a web server in AWS using your Free Tier account.

CHAPTER 6

Creating and Using an AWS Free Tier Account

It is important for you to understand the options around the *Free Tier* account in AWS. This chapter educates you on this powerful option from AWS. It also ensures that you can use this account to create a fully functional web server in AWS.

"Do I Know This Already?" Quiz

The "Do I Know This Already?" quiz allows you to assess whether you should read the entire chapter. Table 6-1 lists the major headings in this chapter and the "Do I Know This Already?" quiz questions covering the material in those sections so you can assess your knowledge of these specific areas. The answers to the "Do I Know This Already?" quiz questions appear in Appendix A, "Answers to the 'Do I Know This Already?' Quizzes and Q&A Sections."

Table 6-1 "Do I Know This Already?" Foundation Topics Section-to-Question Mapping

Foundation Topics Section	Questions
Creating Your Free Tier Account	1–2
Building a Web Server with the Free Tier	3–4

CAUTION   The goal of self-assessment is to gauge your mastery of the topics in this chapter. If you do not know the answer to a question or are only partially sure of the answer, you should mark that question as wrong for purposes of the self-assessment. Giving yourself credit for an answer you correctly guess skews your self-assessment results and might provide you with a false sense of security.

1. How long is the Free Tier period by default?

   a. 2 years

   b. 1 year

   c. 6 months

   d. 3 months

2. Which of these services does not remain free after the Free Tier expiration?

   a. SNS

   b. Lambda

   c. EC2

   d. CloudWatch

3. When selecting an instance from the Quick Start options in EC2, how can you tell if an Amazon Machine Image (AMI) is included as part of your Free Tier membership?

   a. The AMI is noted as "Free Tier Eligible."

   b. All of the Quick Start AMIs are part of the Free Tier.

   c. Only Linux AMIs are part of the Free Tier.

   d. None of the Quick Start AMIs are part of the Free Tier.

4. What is used to authenticate access to an EC2 instance?

   a. Lambda

   b. PPTP

   c. Key pair

   d. Telnet

Foundation Topics

Creating Your Free Tier Account

Let's start by looking at the incredible resources you receive with the Free Tier for 1 year. We will follow this up with the components that remain free after the 1-year period.

> **NOTE**   The exact terms of the Free Tier account could change at any time.

Here are the "free for a year" components, listed in alphabetical order for your convenience:

- **Amplify Hosting:** This is a fully managed continuous integration and continuous delivery (CI/CD) and hosting service for web applications, with 15 GB served per month.

- **API Gateway:** This service enables you to publish, maintain, monitor, and secure your APIs, all while providing global scalability, with 1 million free API calls per month.

- **AppSync:** This service permits you to develop, secure, and run GraphQL APIs at any required scale, with 250,000 query or data modifications per month.

- **Augmented AI:** This service helps build the workflows required for human review of machine learning predictions, with 500 free objects.

- **Cloud Directory:** This is a fully managed, cloud-native directory-building service for data with multiple hierarchies, with 1 GB of storage per month.

- **Comprehend:** This is continuously trained and fully managed natural language processing (NLP), with 50,000 units of text (5M characters) for each API per month.

- **Connect:** This simple-to-use, cloud-based contact center scales to support any size business and is available for 90 minutes per month at this tier.

- **Data Pipeline:** This service provides orchestration for data-driven workflows, with three low-frequency preconditions.

- **EBS:** The Elastic Block Storage service of AWS provides block-based storage for EC2 instances, with 30 GB of general-purpose solid state drives (SSDs).

- **EC2:** This is your virtual machine compute service in the cloud, available for 750 hours per month at this tier.

- **EFS:** The Elastic File Service of AWS provides scalable shared file storage services and 5 GB of total storage.

- **Elastic Container Registry:** This is a registry service for Docker images, available with 500 MB of storage per month.

- **Elastic Transcoder:** This is the AWS fully managed media transcoding service, with 20 minutes of audio transcoding.

- **ElastiCache:** This in-memory, cloud-based cache service is based on industry standard caching protocols and is available for 750 hours of single-node usage.

- **ELB:** The Elastic Load Balancing service of AWS can automatically distribute requests across multiple EC2 instances, with 750 hours per month shared between Classic and Application Load Balancers.

- **GameLift:** GameLift provides simple, fast, cost-effective dedicated game server hosting. The Free Tier comes with 125 hours per month of Amazon GameLift on-demand instance usage, plus 50 GB EBS general-purpose SSD storage.

- **HealthImaging:** This service assists clients in building cloud-native medical imaging applications, with 20 GB of storage.

- **Interactive Video Service:** This service provides easy setup of live, interactive video streams, with 100 hours of SD video output per month.

- **IoT Core:** This service seeks to connect your IoT devices to the cloud, allowing 500,000 messages published or delivered per month.

- **IoT Device Management:** This service helps you onboard, organize, monitor, and remotely manage your connected IoT devices, allowing 50 remote actions per month.

- **IoT Events:** This service seeks to simplify IoT message detection and response, with 2,500 message evaluations per month.

- **IoT Greengrass:** This service provides local compute, messaging, data caching, and sync capabilities for your IoT connected devices, allowing three connected devices for free.

- **Lex:** This service permits you to build voice and chat text chatbots, allowing 10,000 text requests per month.

- **MQ:** Amazon MQ is a managed message broker service for Apache ActiveMQ, and the Free Tier allows 750 hours of a single-instance broker per month.

- **OpenSearch:** This AWS managed service aims to simplify log analytics and real-time application monitoring, with 750 hours free per month.

- **OpsWorks for Chef Automate:** This cloud service provides configuration management with Chef Automate and Chef Server, available for 10 nodes per month.

- **OpsWorks for Puppet Enterprise:** This service provides configuration management in a Puppet Enterprise environment, available for 10 nodes per month.

- **Pinpoint:** Pinpoint enables targeted push notifications for mobile apps, with 5,000 free targeted users per month.

- **Polly:** This service turns text into speech, allowing 5 million characters per month.

- **RDS:** The relational database service of AWS is available for 750 hours per month of applicable database engine usage.

- **Rekognition:** This is a deep learning-based image recognition service, available for 5,000 images per month.

- **S3:** The Simple Storage Service of AWS provides object-based storage to an unlimited scale, with 5 GB of standard storage.

- **SES:** This is the cost-effective cloud-based email service provided by AWS, and it is available for 3,000 messages per month.

- **Transcribe:** This service can add speech-to-text capability to your applications with automatic speech recognition and is available for 60 minutes per month.

- **Translate:** This service provides fast, high-quality, and affordable neural machine translation for 2 million characters per month.

These services are included with a Free Tier account and will remain free for you after the 1 year is up:

- **Application Discovery Service:** This service collects server-specific information for network connections and is available for 1,000 applications per account.

- **Application Migration Service:** This service seeks to simplify and expedite application migrations, and use of this service is unlimited.

- **Chime:** This modern unified communications (UC) service offers meetings with high-quality audio and video. Use of Amazon Chime Basic is unlimited.

- **CloudFormation:** This service permits the creation of infrastructure from code for 1,000 handler operations per month.

- **CloudFront:** This service distributes content to ensure low-latency access to web-based resources, and you are allowed 1 TB of data transfer out.

- **CloudTrail:** This service permits the careful auditing of API calls and activities within AWS and can be used for one trail.

- **CloudWatch:** This service provides simple yet powerful monitoring capabilities for your cloud services in AWS, and you are allowed 10 custom metrics and 10 alarms.

- **CodeArtifact:** This service is a cloud-based artifact repository that assists in the storage and distribution of software packages, with 2 GB of storage available per month.

- **CodeBuild:** This service seeks to simplify the application building and delivery process in AWS, with 100 build minutes.

- **CodeCatalyst:** This fully managed service permits you to build and test your code in the cloud for 2,000 build minutes.

- **CodeCommit:** This highly scalable managed source control service allows five active users per month at this tier.

- **CodePipeline:** This is a continuous delivery service that permits fast and reliable delivery of application updates, with one active pipeline per month.

- **Cognito:** This service provides simple and secure sign-up and sign-in services as well as access control and is available for 50,000 monthly active users (MAUs) each month.

- **Control Tower:** This service assists in setting up multi-account AWS environments, with unlimited free access.

- **Data Exchange:** This service helps you find and use third-party data sets delivered by APIs, files, or Amazon Redshift tables and can be used with 1,600 data sets.

- **Database Migration Service:** This service seeks to make database migrations to or from the cloud very simple, allowing 750 hours of Amazon DMS single-instance usage.

- **DynamoDB:** This service provides fast and flexible NoSQL database access to any scale required, offering 25 GB of storage.

- **Glue:** This is a simple, flexible, and cost-effective extract, transform, and load (ETL) service, allowing 1 million objects to be stored in the AWS Glue Data Catalog.

- **Honeycode:** This service helps you build mobile and web applications with zero programming for 20 users.

- **Key Management Service:** This is a fully managed service that assists you with encryption key management, allowing 20,000 free requests per month.

- **Lambda:** This serverless compute service runs your code in response to events, allowing 1 million free requests per month.

- **License Manager:** This service allows you to set rules to discover and manage third-party license usage, and its usage is unlimited.

- **Managed Service for Prometheus:** This service works with Prometheus to provide monitoring and alerting for these containerized environments, offering 40 million metric samples.

- **Migration Evaluator:** This service helps customers rapidly see projected costs of running their on-premises solutions in the cloud, offering unlimited assessments.

- **Migration Hub:** This is a central location for gaining information about application migrations, with unlimited free usage.

- **Organizations:** This is a centrally managed billing and access control system for your AWS resources, with unlimited free usage.

- **re:Post:** This is a community-driven Q&A service that seeks to eliminate technical roadblocks for AWS customers, with unlimited free usage.

- **Resource Access Manager:** This service helps you securely share your resources across AWS accounts, with unlimited free usage.

- **Resource Explorer:** This service permits you to easily find your AWS resources across AWS regions, with unlimited free usage.

- **Route 53:** This is the highly available and scalable DNS service of AWS, allowing 1,000 IP CIDR blocks per month.

- **Security Hub:** This service automates AWS security checks and centralizes security alerts; it is available as an unlimited trial for 30 days.

- **Service Catalog:** This service permits you to create a catalog of IT services approved for use in your AWS cloud, with 1,000 API calls per month.

- **SNS:** The Simple Notification Service of AWS provides a fast and flexible messaging service for many potential application and service usages, allowing 1 million publishes.

- **SQS:** The Simple Queue Service of AWS provides scalable queueing for message storage between systems and is available for 1 million requests.

- **Step Functions:** This service seeks to coordinate components of distributed applications, allowing 4,000 state transitions per month.

- **Storage Gateway:** This service provides hybrid storage with local integration possible and optimized data transfers, with 100 GB free per account.

- **SWF:** The Simple Workflow Service of AWS can assist you with task coordination and state management services for your cloud applications, allowing 10,000 activity tasks.

- **Systems Manager:** This service allows you to centralize operational data from multiple AWS services, offering free use of 12 of the available features.

- **WAF Bot Control:** This service protects your web applications from common and preservice web bots, allowing 10 million bot control requests per month.

- **Well-Architected Tool:** This service reviews your architecture and helps you adopt well-architected best practices, with unlimited workload reviews.

- **X-ray:** This service helps analyze and debug your applications, allowing 100,000 traces to be recorded per month.

Lab: Creating Your Free Tier Account

If you do not already have a Free Tier account with AWS, it is time for you to create one. Follow these steps:

Step 1.   Search online for **AWS Free Tier**. Select the link from Amazon for the Free Tier account.

Step 2.   Click the **Create a Free Account** button, as shown in Figure 6-1.

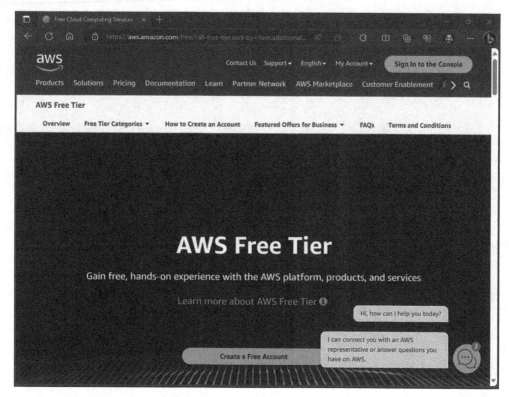

Figure 6-1 The Create a Free Account Button

Step 3. On the Sign Up for AWS page (shown in Figure 6-2), provide your root user email address and your AWS account name. The root user email address is critical and will be the username entry when you log in to this all-powerful root account. You should select an email address that you will have uninterrupted access to for the foreseeable future. The account name is how your account will display in AWS. This is not nearly as critical and can be changed at any time. When you have completed the two fields, click the **Verify Email Address** button.

Step 4. Enter your verification code that was emailed to your root account email address you provided in Step 3. Click **Verify**.

Step 5. Enter and confirm the root user password and click **Continue (step 1 of 5)**.

Step 6. Choose **Business** or **Personal** for your account and fill in your basic contact information. Click **Continue (step 2 of 5)**.

Figure 6-2 The Sign Up for AWS Page

Step 7.   Provide your payment information. Keep in mind that you are not charged anything in the first year provided that you do not exceed your Free Tier limits. This payment method is charged for services in excess of the free tier and will be charged when your account leaves the Free Tier duration of 1 year. Click **Continue (step 3 of 5)**.

Step 8.   Provide the phone number for your phone verification and input the security check to confirm your identity. Click **Continue (step 4 of 5)**.

Step 9.   In the Select a Support Plan window, choose your support option. Note that there is only one free plan: the Basic Support plan. When you are finished, click **Complete Sign Up**.

Step 10.   Sign in to your new AWS account, using the email address you specified during the account creation. Remember that this is your root AWS account. You should use this account to create "standard" admin accounts for management of AWS, and you should very rarely need to log in to this powerful root account.

You are now ready to explore the wonders of AWS. Figure 6-3 shows the welcome screen for the AWS Management Console.

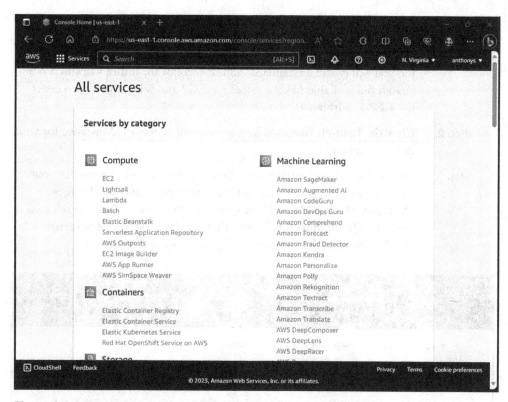

Figure 6-3   The AWS Management Console

Building a Web Server with the Free Tier

Now that you have your Free Tier account, it is time to have some fun and learn a lot in the process. In this section, you will build a fully functional web server in AWS by following some simple steps. You will use EC2 in this lab to create an Amazon Linux instance.

NOTE   Amazon is now naming its Linux instances after the calendar year, so be sure to choose the current image when you are stepping through this lab.

Lab: Building a Web Server with the Free Tier

Follow these steps to build a free web server using AWS EC2:

Step 1.   Log in to the AWS Management Console using the root account you created in the previous lab. While you would not ordinarily use the root account for such a task, you will use this account here. In the next chapter, you will create a "standard" admin account for future work in AWS. Search the available AWS services for **EC2** and select the link to enter the **EC2 Dashboard**.

Step 2.   Click the **Launch Instance** button to create a new EC2 instance for your new web server.

Step 3.   On the Launch an Instance page that appears, provide a name for your web server in the **Name** field. In the **Application and OS Images (Amazon Machine Image)** area, ensure that Amazon Linux is selected from the **Quick Start** tab. Notice that this Amazon Machine Image (AMI) is marked "Free Tier eligible," as shown in Figure 6-4.

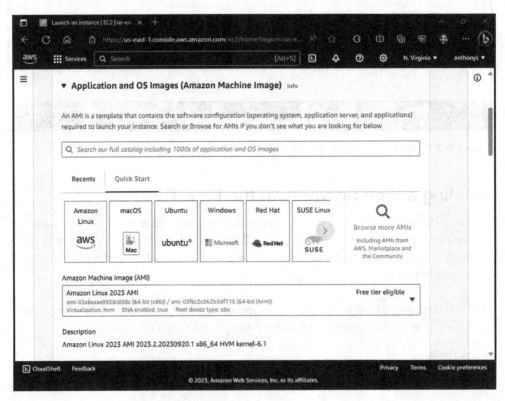

Figure 6-4   The Launch an Instance Page

Step 4.   In the Instance Type area, select the hardware configuration of your instance. Notice that the **t2.micro** type has been selected for you, and this instance type is marked "Free Tier eligible." Figure 6-5 shows this step.

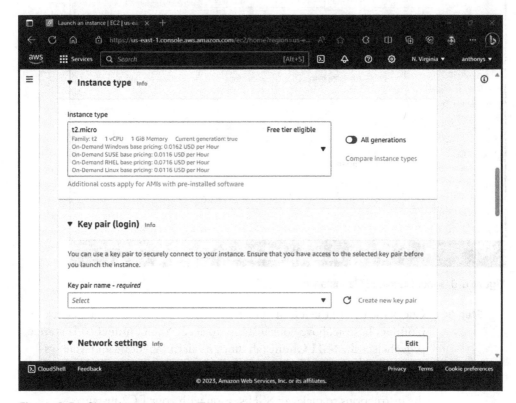

Figure 6-5   Choosing an Instance Type

Step 5.   In the Key Pair (Login) area, click the **Create a New Key Pair** link. Provide a **Key Pair Name** and leave the defaults selected for **Key Pair Type** and the **Private Key File Format**. Click the **Create Key Pair** button.

Step 6.   In the lower right of the Launch an Instance page, click the **Launch Instance** button.

Step 7.   On the Next Steps page, click the **View All Instances** button. You should see your EC2 instance listed on this page. Notice that the instance state is running, as shown in Figure 6-6.

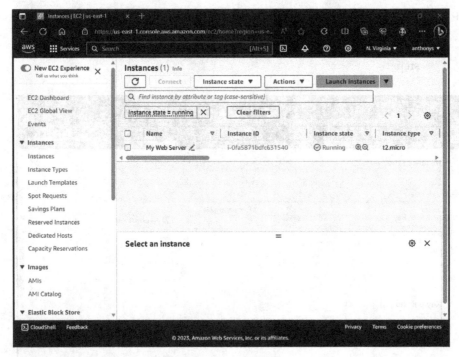

Figure 6-6 Your Running EC2 Instance

Step 8. Check the box to the left of your EC2 instance to select it. Then click the **Connect** button above your instance to access the **Connect to Instance** page. Select the **SSH Client** tab. Both modern Windows and Mac systems ship with enabled SSH clients. On a Windows system, launch a Command Prompt, and on a Mac, launch a Terminal session and follow the instructions to make an SSH session with your EC2 instance.

NOTE If you are having issues making an SSH connection using the instructions in step 8, you can try connecting to your instance in a web browser. On the Connect to Instance page, choose the EC2 Instance Connect tab. Then click the Connect button in the lower-right corner, and you should connect to your Linux instance in the web browser, as shown in Figure 6-7.

Step 9. After logging in to your instance as the user account **ec2-user**, ensure that all of your software packages are up to date by performing a quick software update on your instance. This process may take a few minutes, but it is important to make sure that you have the latest security updates and bug fixes. Use the following command:

[ec2-user ~]$ **sudo yum update -y**

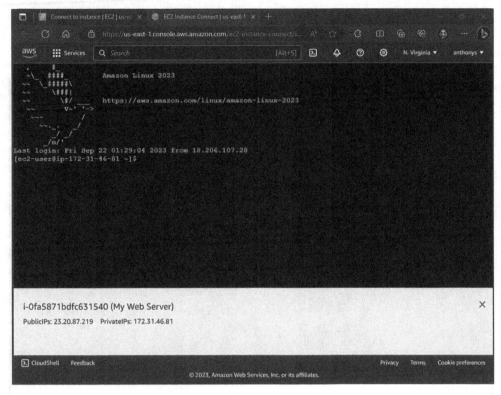

Figure 6-7   The EC2 Instance Connect Option

Step 10.   Use the following command to install the latest versions of the Apache web server and PHP packages for Amazon Linux:

[ec2-user ~]$ **sudo dnf install -y httpd wget php-fpm php-mysqli php-json php php-devel**

Step 11.   Start the Apache web server:

[ec2-user ~]$ **sudo systemctl start httpd**

Step 12.   Use the **systemctl** command to configure the Apache web server to start at each system boot:

[ec2-user ~]$ **sudo systemctl enable httpd**

Step 13.   Test your web server by obtaining the public IP address of your EC2 instance. You can get the public DNS address for your instance by using the Amazon EC2 console. Revisit the EC2 Dashboard and check the properties of your instance. There is a **Public IPv4 Address** column that contains your public IP address. Copy this address to the clipboard. In a web browser address bar, type **http://<your-ip>**. Notice that you cannot use https:// to connect since you have not set up your Apache web server for secure access. By using **http**, you will access the default page on your Apache Web server via the public Internet, as shown in Figure 6-8.

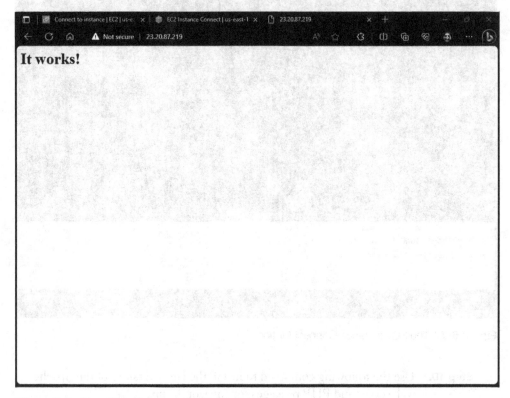

Figure 6-8   Your Web Server on the Public Internet

Step 14.   It's now time to shut down your handy web server, so issue the following command:

[ec2-user ~]$ **sudo shutdown -h now**

NOTE   You can also shut down instances by using the AWS Management Console with the EC2 Dashboard. I always prefer to shut down systems from their own interface when I am working within them. Why is it important to shut down your instance when you are done using it? Because doing so ensures that you are no longer being charged for the instance. Remember that even if you are in the Free Tier of AWS access, you are permitted only 750 hours per month of free EC2 usage.

Exam Preparation Tasks

As mentioned in the section "How to Use This Book" in the Introduction, you have a few choices for exam preparation: the exercises here, Chapter 22, "Final Preparation," and the exam simulation questions in the Pearson Test Prep Software Online.

Review All Key Topics

Review the most important topics in this chapter, noted with the Key Topics icon in the outer margin of the page. Table 6-2 lists these key topics and the page number on which each is found.

Table 6-2 Key Topics for Chapter 6

Key Topic Element	Description	Page Number
List	Free Tier components	77
Lab	Creating a Free Tier account	82
Lab	Creating a web server with a Free Tier account	86

Define Key Term

Define the following key term from this chapter and check your answers in the Glossary:

Free Tier

Q&A

The answers to these questions appear in Appendix A. For more practice with exam format questions, use the Pearson Test Prep Software Online.

1. Provide at least three examples of Free Tier services that can remain forever free.

2. Why should you shut down your EC2 instances in AWS when practicing with the Free Tier account?

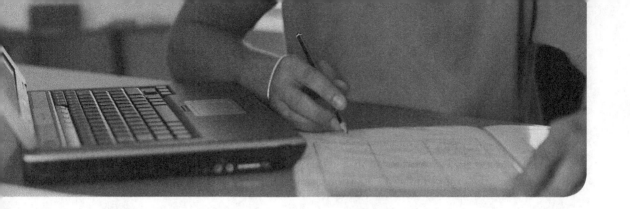

This chapter covers the following subjects:

- **Understanding the Shared Responsibility Model:** This part of the chapter introduces you to the shared responsibility model. Basically, the model indicates that you (the customer) and AWS (the provider) share security responsibilities.

- **AWS Responsibilities:** This section provides examples of Amazon's responsibilities for security in your AWS implementation. The fact that there are many examples of these responsibilities is great news for you. AWS and its parent Amazon have amazing financial resources and incredible engineering talent that you get to take advantage of with the shared responsibility model in place.

- **Customer Responsibilities:** This section provides examples of customer responsibilities for securing the resources in AWS. This is where you need to do your homework when it comes to securing AWS. You need to be aware of the configuration options that are in your control for securing your workloads.

CHAPTER 7

The AWS Shared Responsibility Model

Whereas some organizations are hesitant to move to the cloud due to, sometimes false, fears that their security will suffer, other organizations embrace the opportunities for greatly enhanced security. One major reason this is a reality is the existence of the AWS shared responsibility model. This model helps you fully understand the security environment when you operate in AWS. This chapter makes this subject simple and provides excellent examples of the various parts of the model.

"Do I Know This Already?" Quiz

The "Do I Know This Already?" quiz allows you to assess whether you should read the entire chapter. Table 7-1 lists the major headings in this chapter and the "Do I Know This Already?" quiz questions covering the material in those sections so you can assess your knowledge of these specific areas. The answers to the "Do I Know This Already?" quiz questions appear in Appendix A, "Answers to the 'Do I Know This Already?' Quizzes and Q&A Sections."

Table 7-1 "Do I Know This Already?" Foundation Topics Section-to-Question Mapping

Foundation Topics Section	Questions
Understanding the Shared Responsibility Model	1–3
AWS Responsibilities	4
Customer Responsibilities	5–6

CAUTION The goal of self-assessment is to gauge your mastery of the topics in this chapter. If you do not know the answer to a question or are only partially sure of the answer, you should mark that question as wrong for purposes of the self-assessment. Giving yourself credit for an answer you correctly guess skews your self-assessment results and might provide you with a false sense of security.

1. The AWS shared responsibility model divides security responsibilities between which two parties? (Choose two.)

   a. The AWS customer

   b. The AWS partner

   c. The community cloud vendor

   d. Amazon AWS

2. Customer responsibilities vary in the shared responsibility model based on what major factor?

   a. The number of AWS employees in the region used by the customer

   b. The amount of customer data intended for cloud storage

   c. Which AWS services the customer chooses to use

   d. How much money the customer is willing to spend on support

3. Which is not a common category of IT security controls in the AWS shared responsibility model?

   a. Inherited

   b. Deferred

   c. Customer specific

   d. Shared

4. Which of the following is not an example of an Amazon responsibility in the AWS shared responsibility model?

   a. Physical security of the data center

   b. Cloud software

   c. Edge locations

   d. IAM policies

5. Which of the following is not an example of a customer responsibility in the AWS shared responsibility model?

   a. Data integrity authentication

   b. Guest operating system

   c. Virtualization software on the host

   d. Customer data

6. Who is responsible for the security and patching of the database software with AWS RDS?

   a. The AWS partner

   b. The database software vendor

   c. The customer

   d. AWS

Foundation Topics

Understanding the Shared Responsibility Model

The *AWS shared responsibility model* divides the security responsibilities between two parties: the AWS customer (you) and Amazon (AWS). The fact that you are no longer responsible for a massive portion of the security required for scalable data centers is a huge advantage. You can leverage the massive budgets of Amazon and its intense expertise.

The next two sections of this chapter provide examples of responsibilities in each part of the model. But for now, in general, it's important to realize that Amazon's responsibilities include the host operating system and virtualization layer down to the physical security of the facilities in which the service operates. It is your responsibility as the customer to secure the guest operating system (including updates and security patches), application software, and the AWS network security group firewall.

Be aware that the customer responsibilities vary depending on which services the customer chooses to use. The customer responsibilities further vary based on the level of integration of AWS services consumed and their IT infrastructure. Laws and regulations that must be followed also vary. Examples of the different responsibility levels for different services used are given later in the chapter.

As shown in Figure 7-1, AWS is considered *security of the cloud*, and the customer's responsibility is considered *security in the cloud*.

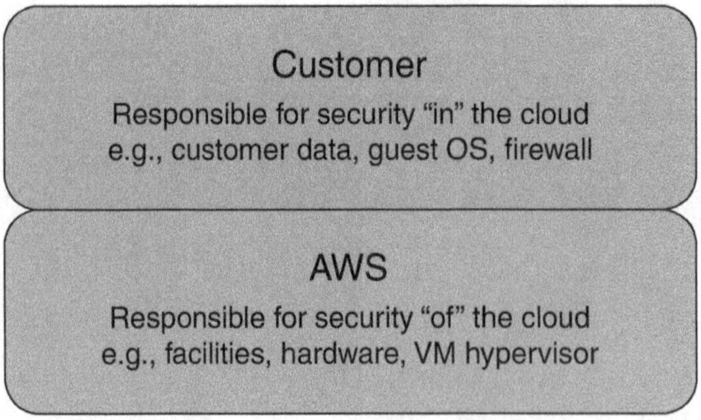

Customer
Responsible for security "in" the cloud
e.g., customer data, guest OS, firewall

AWS
Responsible for security "of" the cloud
e.g., facilities, hardware, VM hypervisor

Figure 7-1   The AWS Shared Responsibility Model

In addition to partitioning the operational security concerns between the customer and AWS, the shared responsibility model also applies to IT controls that are in use. Amazon groups these controls into three categories:

- **Inherited controls:** These are security controls the customer fully inherits from AWS. Perfect examples are the physical and environmental security controls used by Amazon.

- **Shared controls:** These are controls that apply to both the infrastructure layer of Amazon and the customer responsibilities. Note that these shared controls apply to each domain in completely separate contexts or perspectives. AWS provides the requirements for the infrastructure, and the client must provide their own control implementation within their use of the services. A great example is Identity and Access Management (IAM). The IAM service must be secured, meet regulatory compliance, and function as intended, and the customer should create well-crafted policies.

- **Customer-specific controls:** These are security controls the customer is solely responsible for, and they vary based on the services the customer selects, of course. A great example would be applying specific patches to one of your operating systems on an EC2 instance.

AWS Responsibilities

Remember that Amazon is considered responsible for security *of* the cloud. That is, AWS is responsible for protecting the infrastructure that runs the services chosen, including the hardware and software required to power the AWS service as well as the networking and facilities used.

Specific Amazon responsibilities include the following:

- Cloud software, including compute, storage, networking, and database software

- Hardware

- AWS global infrastructure, including Regions, Availability Zones, and Edge Locations

As we will elaborate on in the next section, it is important to remember that these AWS responsibilities will shift based on the AWS service selected. While it might seem like it would be difficult to track and configure these responsibilities, AWS makes it fairly simple. The configuration options available in the GUI of the Management Console make the shared responsibilities obvious.

Customer Responsibilities

Remember that the customer is responsible for security *in* the cloud. Specific examples of client responsibilities include the following:

- Customer data

- Platform, applications, IAM

- Guest operating systems

- Network and firewall configurations

- Client-side data encryption

- Server-side encryption (file system and/or data)

- Network traffic protection (encryption, integrity, and identity)

Figure 7-2 shows an example of a customer checking the security group settings that apply to an EC2 instance. This is a perfect example of customer responsibilities. AWS is responsible for making sure the security group functions as intended, but it is the customer's responsibility to configure it correctly.

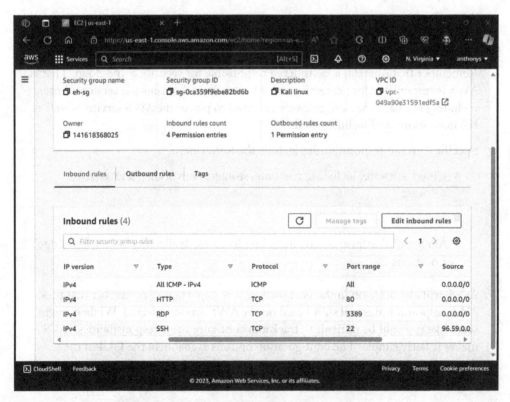

Figure 7-2   Checking the Security Group Settings for an EC2 Instance

Also remember that your customer responsibilities vary based on the specific services selected. Here are some examples you should consider:

- If you are relying heavily on Simple Storage Service (S3) for storage, you will be responsible for knowledge and proper configuration of the security permissions for your resources.

- If you choose to use EC2, you are required to keep the operating system updated and patched, and you are also responsible for the application software required on the guest operating system. You are responsible for the appropriate security group configuration for the EC2 instance as well, as shown earlier in the chapter.

- If you choose to use the managed AWS Relational Database Service (RDS), you are responsible for securing your data, but AWS bears the responsibility of securing the underlying database technology and patching it as required.

- If you choose to use the serverless compute service of Lambda, once again you are responsible for securing the data outputs of Lambda, but AWS is responsible for all security on the actual compute resources that make up the pool.

Exam Preparation Tasks

As mentioned in the section "How to Use This Book" in the Introduction, you have a few choices for exam preparation: the exercises here, Chapter 22, "Final Preparation," and the exam simulation questions in the Pearson Test Prep Software Online.

Review All Key Topics

Review the most important topics in this chapter, noted with the Key Topics icon in the outer margin of the page. Table 7-2 lists these key topics and the page number on which each is found.

Table 7-2 Key Topics for Chapter 7

Key Topic Element	Description	Page Number
Overview	The AWS shared responsibility model	97
List	Examples of Amazon responsibilities	97
List	Examples of customer responsibilities	98

Define Key Terms

Define the following key terms from this chapter and check your answers in the Glossary:

AWS shared responsibility model, security of the cloud, security in the cloud

Q&A

The answers to these questions appear in Appendix A. For more practice with exam format questions, use the Pearson Test Prep Software Online.

1. What would be an example of IT security controls that a customer inherits from Amazon?

2. Provide at least three examples of client responsibilities under the AWS shared responsibility model.

3. Provide at least two examples of Amazon responsibilities under the AWS shared responsibility model.

This chapter covers the following subjects:

- **An Introduction to AWS Security:** This section discusses the major aspects of the AWS approaches to securing your infrastructure and resources.

- **AWS Security Compliance Programs:** This section of the chapter ensures that you understand the many efforts that AWS engages in to ensure you can maintain compliance in security with laws and regulations you might face.

CHAPTER 8

AWS Cloud Security, Governance, and Compliance

It is important that you understand the approaches that Amazon takes to security when it comes to AWS. It is also important to know specifics regarding the levels of compliance and attestation that AWS believes are important. This chapter discusses these points in detail, describing specific technologies that AWS uses to help ensure that you can create the most secure architecture possible in the cloud and beyond.

"Do I Know This Already?" Quiz

The "Do I Know This Already?" quiz allows you to assess whether you should read the entire chapter. Table 8-1 lists the major headings in this chapter and the "Do I Know This Already?" quiz questions covering the material in those sections so you can assess your knowledge of these specific areas. The answers to the "Do I Know This Already?" quiz questions appear in Appendix A, "Answers to the 'Do I Know This Already?' Quizzes and Q&A Sections."

Table 8-1 "Do I Know This Already?" Foundation Topics Section-to-Question Mapping

Foundation Topics Section	Questions
An Introduction to AWS Security	1–2
AWS Security Compliance Programs	3–5

CAUTION The goal of self-assessment is to gauge your mastery of the topics in this chapter. If you do not know the answer to a question or are only partially sure of the answer, you should mark that question as wrong for purposes of the self-assessment. Giving yourself credit for an answer you correctly guess skews your self-assessment results and might provide you with a false sense of security.

1. Amazon is interested in offering you high levels of confidentiality with your data in AWS. What is a key technology area that accommodates this?

   a. Authentication

   b. Hashing

   c. Encryption

   d. Fault tolerance

2. What service in AWS assists your security efforts by using roles, users, and groups?

   a. S3

   b. IAM

   c. EC2

   d. Glacier

3. Amazon seeks out attestations from _____ organizations. (Choose two.)

   a. dependent

   b. independent

   c. third-party

   d. subsidiary

4. Which of the following is not something Amazon typically provides to AWS customers in the area of compliance?

   a. Mapping documents

   b. Compliance playbooks

   c. Security features

   d. Physical host security playbooks

5. Which of the following services can automate the process of assessing and managing the compliance of AWS resources against industry standards and regulations?

   a. CloudTrail

   b. Audit Manager

   c. AWS Config

   d. CloudWatch

Foundation Topics

An Introduction to AWS Security

Amazon understands that a major concern for many organizations considering moving to public (or hybrid) clouds is security. As a result, it has taken great pains to ensure that incredible levels of security are available for your organization, including massive efforts around *confidentiality*, *integrity*, and *availability* (CIA). The CIA triad, or security triad, is illustrated in Figure 8-1.

The Security Triad

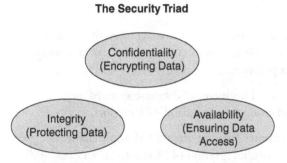

Figure 8-1 The Security Triad

Next, we'll look at some of the main approaches that Amazon takes to secure AWS.

The first is keeping customer data as safe as possible. Amazon ensures a resilient and highly available infrastructure. High levels of the latest security technologies are deployed, and strong safeguards are in place for every aspect of Amazon's security responsibilities.

With AWS, you can take advantage of rapid innovations in security technology at scale. This includes the robust Identity and Access Management (IAM) system, encryption of data at rest and in transit, and segmentation services.

With AWS security, you pay for what you need. This permits high levels of security with controlled and elastic capacity and costs.

AWS also ensures diverse *compliance* support to offer adherence to governance, oversight, and automation.

In addition, AWS follows the Shared Responsibility Model, which divides responsibility clearly between the customer (you) and Amazon. This allows you to leverage Amazon's incredible expertise in secure infrastructures and technology knowledge. However, you must have expertise in securing components within AWS services. For example, you would be responsible for patching some of your virtual machine (EC2) deployments.

> **NOTE** Amazon keeps the hardware on which your virtual machines reside highly secure.

Specific security products and features encompass a variety of tools and monitoring resources, including the following:

- **Robust network security:** Amazon provides built-in firewalling, encryption in transit, private connectivity options, and built-in distributed denial-of-service (DDoS) mitigation.

- **Efficient security tools:** Tools are available for management of resource commissioning and decommissioning, inventory and configuration management, and implementing best practices.

- **Data encryption at every level:** This includes database systems, key management, hardware-based storage options, and API support.

- **Access control and management:** Amazon offers IAM, multifactor authentication, federation support, integration of IAM into all services, and API support.

- **Monitoring and logging tools:** Amazon provides deep visibility into API calls, log aggregation tools, alerts, and reduced risks. You can use AWS CloudTrail to monitor all actions that have transpired in and around your AWS solutions.

- **AWS Marketplace:** Amazon offers anti-malware, intrusion prevention systems (IPSs), and policy management tools in the AWS Marketplace (see Figure 8-2).

AWS gives you the ability to encrypt data at every phase of its use: at rest, in transit, and in use. It also provides services that specialize in securing your workloads. Here are just some of them:

- *Amazon Inspector*: This security assessment service helps users identify potential vulnerabilities and security issues in EC2 instances and applications. The service automates the process of assessing security and compliance by analyzing the behavior of applications, identifying common security misconfigurations, and generating detailed findings reports. Amazon Inspector simplifies the task of maintaining a secure environment by providing actionable insights, allowing you to proactively address security concerns and enhance the overall resilience of your AWS resources.

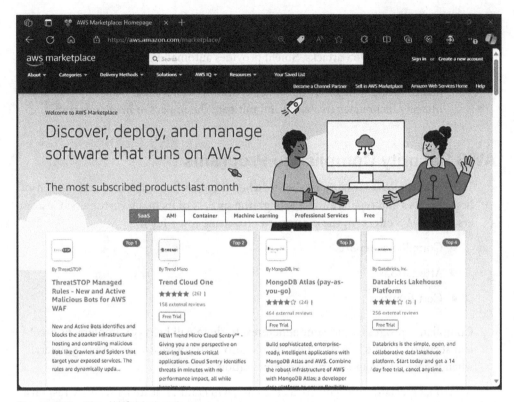

Figure 8-2   The AWS Marketplace

- *AWS Security Hub*: This comprehensive security service provides a centralized view of security alerts and compliance status across multiple AWS accounts. It aggregates, organizes, and prioritizes findings from various AWS services, as well as supported third-party security tools, enabling users to efficiently manage and respond to potential security threats within AWS environments.

- *Amazon GuardDuty*: This is a managed threat detection service that continuously monitors and analyzes the network and account activities within your AWS environment. Leveraging machine learning and threat intelligence, GuardDuty detects unusual or suspicious behavior, such as unauthorized access or malicious activity, providing real-time alerts to help you quickly respond to potential security threats. By automating the detection of security anomalies, GuardDuty helps users enhance the overall security posture of AWS resources and helps protect them against various cyber threats.

- *AWS Shield*: AWS Shield is a managed DDoS protection service that is designed to safeguard your applications and websites from malicious and volumetric DDoS attacks. Shield provides automatic detection and mitigation of DDoS attacks, helping to ensure the availability and uninterrupted performance of applications by dynamically scaling resources and applying advanced filtering techniques to absorb and mitigate the impact of malicious traffic.

AWS Security Compliance Programs

How does Amazon measure its success when it comes to compliance with security best practices and regulations? Through the success of its many customers! Customers drive AWS efforts in these categories (to name just a few):

- Compliance reports
- Attestations
- Certifications

Compliance programs and your adherence to them will help you implement excellent security at scale in AWS. This should also help you realize cost savings overall when it comes to your security implementation.

Amazon, especially once you are a customer, will communicate its security responsibilities, successes, failures, and overall efforts using the following means:

- Obtaining industry certifications
- Obtaining independent, third-party attestations
- Publishing security information white papers and web content
- Providing certificates, reports, and other documents to customers, sometimes under a nondisclosure agreement (NDA)

Amazon also provides the following to customers:

- Functionality through security features
- Compliance playbooks
- Mapping documents

AWS also offers a robust risk and compliance program that helps with the following:

- Risk management
- Control environments
- Information security

Amazon regularly scans all public-facing points for vulnerabilities. It even uses independent, third-party firms to perform threat assessments against its technologies and infrastructure. If you (as a customer) are interested in performing penetration (pen) testing against your resources, you may do so, but you must be careful to pen test only your resources. You are not permitted to perform penetration tests against other customers or AWS. So, for example, you can freely pen test one of your own EC2 servers, but you cannot penetration test the EC2 service itself.

Remember, as a customer of AWS, you must do the following:

- Engage in a robust security lifecycle approach that includes a review phase, a design phase, and phases of identification and verification. The identification phase should include external controls that are required to secure the customer resources.

- Understand the required compliance objectives.

- Establish a control environment.

- Understand the validation based on risk tolerances.

- Consistently verify the effectiveness of the security measures deployed.

A product to help you with compliance in AWS is AWS Artifact. This service offers on-demand access to AWS compliance reports and other documentation. AWS Artifact makes it easier for customers to understand the security and compliance posture of the AWS services they use, as well as to meet their own compliance requirements.

Fortunately, there are many other services to assist with governance and compliance in your AWS solutions, including the following:

- *CloudWatch*: This monitoring and observability service allows you to collect, analyze, and visualize data from various AWS resources and applications in real time. With features like customizable dashboards, alarms, and logs, CloudWatch enables you to gain insights into the performance, health, and operational efficiency of your AWS infrastructure, facilitating proactive management and optimization of resources.

- *CloudTrail*: This logging service records and monitors all API calls made on the AWS platform, offering a comprehensive audit trail of activities across an AWS account. By capturing information such as the identity of the caller, the time of the call, and the parameters used, CloudTrail aids in security analysis, resource change tracking, and compliance management by providing a detailed history of account activity and resource modifications.

■ *AWS Audit Manager:* This compliance management service automates the process of assessing and managing the compliance of AWS resources against industry standards and regulations. It enables users to streamline audit preparations, conduct risk assessments, and generate comprehensive reports, helping an organization maintain a secure and compliant environment by providing a centralized tool for tracking and managing compliance controls. Figure 8-3 shows AWS Audit Manager in the AWS Management Console.

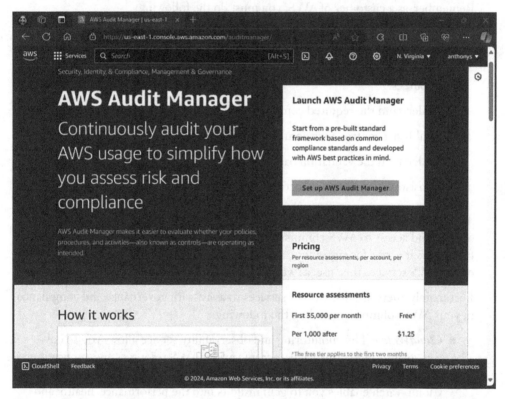

Figure 8-3   The AWS Audit Manager

■ *AWS Config:* This service allows you to assess, audit, and evaluate the configurations of your AWS resources over time. By providing a detailed inventory of resource configurations and recording configuration changes, AWS Config enables you to maintain compliance, troubleshoot issues, and gain insights into resource relationships and dependencies in your AWS environment.

For more information regarding AWS and security compliance, you can visit the AWS Compliance page at https://aws.amazon.com/compliance, which provides links to a wealth of valuable resources.

Exam Preparation Tasks

As mentioned in the section "How to Use This Book" in the Introduction, you have a few choices for exam preparation: the exercises here, Chapter 22, "Final Preparation," and the exam simulation questions in the Pearson Test Prep Software Online.

Review All Key Topics

Review the most important topics in this chapter, noted with the Key Topics icon in the outer margin of the page. Table 8-2 lists these key topics and the page number on which each is found.

Table 8-2   Key Topics for Chapter 8

Key Topic Element	Description	Page Number
List	Security features in AWS	106
List	Security services in AWS	106
Overview	Penetration testing	109

Define Key Terms

Define the following key terms from this chapter and check your answers in the Glossary:

confidentiality, integrity, availability, compliance, Amazon Inspector, AWS Security Hub, Amazon GuardDuty, AWS Shield, CloudWatch, CloudTrail, AWS Audit Manager, AWS Config

Q&A

The answers to these questions appear in Appendix A. For more practice with exam format questions, use the Pearson Test Prep Software Online.

1. Why might you turn to AWS Marketplace when working on your security infrastructure in AWS?

2. Name at least three services that you can use to secure your AWS environment.

This chapter covers the following subjects:

- **Identity and Access Management:** Where would your AWS architecture be if you didn't have the ability to secure it? It would be in a very, very bad place. IAM is a key ingredient for AWS security, and this section of the chapter ensures that you understand the components of IAM in AWS and how the parts work together to help secure your environment.

- **Best Practices with IAM:** While AWS makes IAM pretty simple, you should always follow the generally accepted best practices. This part of the chapter describes these best practices for you.

- **Other Access Management-Related AWS Services:** While IAM is the star of this chapter, there are many other important AWS services you need to be aware of around identity and access management.

CHAPTER 9

AWS Access Management

You need your users and your colleagues to be able to authenticate against AWS and then have their access strictly defined. AWS Identity and Access Management (IAM) is the primary tool for these responsibilities. This chapter takes a deep dive into IAM.

"Do I Know This Already?" Quiz

The "Do I Know This Already?" quiz allows you to assess whether you should read the entire chapter. Table 9-1 lists the major headings in this chapter and the "Do I Know This Already?" quiz questions covering the material in those sections so you can assess your knowledge of these specific areas. The answers to the "Do I Know This Already?" quiz questions appear in Appendix A, "Answers to the 'Do I Know This Already?' Quizzes and Q&A Sections."

Table 9-1 "Do I Know This Already?" Foundation Topics Section-to-Question Mapping

Foundation Topics Section	Questions
Identity and Access Management	1–2
Best Practices with IAM	3–4
Other Access Management-Related AWS Services	5–6

CAUTION The goal of self-assessment is to gauge your mastery of the topics in this chapter. If you do not know the answer to a question or are only partially sure of the answer, you should mark that question as wrong for purposes of the self-assessment. Giving yourself credit for an answer you correctly guess skews your self-assessment results and might provide you with a false sense of security.

1. IAM can permit access to accounts that have already been authenticated in another domain or application. What is this called?

    a. Proxy trust

    b. Role sharing

    c. Proxy

    d. Federation

2. What identity in IAM is very similar to a user account but has no login credentials associated with it?

   a. Group

   b. Role

   c. Proxy user

   d. Principal

3. Why might you create many different accounts for one of your AWS engineers?

   a. To follow the concept of least privilege

   b. To reduce the resources required by IAM

   c. To provide back doors into the system

   d. To ensure that you can log activity

4. In a high-security environment, what should you do with privileged user accounts?

   a. Store credentials in an S3 bucket

   b. Create roles that mimic the accounts

   c. Use MFA with these accounts

   d. Share the access keys with other accounts that require access

5. You would like to simplify account access for your IT team working in AWS. What service permits the creation of a single sign-on type of environment for your AWS workloads?

   a. Secret Manager

   b. IAM

   c. Systems Manager

   d. IAM Identity Center

6. You are building a large, scalable web-based application hosted in AWS. What service can help you with the storage of passwords required by this program and can provide automated rotation of secrets?

   a. IAM

   b. Secrets Manager

   c. Systems Manager

   d. IAM Identity Center

Foundation Topics

Identity and Access Management

When it comes to accessing your AWS account and working inside it, you need the *Identity and Access Management* (*IAM*) services of AWS. IAM allows you to grant access to other individuals for team management of the services. IAM permits extremely granular permissions. For example, you might grant someone read access to only a single bucket of objects in S3. Other features of IAM include the following:

- **Access from service to service in AWS:** For example, you can have an application running on an EC2 instance access an S3 bucket. As you will learn later in this chapter, roles are commonly used for such access.

- *Multifactor Authentication* (*MFA*): Access can be permitted using a password and a code from an approved device to greatly strengthen security. Figure 9-1 shows the configuration area for MFA in the IAM Management Console.

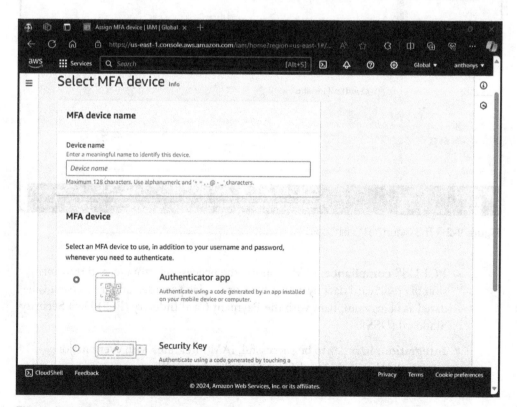

Figure 9-1 Configuring MFA for an Account

- **Identity federation:** With *federation*, users who have already authenticated with another service can gain temporary access to resources and services in your account.

- **Identity information for assurance:** CloudTrail can trace and log all SPI activity against every service and resource in your account. Figure 9-2 shows the CloudTrail Dashboard in AWS.

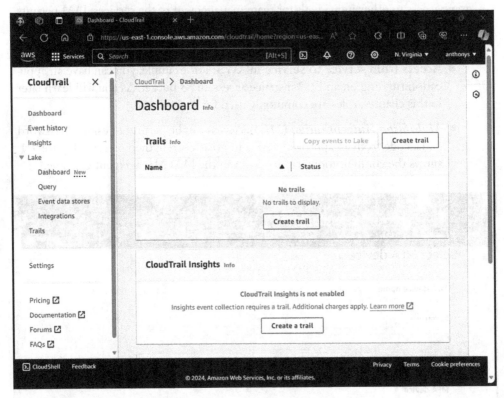

Figure 9-2   The CloudTrail Dashboard

- **PCI DSS compliance:** IAM supports the processing, storage, and transmission of credit card data by a merchant or service provider, and it has been validated as being compliant with the Payment Card Industry (PCI) Data Security Standard (DSS).

- **Integration:** In order to be successful, IAM integrates with every major service of AWS, including EC2, EFS, VPC, and RDS.

- **Always free:** While some services of AWS can be free for one year (using the Free Tier account), IAM services remain free for the life of your account.

- **Accessibility options:** You can access the components of IAM in a variety of ways, including using the AWS Management Console, AWS command-line tools, AWS SDKs, and the IAM HTTPS API.

It is critical that you understand the main identities you'll use in IAM. Please realize that there is much more to IAM than these identities, but at this point in your AWS education, you need to know the main foundational components.

Identities consist of the following:

- **AWS account root user:** This is the account you established when you signed up for AWS, and the username for this account is the email address used for signup. We discuss this account in greater detail later in the chapter.

- **Users:** A *user* is an entity that you create in AWS to represent a person or service that interacts with AWS. When you create an IAM user, you grant it permissions by making it a member of a group that has appropriate permissions policies attached (which is the recommended method) or by directly attaching policies to the user. You can also clone the permissions of an existing IAM user, which automatically makes the new user a member of the same groups and attaches all the same policies. Figure 9-3 shows a user in AWS.

- **Groups:** A *group* is a collection of IAM users. You can use a group to specify permissions for a collection of users, which can make those permissions easier to manage for those users.

- **Roles:** A *role* is similar to a user account, but it does not have any credentials (password or access keys) associated with it. One powerful use of roles in AWS is to use them to enable one service to securely access another service within AWS.

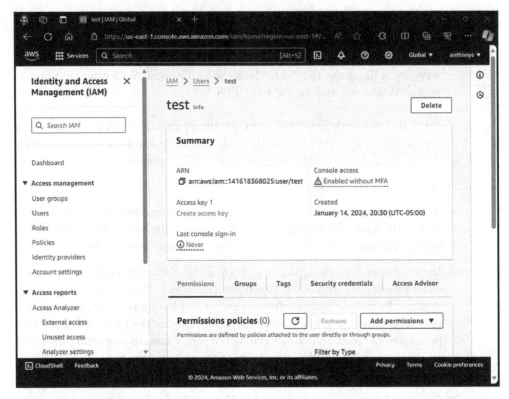

Figure 9-3 A User in AWS IAM

Best Practices with IAM

While IAM in AWS provides many exciting capabilities, its complexity can cause organizations to make fatal mistakes when working with the service. This section highlights some best practices that can save you from making such mistakes.

You should consider following most (if not all) of these recommendations:

- **Use the root account for as little as possible:** This is the account you established when you signed up for AWS. The root account is the all-powerful administrator account: It has the power to delete the whole AWS account! In addition to being able to delete (cancel) the AWS account itself, the root account might be needed to change account settings, restore IAM user permissions, activate IAM access to the Billing and Cost Management console, or sign up for AWS GovCloud. You should therefore use it as infrequently as possible. A best practice is to create AWS admin accounts of varying privilege levels and use them instead of using the root account.

- **Store root user access keys securely:** You have already seen how important it is to use the root user account for your AWS implementation infrequently. In addition, it is critical that you protect the access key ID and secret access key for this account. You must ensure that you have these credentials protected in your own infrastructure and treat them with the utmost care. In fact, in a high-security environment, you should consider not defining access keys for the root account. Instead, use the email address, a complex password, and physical multifactor authentication instead for the rare times this account must be used.

- **Create individual IAM users:** Because it is a best practice to use the root account for your AWS implementation infrequently, it is critical that you create additional user accounts, including one for yourself so that you are not left using the root account. In larger organizations, you will have a large team working on AWS. You must create multiple accounts for your staff to ensure that everyone is authenticating and being authorized for only those resources and permissions that are required for the members to do their jobs. You will most likely have at least one account in IAM for every person who requires administrative access.

- **Use groups to assign permissions to IAM users:** Even though it might seem silly, if you are the sole administrator of your AWS implementation, you will want to create a group and assign permissions to this group. Why? If you ever need to grow and hire another administrator, you can just add that user account to the group you created. You always want your AWS implementations to scale, and using groups helps ensure scalability. It should also be noted that applying permissions to groups instead of to individual user accounts will help eliminate assignment errors, as it minimizes the number of permissions you must grant.

- **Use AWS-defined policies for permissions:** Amazon was very kind in defining a ton of policies you can easily leverage when working with IAM. What's more, AWS maintains and updates these policies as it introduces new services and API operations. The policies that AWS has created are defined around the tasks you most commonly need to perform. They make up an excellent starting place for your own policies. You can copy a given policy and customize it to make it even more secure. Oftentimes, you will find that the default defined policies are too broad with access.

- **Grant the least privileges possible:** One reason you are likely to end up with many different accounts for yourself in AWS is that you always want to sign in with the account that provides the least privileges for what you are trying to accomplish. That way, if an attacker manages to capture your security credentials and begins acting as you in the AWS architecture, they can do a limited amount of damage. For example, if you need to simply monitor the files in AWS S3 buckets, you can use an account with only read permissions on these buckets. This would certainly limit the damage an attacker could carry out if they obtained your credentials.

- **Review IAM permissions:** You should not use a "set and forget" policy when it comes to your permissions in IAM. You should consistently review the permissions level assigned to ensure that you are following least privilege concepts and that you are still granting those permissions to the groups that require them. There is even a policy summary option within IAM to facilitate this.

- **Always configure a strong password policy for your users:** It is a sad fact of human nature: Your users will tend to be lazy about setting (and changing) their passwords. They will tend to use simple passwords that are easy for them to remember. Unfortunately, these simple passwords are also easy to crack. Improve your security by setting a strong password policy that your users must adhere to. Figure 9-4 shows the configuration of a password policy for user accounts in the IAM Management Console.

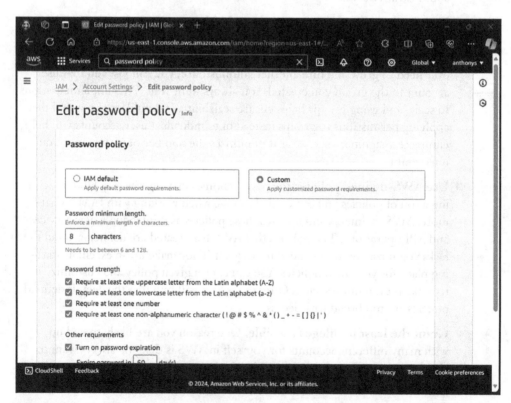

Figure 9-4   Configuring a Password Policy

- **Enable multifactor authentication for privileged user accounts:** Of course, you already know to use MFA for the seldom-used AWS root account, but you should also protect key admin accounts you have created in AWS. Using MFA ensures that the user knows something (like a password) and also possesses something (like a smartphone). With most AWS environments today, MFA is considered mandatory.

- **Use roles:** You should consider using roles in AWS when you have applications or services running on EC2 instances that need to access other services or resources.

- **Use roles to delegate permissions:** Roles can also be very valuable when you need to permit one AWS account to access resources in another AWS account. This is a much more secure option than providing the other AWS account with username and password information for your account.

- **Do not share access keys:** It might be tempting to share the access keys that permit programmatic access to a service or resource with another account that needs the same access. Resist this temptation. Remember that you can create a role that encompasses the required access.

- **Rotate credentials:** Be sure to change passwords and access keys regularly in AWS. The reason for this, of course, is that if these credentials are compromised, you will have minimized the damage that can be done when the stolen credentials no longer function.

- **Remove unnecessary credentials:** Because it is so easy to learn and test new features in AWS, it can get messy when you leave in place IAM components that are no longer needed. Be sure to routinely audit your resources for any "droppings" that are no longer needed. AWS even assists in this regard by structuring reports around credentials that have not been recently used.

- **Use policy conditions:** Always consider building conditions into your security policies. For example, access might have to come from a select range of IP addresses. Or MFA might be required. Or there might need to be time-of-day or day-of-week conditions.

- **Monitor, monitor, monitor:** AWS services provide the option for an intense amount of logging. Here are just some of the services where careful logging and analysis can dramatically improve security:

  - CloudFront
  - CloudTrail

■ CloudWatch

■ AWS Config

■ S3

Other Access Management-Related AWS Services

At this point in this text, I am sure you are not surprised to learn that there are plenty of services available in AWS to assist with identity and access management. Let's look at just some of them here:

■ *AWS IAM Identity Center*: This service was previously named AWS Single Sign-On, and so it isn't surprising that one of the main purposes of IAM Identity Center is single sign-on: You can use the service to connect your on-premises directory service to AWS so that your users can use a single set of sign-on credentials to operate within AWS. As you might guess, the IAM Identity Center offers its own directory service in case you want to transition to a fully cloud-based directory service.

■ *AWS Secrets Manager*: This service does just what is sounds like it might do: It manages your secrets (passwords). Secrets Manager securely stores and manages sensitive information such as API keys, database passwords, and other credentials used by applications. With Secrets Manager, you can centralize and rotate these secrets automatically. This can help to enhance security by reducing the risk associated with long-lived credentials. Figure 9-5 shows the AWS Secrets Manager.

■ *AWS Systems Manager*: This is a comprehensive management service that facilitates the automation and control of operational tasks across an AWS environment. This service provides a unified user interface that allows you to view and manage operational data from multiple AWS services. With AWS Systems Manager, you can automate common and repetitive tasks, such as software patching, configuration management, and instance inventory tracking. It also offers features like Run Command, which allows users to execute commands on instances remotely, and State Manager, which makes it possible to define and enforce desired system configurations.

You are probably seeing another theme regarding AWS at this point: If there is a need for a feature in your on-premises environment, AWS most likely offers it in the cloud, pulling more and more customers into the cloud giant's offerings.

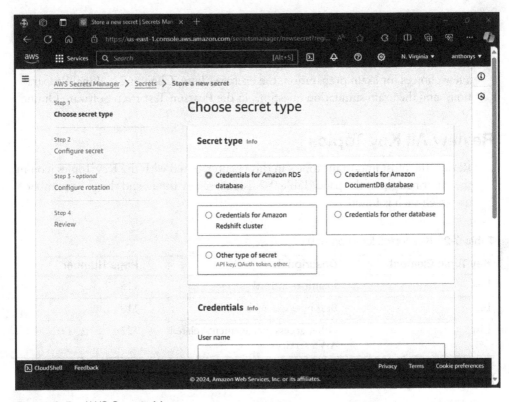

Figure 9-5   AWS Secrets Manager

Exam Preparation Tasks

As mentioned in the section "How to Use This Book" in the Introduction, you have a few choices for exam preparation: the exercises here, Chapter 22, "Final Preparation," and the exam simulation questions in the Pearson Test Prep Software Online.

Review All Key Topics

Review the most important topics in this chapter, noted with the Key Topics icon in the outer margin of the page. Table 9-2 lists these key topics and the page number on which each is found.

Table 9-2 Key Topics for Chapter 9

Key Topic Element	Description	Page Number
List	Identities in IAM	115
List	Best practices with IAM	118
List	Other access management-related AWS services	122

Define Key Terms

Define the following key terms from this chapter and check your answers in the Glossary:

Identity and Access Management (IAM), multifactor authentication (MFA), federation, user, group, role, AWS IAM Identity Center, AWS Secrets Manager, AWS Systems Manager

Q&A

The answers to these questions appear in Appendix A. For more practice with exam format questions, use the Pearson Test Prep Software Online.

1. What do you often use when you need to provide access from an application running on an EC2 instance to other resources within AWS?

2. What account is created when you sign up for AWS but should be used very sparingly after that point?

This chapter covers the following subjects:

- **Some AWS Security Features:** This section of the chapter covers several critical tools for securing AWS resources.

- **Tools for Security Support:** This section of the chapter details various important tools designed for security support in AWS.

- **Additional Security Support Resources:** This section of the chapter provides even more security support resource ideas that are available to you as a potential or existing AWS customer.

CHAPTER 10

Components and Resources for Security

AWS makes possible greater security than ever before in your infrastructure and architectures. In order to achieve the highest levels of security and the lowest levels of risk, you should be ready to take advantage of the tremendous resources AWS makes available for security support. This chapter gives you the information you need to do this.

"Do I Know This Already?" Quiz

The "Do I Know This Already?" quiz allows you to assess whether you should read the entire chapter. Table 10-1 lists the major headings in this chapter and the "Do I Know This Already?" quiz questions covering the material in those sections so you can assess your knowledge of these specific areas. The answers to the "Do I Know This Already?" quiz questions appear in Appendix A, "Answers to the 'Do I Know This Already?' Quizzes and Q&A Sections."

Table 10-1 "Do I Know This Already?" Foundation Topics Section-to-Question Mapping

Foundation Topics Section	Questions
Some AWS Security Features	1–2
Tools for Security Support	3–4
Additional Security Support Resources	5–6

CAUTION The goal of self-assessment is to gauge your mastery of the topics in this chapter. If you do not know the answer to a question or are only partially sure of the answer, you should mark that question as wrong for purposes of the self-assessment. Giving yourself credit for an answer you correctly guess skews your self-assessment results and might provide you with a false sense of security.

1. Where does AWS apply a security group in your cloud infrastructure?

    a. Your subnet

    b. Your elastic IP address

c. Your virtual network interface card

d. Your RDS database

2. Where does AWS apply a network ACL in your cloud infrastructure?

a. Your subnet

b. Your elastic IP address

c. Your virtual network interface card

d. Your RDS database

3. What tool should you use if you are interested in reading the latest information about security enhancements to AWS?

a. Knowledge Center

b. Security Blog

c. Trusted Advisor

d. CloudWatch

4. Which of the following tools provides real-time monitoring?

a. Security Center

b. Security Blog

c. Knowledge Center

d. Cognito

5. What acts like your own cloud expert in AWS, providing recommendations for greater security based on your existing configurations?

a. Trusted Advisor

b. Artifact

c. EC2

d. Cognito

6. Which statement about Trusted Advisor is correct?

a. There are no cost optimization checks.

b. The tool is not available with a Free Tier account.

c. Only the root account has Trusted Advisor access.

d. Not all checks are available with a Free Tier account.

Foundation Topics

Some AWS Security Features

I want to be perfectly clear: There are currently a *ton* of security services and tools in the AWS portfolio of products. In this section of the chapter, we will explore two that are fundamental to the operation of AWS: security groups and network access control lists (NACLs). We will also examine a third tool that is considered critical for organizations that are making web services and applications available via AWS: the Web Application Firewall (WAF) service.

Security Groups

Because security of your resources in the cloud is a prime concern for both you and Amazon, it is no big surprise that AWS provides built-in firewalls with your compute resources. These *security groups* help you easily control the accessibility of your EC2 virtual machine resources. Figure 10-1 shows an example of a security group assigned to a virtual network interface card in AWS.

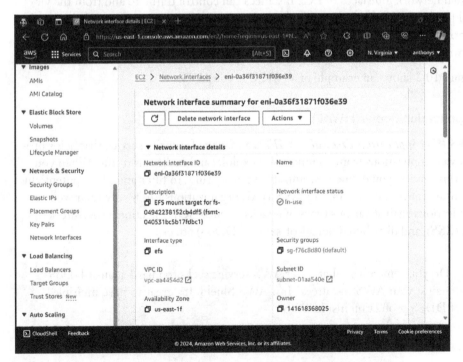

Figure 10-1   A Security Group Assigned to a virtual network interface card

Perhaps you have a web tier in your AWS architecture. You can configure the security group for this tier to permit HTTP and HTTPS traffic from customers using the web tier, and at the same time you can permit your team of support engineers to access the web tier using SSH and RDP. All other protocol attempts at accessing the web tier are denied by the security group.

You might wonder where security group are applied in AWS. AWS applies a security group by attaching it to the virtual network interface card (vNIC) of an EC2 virtual machine. This allows the security group to easily control (firewall) the traffic entering and exiting the EC2 instances.

Network ACLs (NACLs)

Network access control lists (NACLs) allow you to control access to your Virtual Private Cloud (VPC) subnets. NACLs are stateless constructs, which means you must configure inbound and outbound rules, as there is no automatic recognition of state with traffic flows, and there are no automated access entries.

Students are often puzzled about why these "firewalls" exist when there are already security groups inside AWS. Remember that security groups that are attached to virtual network interfaces of EC2 instances can control traffic to and from the virtual machines. NACLs are attached to subnets in a VPC to control traffic into and out of the entire subnet. Having multiple levels of built-in firewalls within the AWS network infrastructure permits fine-grained control of security.

Figure 10-2 shows an example of a NACL inside AWS.

Web Application Firewall (WAF)

AWS *Web Application Firewall (WAF)* is a managed security service that helps protect web applications from common web exploits and malicious traffic. When you use this service, you define customizable security rules to filter and block potentially harmful requests. By leveraging AWS WAF, organizations can fortify their web applications against various types of attacks, such as SQL injection, cross-site scripting (XSS), and distributed denial-of-service (DDoS) attacks.

NOTE Do you remember what other AWS service seeks to guard against DDoS attacks against your AWS resources? It is AWS Shield. It's great to have multiple levels of DDoS protection inside AWS.

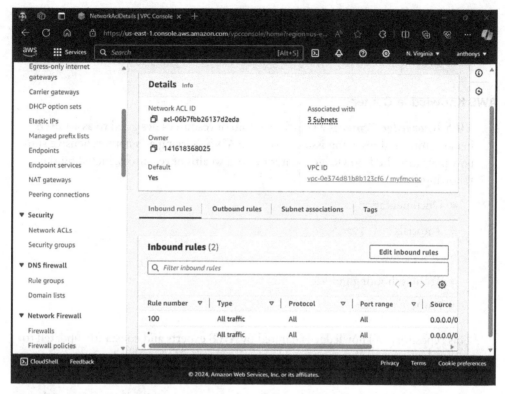

Figure 10-2   A NACL in AWS

AWS WAF also offers the following benefits and capabilities:

- **Flexibility:** You have a lot of flexibility when you are creating rules. Users can create rules based on IP addresses, HTTP headers, URI strings, and other customizable conditions to precisely control which traffic is allowed or blocked. This adaptability makes it possible to tailor security policies to the specific needs of different applications, ensuring a fine-grained level of protection.

- **Integration:** AWS WAF integrates seamlessly with other AWS services, allowing you to combine it with services like AWS CloudFront, Amazon API Gateway, or Application Load Balancer.

- **Monitoring:** AWS gives you actionable insights and real-time monitoring capabilities. Thanks to WAF, you can gain visibility into your web traffic, monitor the effectiveness of security rules, and receive detailed logs and metrics.

Tools for Security Support

When you have a topic as critical as security, you need a wealth of tools to assist you. With AWS, that is exactly what you get. Let's look at some of them.

AWS Knowledge Center

AWS Knowledge Center is a centralized hub of resources designed to assist users in navigating and resolving issues related to AWS. Serving as a comprehensive support platform, the Knowledge Center offers a wealth of resources, including the following:

- Documentation
- Tutorials
- Best practices
- Troubleshooting guides
- FAQs

This repository of knowledge is curated by AWS experts and constantly updated to reflect the latest developments and improvements in AWS technologies to ensure that you have access to accurate and timely information.

Like AWS itself, AWS Knowledge Center features a user-friendly interface and search functionality. Whether users are seeking guidance on specific AWS services, troubleshooting technical issues, or exploring best practices for implementation, the Knowledge Center provides a structured and easily accessible resource to enhance understanding and proficiency in utilizing AWS.

AWS Security Center

AWS Security Center is a centralized hub within the AWS console that is dedicated to providing comprehensive insights and tools to enhance the security of your AWS environments. It serves as a command center for security operations, offering a unified dashboard that consolidates security-related information and resources. This powerful tool includes these features:

- **Automated tools:** Users can leverage automated tools for security assessment and compliance monitoring.
- **Posture improvement:** The Security Center provides a holistic view of security-related alerts, findings, and compliance status. You can streamline your

approach to managing and improving the security posture of your AWS workloads by using the wealth of information discovered by Security Center.

- **Real-time monitoring:** As with many of the other AWS security tools, with the Security Center, you have the luxury of real-time monitoring of security events in your AWS solutions.

The AWS Security Center can play a crucial role in helping you maintain a robust and secure cloud environment on AWS.

AWS Security Blog

The *AWS Security Blog* is a dedicated platform that provides valuable insights, best practices, and updates on security within the AWS ecosystem. Its goal is to allow AWS customers to enhance their understanding of security measures and practices specific to AWS Cloud services. These are some of the topics covered:

- Security architecture
- Compliance
- Threat detection
- Identity and access management
- Encryption
- Security automation

One of the many great things about the AWS Security Blog is its commitment to staying current with the ever-evolving landscape of cybersecurity. The blog regularly publishes articles authored by AWS security experts, detailing real-world scenarios, case studies, and practical tips to address emerging security challenges.

Additional Security Support Resources

Believe it or not, there are even more security support resources than we have mentioned thus far in the chapter. This section explores more of them.

AWS Trusted Advisor

Wouldn't it be nice if you had your own cloud expert working for you at AWS? This is the concept behind the *Trusted Advisor* tool. This management tool ensures that you are following security best practices and helps you close security gaps. But security is not the only expertise of Trusted Advisor. The tool also analyzes your

AWS usage and makes recommendations in other categories as well, including the following:

- Cost optimization
- Performance
- Fault tolerance
- Service limits
- Operational excellence

NOTE Not all of the possible Trusted Advisor checks are available without an additional payment. The Free Tier account provides only limited (yet still valuable) access to the various checks.

Lab: Using the Trusted Advisor

This lab walks you through the steps of using the Trusted Advisor to learn about security issues and improvements you might be able to make to enhance your AWS security.

NOTE This lab assumes that you have an AWS account. If you do not, go back to Chapter 6, "Creating and Using an AWS Free Tier Account," and find the lab that walks you through the creation of an AWS Free Tier account.

Follow these steps to use Trusted Advisor:

Step 1. In the AWS Management Console, search for **Trusted Advisor**. Select the **Trusted Advisor** link that appears.

Step 2. In the dashboard on the left side of the page, click **Security**.

Step 3. Note the security checks that have been performed and the results. Also note the other security checks that may be purchased. Figure 10-3 shows an example of these security checks.

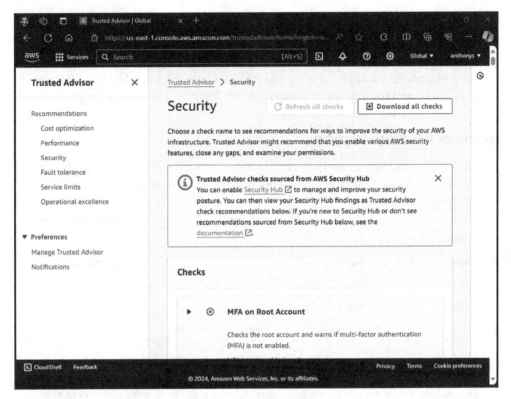

Figure 10-3 Using the Trusted Advisor for Security Guidance

AWS Marketplace

What if you have security needs that AWS cannot address? One possibility is to turn to the *AWS Marketplace*. This is an online platform that facilitates the discovery, procurement, and deployment of a wide array of software, solutions, and services.

The AWS Marketplace is a digital marketplace where you can explore, purchase, and instantly deploy third-party applications that run on the AWS Cloud infrastructure. With a diverse selection of products spanning categories such as machine learning, security, analytics, and more, the AWS Marketplace provides users with a convenient and scalable way to find and integrate solutions into their AWS environments, streamlining the process of software acquisition and enabling rapid innovation in the cloud.

Exam Preparation Tasks

As mentioned in the section "How to Use This Book" in the Introduction, you have a few choices for exam preparation: the exercises here, Chapter 22, "Final Preparation," and the exam simulation questions in the Pearson Test Prep Software Online.

Review All Key Topics

Review the most important topics in this chapter, noted with the Key Topics icon in the outer margin of the page. Table 10-2 lists these key topics and the page number on which each is found.

Table 10-2   Key Topics for Chapter 10

Key Topic Element	Description	Page Number
Overview	Security groups	129
Overview	Network access control lists (NACLs)	130
Lab	Using the AWS Trusted Advisor	134

Define Key Terms

Define the following key terms from this chapter and check your answers in the Glossary:

security group, network access control list (NACL), Web Application Firewall (WAF), AWS Knowledge Center, AWS Security Center, AWS Security Blog, Trusted Advisor, AWS Marketplace

Q&A

The answers to these questions appear in Appendix A. For more practice with exam format questions, use the Pearson Test Prep Software Online.

1. What resource should you use if you are interested in browsing third-party security products that you can integrate into your AWS solutions?

2. What AWS security component acts as a firewall for subnets in a virtual private cloud?

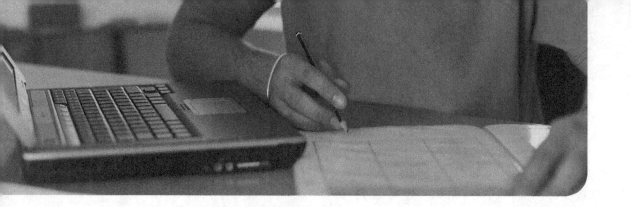

This chapter covers the following subjects:

- **Automation:** Automation is a key driver in the adoption of cloud technologies. This section of the chapter discusses many of the technologies of AWS and the approaches taken to automation.

- **Orchestration:** Orchestration takes automation even further, permitting the coordination and scheduling of many different automation events. This part of the chapter walks you through some of the orchestration that is possible with AWS.

- **Management Options:** There are many ways to manage AWS effectively. This section of the chapter lays them out for you in detail.

- **Deployment and Connectivity Options:** In this section of the chapter, you will learn about common cloud deployment models and specific methods of connecting to the AWS Cloud.

CHAPTER 11

Methods of Deploying and Operating in AWS

This chapter focuses on getting things done in AWS in the most efficient and cost-effective manner. Using automation and orchestration can also dramatically improve performance and security by reducing errors and improving consistency in configurations. This chapter ensures that you know details about the many methods you can use to manage AWS and to deploy and connect to your AWS Cloud solution.

"Do I Know This Already?" Quiz

The "Do I Know This Already?" quiz allows you to assess whether you should read the entire chapter. Table 11-1 lists the major headings in this chapter and the "Do I Know This Already?" quiz questions covering the material in those sections so you can assess your knowledge of these specific areas. The answers to the "Do I Know This Already?" quiz questions appear in Appendix A, "Answers to the 'Do I Know This Already?' Quizzes and Q&A Sections."

Table 11-1 "Do I Know This Already?" Foundation Topics Section-to-Question Mapping

Foundation Topics Section	Questions
Automation	1–2
Orchestration	3–4
Management Options	5–6
Deployment and Connectivity Options	7–8

CAUTION The goal of self-assessment is to gauge your mastery of the topics in this chapter. If you do not know the answer to a question or are only partially sure of the answer, you should mark that question as wrong for purposes of the self-assessment. Giving yourself credit for an answer you correctly guess skews your self-assessment results and might provide you with a false sense of security.

1. Why is automation so easily accommodated in AWS?

   a. Because CloudTrail provides automation templates automatically for you

   b. Because multiple regions facilitate code deployment

   c. Because physical systems host the EC2 instances you work with daily

   d. Because all actions can be implemented through API calls

2. Which of the following is not considered a benefit of automation?

   a. Reduction in required security measures

   b. Lowered operating costs

   c. Simpler and faster code deployment

   d. Reduction in the potential for errors

3. What is a tool that can assist with orchestration in your AWS environment?

   a. Kinesis

   b. CloudWatch

   c. CloudTrail

   d. CloudFormation

4. Which is not considered a benefit of orchestration?

   a. Reduction in overall IT costs

   b. Elimination of the need for experimentation

   c. Improved delivery times

   d. Reduced friction between different teams

5. CloudWatch falls into which category of management options?

   a. Provisioning

   b. Managed services for configuration

   c. Operations management

   d. Monitoring and logging

6. What is the fully managed configuration management service in AWS?

   a. CloudTrail

   b. OpsWorks

   c. CloudFormation

   d. CloudWatch

7. What deployment model is often the first step for an organization that is beginning to adopt cloud technologies?

    a. Cloud

    b. On premises

    c. Hybrid

    d. Green

8. What connectivity option to AWS would you recommend if your organization wants to enhance the security of a public Internet connection to its AWS Cloud?

    a. AWS VPN

    b. Public Internet

    c. AWS Direct Connect

    d. AWS CloudTrail

Foundation Topics

Automation

Automation is one of the reasons many technical engineers love cloud technologies. With AWS, there is a huge emphasis on using API calls to configure the architecture. This permits automation of everything associated with AWS.

Automation incorporates elements and benefits such as the following:

- Configuration templates

- Code deployment automation

- Self-healing infrastructures

- Reduction in the need for manual interventions

- Reduction in the potential for errors

- Lowered operating costs for managed service providers (MSPs)

For many organizations relying on AWS today, approaching any challenge for their IT organization begins with the question "How can we automate the solution?" Let's look at a specific case. Perhaps your organization's corporate policy says you cannot use any of the default resources created for you in AWS. For example, you must create a completely unique VPC with your own unique security constraints. Sure, you could go into the Management Console and do lots of potentially error-prone mouse clicking, but things are much easier (and more accurate) when you can automate such actions with a script.

Automation tends to play a huge role in a number of areas is AWS. Here are just a few:

- Backup generation and retention

- Security compliance

- Code deployment

- AWS infrastructure changes

Because AWS takes an API-centric approach, there is really nothing you cannot automate. The short list given here just highlights areas where automation is frequently in use by AWS customers.

Orchestration

A huge point of confusion for many engineers who are new to AWS and cloud technology is understanding the differences between cloud automation and cloud *orchestration*. One of the reasons is related to the fact that the two terms are often used interchangeably, which is often incorrect. The differences between these concepts highlight a key challenge for teams looking to improve IT processes.

Recall that *automation* involves accomplishing a task or function without human intervention. *Orchestration*, on the other hand, is the process of arranging and coordination of automated tasks, ultimately resulting in a consolidated process or workflow. Automation and orchestration go hand in hand, but note that they are technically different concepts.

With AWS, you are encouraged to create standard processes to spin up full environments to host new and exciting applications. You accomplish this by orchestrating many automated tasks, such as the following:

- Automating new instances with Auto Scaling

- Load balancing with automated ELB configurations

- Deploying automation by using a tool like CodeDeploy in AWS (Figure 11-1 shows the Getting Started page of CodeDeploy in the AWS Management Console.)

- Using Puppet scripts to automate the configuration of the operating system

While individually the tasks in the preceding list might be fairly simple to automate with the robust tools and capabilities of AWS, taken together, these tasks can be very tricky to orchestrate. After all, these activities must occur in a particular order, under certain security groups/tools, and must be given roles and granted permissions. In other words, engineers must complete hundreds of manual tasks to deliver the new environment, even when the building blocks of that environment are automated. This is where orchestration is key.

Cloud orchestration tools, whether native to the IaaS (infrastructure as a service) platform or third-party software tools, enumerate the resources, instance types, IAM roles, and other resources required. Orchestration can also enumerate the configuration of these resources and the interconnections between them.

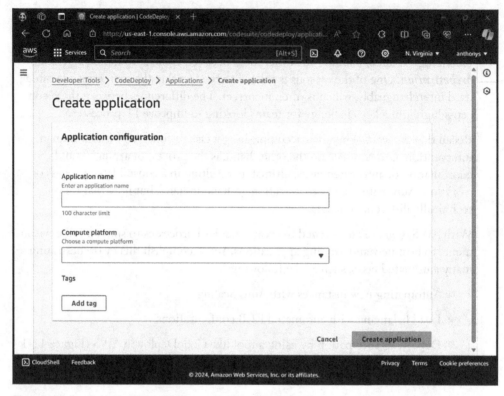

Figure 11-1   CodeDeploy in AWS

AWS engineers can use tools like CloudFormation to create declarative templates that orchestrate these processes into a single workflow so that the "new environment" workflow previously described becomes a single API call.

Well-orchestrated IT processes enable and empower continuous integration and continuous delivery, uniting teams in the creation of a set of templates that meet developer requirements. Such templates are in many ways living documents that embody the celebrated and popular DevOps philosophy.

The benefits of orchestration tools far outweigh any potential drawbacks. For organizations today, they celebrate advantages such as the following:

- Reduced overall IT costs

- Gained time for new or experimental projects

- Improved delivery times to customers

- Reduced friction between system and development teams

Management Options

There is an incredibly impressive range of options for managing AWS. These tools fall into the following subcategories:

- **Provisioning:** CloudFormation is the primary management service in the provisioning category. It provides a common language for describing and provisioning all the infrastructure resources in a cloud environment. Cloud-Formation allows you to use a simple text file to model and provision all the resources needed for your applications across all regions and accounts—and it can accomplish this in an automated and secure manner. Once everything is modeled in CloudFormation, your text file serves as the single "source of truth" regarding the resources of your cloud environment. It is recommended that you also create a collection of approved CloudFormation files in an AWS Service Catalog to allow your organization to deploy only approved and compliant resources.

- **Operations management:** AWS provides a set of services for systems and operations management that allows you to control your infrastructure resources with proper governance and compliance. You can use AWS Systems Manager to quickly view and monitor all your resources and automate common operational tasks, such as patching and state management. Systems Manager provides a unified user interface that enables you to easily manage your cloud operations activities in one place. You can also use CloudTrail for logging user activities in your organization and AWS Config for inventorying all configurations across your resources.

- **Monitoring and logging:** CloudWatch is the primary monitoring service for AWS Cloud resources and the applications you run on AWS. You can use CloudWatch to collect and track metrics, collect and monitor log files, set alarms, and automatically react to changes in your AWS resources. Cloud-Watch can monitor AWS resources such as EC2 instances, DynamoDB tables, and RDS database instances, as well as any custom metrics or log files generated by your applications. CloudWatch also provides a stream of events that describe changes to your AWS resources that you can use to react to changes in your applications.

- **Managed services for configuration:** The main tool in this area is AWS OpsWorks. OpsWorks is a fully managed configuration management service that hosts and scales Chef Automate and Puppet Enterprise servers. OpsWorks eliminates the need to install and operate your own configuration management systems or worry about scaling its infrastructure. It also works seamlessly with your existing Chef and Puppet tools. OpsWorks can automatically patch, update, and back up your Chef and Puppet servers as well as maintain their availability. OpsWorks is an excellent choice if you are an existing user of Chef or Puppet. Figure 11-2 shows OpsWorks in AWS.

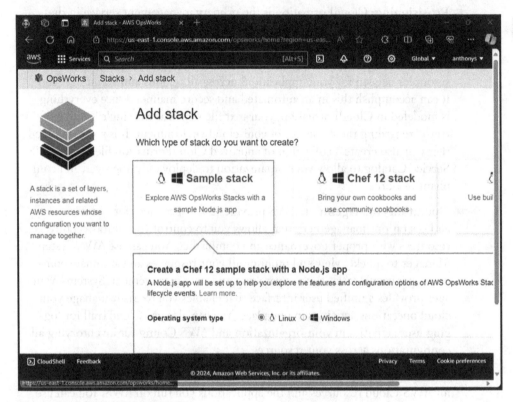

Figure 11-2 OpsWorks in AWS

Remember that to access your AWS resources from a management perspective, you also have many options. Here are the main options you should be aware of:

- **The AWS Management Console:** This is a simple, easy-to-use web-based interface that allows you to easily manage and control your AWS resources. It is the tool you see screen captured throughout this text. The Management Console gives you a centralized platform for tasks such as provisioning and monitoring services, configuring security settings, and accessing various management tools.

- **The AWS command-line interface (CLI):** This is a powerful and flexible tool that enables you to interact with and manage AWS resources directly from the command line. The CLI can help you streamline tasks such as resource provisioning, configuration, and automation tasks. Figure 11-3 shows the AWS CLI installed on my local Windows machine and being accessed from my local command prompt.

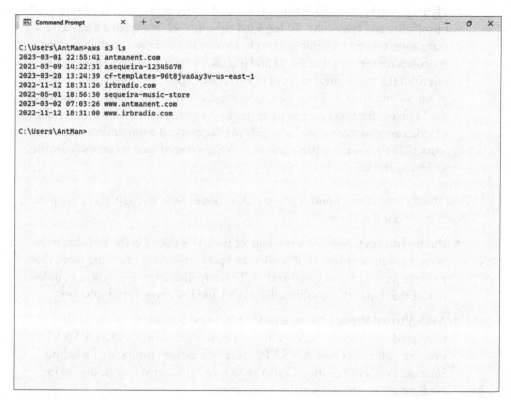

Figure 11-3   The AWS CLI

- **Programmatic access using software development kits (SDKs) and application programming interfaces (APIs):** You can use APIs and SDKs to automate the management of AWS services, which means your developers and administrators can script and code interactions with cloud resources for efficient operations and maintenance.

Deployment and Connectivity Options

What are the options for deployment of your IT solutions in the modern era? There are three you should know as an AWS Cloud practitioner:

- **On premises:** In this model, you are keeping everything fully under the control of your organization. You can consider this the "traditional" approach to IT, where all of the hardware and software you need to run your tech are kept within facilities that your company owns. Notice that if everyone followed this model today, there would be no cloud. Gulp.

- **Cloud:** With the cloud model, you take full advantage of a technology like AWS.

- **Hybrid:** A hybrid model features the use of both on-premises hardware and/ or software and the cloud. Taking a hybrid approach is a typical first step for companies today. With this approach, an organization can use the on-premises approach for services it excels at and use the cloud for services that can benefit from the many advantages of cloud. For example, perhaps your company produces and creates videos for education. Let's say your company handles all the IT needs for this business perfectly fine on premises, with the expectation of video archive storage and a worldwide, high-speed content distribution network (CDN). Your company can use AWS (or one of its competitors) for the archiving and CDN.

What about connectivity options to the AWS Cloud? Sure enough, there are plenty, including options like these:

- **Public Internet:** A major advantage of the AWS Cloud is the fact that your resources can be accessed (if needed and permitted) using nothing more than a simple public Internet connection. This anytime, anywhere access is, in fact, one of the things that qualifies the AWS Cloud as a true cloud solution.

- **AWS Virtual Private Network (VPN):** An organization can establish encrypted connections between its on-premises networks and its AWS VPCs over the public Internet. AWS VPN supports various protocols, including Internet Protocol Security (IPsec) and OpenVPN, providing flexibility in configuring secure and scalable connections.

- **AWS Direct Connect:** AWS Direct Connect gives you your own private connection to the AWS Cloud. We cover this option in detail in Chapter 12, "The AWS Global Infrastructure."

Exam Preparation Tasks

As mentioned in the section "How to Use This Book" in the Introduction, you have a few choices for exam preparation: the exercises here, Chapter 22, "Final Preparation," and the exam simulation questions in the Pearson Test Prep Software Online.

Review All Key Topics

Review the most important topics in this chapter, noted with the Key Topics icon in the outer margin of the page. Table 11-2 lists these key topics and the page number on which each is found.

Table 11-2 Key Topics for Chapter 11

Key Topic Element	Description	Page Number
List	Automation elements	142
List	Common areas that use automation	142
List	Benefits of orchestration	144
List	Management access options in AWS	145

Define Key Terms

Define the following key terms from this chapter and check your answers in the Glossary:

automation, orchestration

Q&A

The answers to these questions appear in Appendix A. For more practice with exam format questions, use the Pearson Test Prep Software Online.

1. Name at least two areas where automation is often used in AWS.

2. Name at least two management access options for AWS.

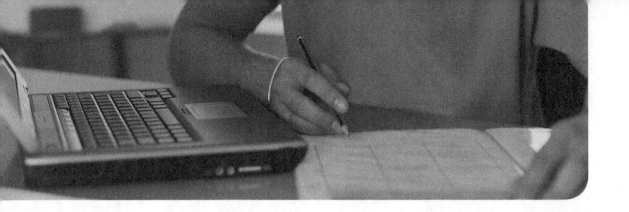

This chapter covers the following subjects:

■ **Regions:** This section describes the concept of Regions and what they contain. Although Regions are constantly being added, this section gives you a look at the current Regions as of this writing and the naming conventions used for them.

■ **Availability Zones:** This section provides valuable information about the Availability Zones that exist within Regions. These AWS global infrastructure components are critical for high-availability designs.

■ **Other Global Infrastructure Components:** This section provides details on other components found in the AWS global infrastructure, including topics like edge locations, CloudFront, and Global Accelerator.

CHAPTER 12

The AWS Global Infrastructure

AWS is a high-tech, high-speed global infrastructure of advanced data centers around the globe. This chapter describes how the AWS global infrastructure is organized and how you can connect to it.

"Do I Know This Already?" Quiz

The "Do I Know This Already?" quiz allows you to assess whether you should read the entire chapter. Table 12-1 lists the major headings in this chapter and the "Do I Know This Already?" quiz questions covering the material in those sections so you can assess your knowledge of these specific areas. The answers to the "Do I Know This Already?" quiz questions appear in Appendix A, "Answers to the 'Do I Know This Already?' Quizzes and Q&A Sections."

Table 12-1 "Do I Know This Already?" Foundation Topics Section-to-Question Mapping

Foundation Topics Section	Questions
Regions	1–3
Availability Zones	4–6
Other Global Infrastructure Components	7–9

CAUTION   The goal of self-assessment is to gauge your mastery of the topics in this chapter. If you do not know the answer to a question or are only partially sure of the answer, you should mark that question as wrong for purposes of the self-assessment. Giving yourself credit for an answer you correctly guess skews your self-assessment results and might provide you with a false sense of security.

1. How many Availability Zones (AZs) are located in each Region in the AWS global infrastructure?

   a. At least two

   b. One

   c. Two

   d. Three

2. What is an Edge Location used for in an AWS Region?

   a. CloudFormation

   b. RDS

   c. S3

   d. CloudFront

3. Which statement regarding Regions in AWS is not correct?

   a. Regions in North America rely on the presence of the other North American Regions.

   b. Regions are connected to other Regions with fast connections.

   c. Edge Locations exist inside Regions.

   d. Availability Zones exist inside Regions.

4. How many discrete data centers are located in an AZ in the AWS global infrastructure?

   a. At least one

   b. At least two

   c. At least three

   d. At least four

5. How does Amazon design each AZ in the AWS global infrastructure?

   a. To be located in the largest city in a Region

   b. To exist outside a Region

   c. As an independent failure domain

   d. As being dependent on at least one other AZ

6. How is a typical AZ given power in the AWS global infrastructure?

   a. Via different grids from independent utilities

   b. From generators powered by Amazon

   c. From a single grid from the highest-performance utility

   d. From a shared public power station

7. What component allows you to connect privately from your on-premises datacenter to the Virtual Private Cloud (VPC) services you need, bypassing the public Internet?

   a. VPC endpoint

   b. Direct Connect

   c. VPN

   d. CloudFront

8. What do you use if you have multiple VPCs in AWS and you need to communicate between them?

   a. Gateway endpoint

   b. VPC peering

   c. Direct Connect

   d. ClassicLink

9. What technology is an attempt by AWS to place compute, storage, database, and other key service resources closer to large population and industry centers around the world?

   a. Local Zone

   b. CloudFront

   c. Global Accelerator

   d. Gateway Endpoints

Foundation Topics

Regions

AWS serves over a million active customers in more than 245 countries and territories. Amazon is steadily expanding its global infrastructure to help customers achieve lower latency and higher throughput and to ensure that their data resides only in the Region they specify.

Amazon builds the AWS Cloud infrastructure around *Regions* and *Availability Zones (AZs)*. A Region is a physical location in the world where there are multiple AZs. Note that a Region, by design, must have at least two or more AZs—and never just one. At the time of this writing, there are 32 Regions around the world and 102 AZs. Note that these numbers are now increasing at a faster rate than ever before.

Figure 12-1 shows the current Regions around the world at the time of this writing.

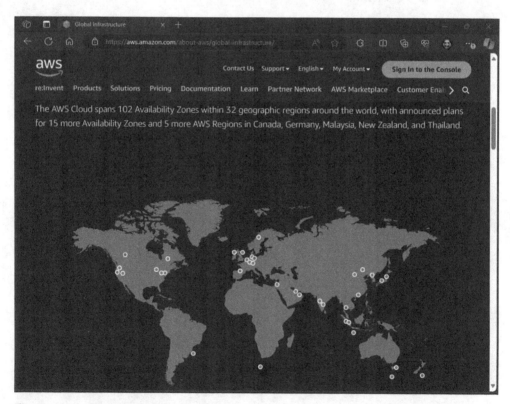

Figure 12-1 The AWS Global Infrastructure

Each Amazon Region is designed to be completely isolated from the other Amazon Regions. This isolation achieves the highest possible fault tolerance and stability. While each AZ is isolated from a fault tolerance perspective, Amazon connects the AZs within a Region through low-latency links.

To give you a sense for Regions in AWS, examine the details for some of the North American Regions:

- **US East (Northern Virginia) Region:** 6 AZs, launched in 2006

- **US East (Ohio) Region:** 3 AZs, launched in 2016

- **US West (Oregon) Region:** 4 AZs, launched in 2011

- **US West (Northern California) Region:** 3 AZs, launched in 2009

- **AWS GovCloud (US-West) Region:** 3 AZs, launched in 2011

- **AWS GovCloud (US-East) Region:** 3 AZs, launched in 2018

- **Canada (Central) Region:** 3 AZs, launched in 2016

When you reference Regions in your AWS code or at the CLI, you use standardized names created by Amazon for the various Regions. Table 12-2 lists just some of the AWS Regions and their official, standardized AWS names that you need to use when referencing them.

Table 12-2 Some AWS Regions and Their Standard Names

Region	Name
US West (Oregon) Region	us-west-2
US West (N. California) Region	us-west-1
US East (Ohio) Region	us-east-2
US East (N. Virginia) Region	us-east-1
Asia Pacific (Mumbai) Region	ap-south-1
Asia Pacific (Seoul) Region	ap-northeast-2
Asia Pacific (Singapore) Region	ap-southeast-1
Asia Pacific (Sydney) Region	ap-southeast-2
Asia Pacific (Tokyo) Region	ap-northeast-1
Canada (Central) Region	ca-central-1

Region	Name
China (Beijing) Region	cn-north-1
EU (Frankfurt) Region	eu-central-1
EU (Ireland) Region	eu-west-1
EU (London) Region	eu-west-2
EU (Paris) Region	eu-west-3
South America (São Paulo) Region	sa-east-1
AWS GovCloud (US)	us-gov-west-1

The AWS infrastructure also hosts AWS Edge Locations. AWS CloudFront uses these locations to deliver content at low latency to local clients requesting the data. There are many Edge Locations in North America; in fact, there are too many to list here.

Availability Zones

Be sure to remember these facts regarding Availability Zones:

- An AZ consists of one or more discrete data centers—each with redundant power, networking, and connectivity—housed in separate facilities.

- AZs enable you to operate production applications and databases that are more highly available, fault tolerant, and scalable than would be possible from a single data center.

AWS gives you the flexibility to place instances and store data within multiple geographic Regions as well as across multiple Availability Zones within each Region. Amazon designs each Availability Zone as an independent failure zone. This independence means that Amazon physically separates Availability Zones within a typical metropolitan Region. Amazon chooses lower-risk floodplains in each Region.

In addition to having discrete uninterruptible power supplies (UPSs) and onsite backup generation facilities, AZs are each fed via different grids from independent utilities to further reduce single points of failure. AZs are all redundantly connected to multiple Tier 1 transit providers. Some AZs have their own power substations; in fact, as I write this, a majority of them are creating their own power.

Other Global Infrastructure Components

While Regions, Availability Zones, and Edge Locations are typically considered the main components of the AWS global infrastructure, they are certainly not the only components. In this section, we examine more components (including connections) that you can work with when using AWS.

AWS Local Zones

AWS *Local Zones* are a relatively new concept for the AWS global infrastructure. These zones are an attempt by Amazon to place compute, storage, database, and other key service resources closer to large population and industry centers around the world. For example, because Chicago is such a bustling US city filled with industry, AWS created the Chicago local zone (us-east-1-chi-1a).

Notice for AWS Local Zones to be truly useful, they must support the most popular and foundational AWS services users tend to rely upon every day, including the following:

- EC2
- VPC
- EBS
- ElastiCache
- RDS

A hugely important aspect of AWS Local Zones is that customers do not pay extra for them. When you use Local Zones, you are still charged on demand for resources, just as you are for your typical AWS resources in typical Availability Zones. In fact, you can even still take advantage of On-Demand Capacity Reservations with AWS Local Zones in an attempt to save even more money.

AWS Wavelength Zones

AWS *Wavelength Zones* are another relatively new part of AWS Regions. These zones exist to carry the new AWS Wavelength infrastructure. AWS Wavelength allows developers to construct apps that deliver ultra-low latency to mobile devices and their end users. The idea here is to place AWS compute and storage resources close to the edge of communications service providers' 5G networks to speed things up for end users. These components are also used with AWS Wavelength Zones:

- **Wavelength subnets:** These are the subnets you create in a Wavelength Zone.

- **Carrier gateway:** This gateway permits inbound traffic from the carrier network and also permits outbound traffic to the carrier network and the Internet.

- **Network border group:** This is a unique set of availability zones, local zones, and wavelength zones from which AWS advertises IP addresses.

- **Wavelength application:** This is an application running in a Wavelength Zone for end-user access.

AWS resources that can be used with Wavelength Zones currently include the following:

- EC2
- EC2 Auto Scaling
- EC2 Systems Manager
- EKS clusters
- ECS clusters
- EBS
- CloudWatch
- CloudTrail
- CloudFormation

AWS CloudFront

As you know, the AWS global infrastructure has many Edge Locations that are scattered around the globe. The primary job of Edge Locations is to power the AWS CloudFront service.

CloudFront is a global content delivery network (CDN) service. This service accelerates delivery of your websites, APIs, video content, or other web assets. By automatically routing requests for your content to the nearest Edge Location, it delivers content with the best possible performance.

Figure 12-2 shows the CloudFront dashboard. Notice that global caching workloads are termed *distributions*. In the figure you can see two active CloudFront distributions for two different websites hosted in AWS.

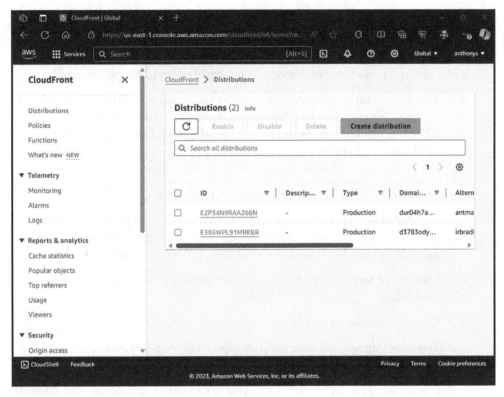

Figure 12-2   AWS CloudFront

AWS Global Accelerator

AWS *Global Accelerator* is a service that helps improve the availability and performance of applications by using static anycast IP addresses and directing traffic over the AWS global network. This service is designed to route traffic over the optimal AWS network path, reducing latency and providing a more consistent user experience.

Anycast IP addressing is a technology that allows the use of identical IP addresses on network nodes. In the case of AWS Global Accelerator, multiple identical static IP addresses advertise services to clients, and the most optimal route is selected to guide incoming AWS user traffic to the closest services needed.

Notice that while technologies like AWS Local Zones and CloudFront seek to move resources closer to users, AWS Global Accelerator focuses on moving incoming client traffic as efficiently as possible to destinations within the global infrastructure.

AWS Direct Connect

AWS *Direct Connect* makes it easy to establish a dedicated network connection from your premises to AWS. With AWS Direct Connect, you get to bypass the public Internet entirely as you connect your organization to the public cloud.

Why would you want to pay extra for this? For one thing, security is enhanced. But for most organizations, the main draw is that more predictable bandwidth is available. When you use a private Direct Connect option for AWS Cloud connectivity, you don't have to fight others for bandwidth on the Internet (which is called *contention*), so you typically experience more consistent throughput.

Features of AWS Direct Connect are numerous and include the following:

- Establishment of private connectivity between AWS and your data center, office, or colocation environment (Keep in mind that you typically work with an AWS partner data center, so the privacy of the connection is still relative.)

- Potential reduction of your network costs (through savings of the AWS transfer-out fee)

- Potential increase in bandwidth throughput

- Typically a more consistent network experience than Internet-based connections

- Use of 802.1Q VLANs that enable you to partition a connection into multiple virtual interfaces that can access different resources

VPC Endpoints

A *VPC endpoint* enables you to privately connect your VPC to supported AWS services and VPC endpoint services powered by PrivateLink without requiring an Internet gateway, NAT device, VPN connection, or AWS Direct Connect connection. Traffic between your VPC and the other service does not leave the Amazon network, and therefore, instances in your VPC do not require public IP addresses to communicate with resources in the service.

Endpoints are virtual devices. They are highly available VPC components that allow communication between instances in your VPC and services without imposing availability risks or bandwidth constraints on your network traffic.

There are two types of VPC endpoints: interface endpoints and gateway endpoints. You should create the type of VPC endpoint required by the supported service.

Interface Endpoints

An *interface endpoint* is an elastic network interface with a private IP address that serves as an entry point for traffic destined for a supported service. Here are just some of the many popular services that are supported:

- API Gateway
- CloudWatch
- CodeBuild
- Config
- EC2
- Elastic Load Balancing API
- Key Management Service
- Kinesis Data Streams
- S3
- SageMaker Runtime
- Secrets Manager
- Security Token Service
- Service Catalog
- SNS
- SQS
- Storage Gateway
- Systems Manager
- Endpoint services hosted by other AWS accounts
- Supported AWS Marketplace partner services

Gateway Endpoints

A *gateway endpoint* is a gateway that is a target for a specified route in your route table and used for traffic destined for a supported AWS service. Gateway endpoints are destinations that are reachable from within Amazon VPC through prefix lists within Amazon VPC's route table. The following AWS services are supported for gateway endpoint usage:

- S3
- DynamoDB

VPC Peering

An AWS *VPC peering* connection is a networking connection between two VPCs that enables you to route traffic between those VPCs privately. Instances in either VPC can communicate with each other as if they are within the same network. You can create a VPC peering connection between your own VPCs, with a VPC in another AWS account, or with a VPC in a different AWS Region.

AWS uses the existing infrastructure of a VPC to create a VPC peering connection; it is neither a gateway nor a VPN connection, and it does not rely on a separate piece of physical hardware. There is no single point of failure for communication or a bandwidth bottleneck. Figure 12-3 shows the configuration of a VPC peering in AWS.

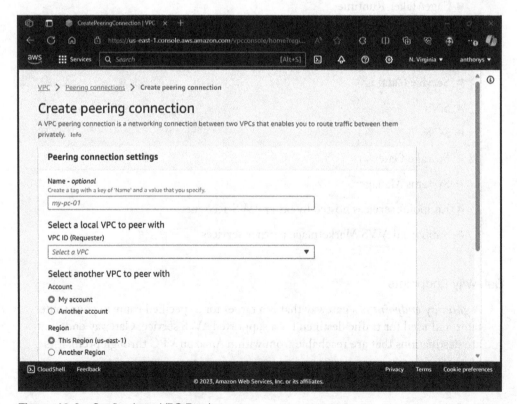

Figure 12-3   Configuring a VPC Peering

Exam Preparation Tasks

As mentioned in the section "How to Use This Book" in the Introduction, you have a few choices for exam preparation: the exercises here, Chapter 22, "Final Preparation," and the exam simulation questions in the Pearson Test Prep Software Online.

Review All Key Topics

Review the most important topics in this chapter, noted with the Key Topics icon in the outer margin of the page. Table 12-3 lists these key topics and the page number on which each is found.

Table 12-3 Key Topics for Chapter 12

Key Topic Element	Description	Page Number
List	Region characteristics	154
List	AZ characteristics	156
Overview	AWS CloudFront	158
Overview	AWS Global Accelerator	159
Overview	AWS Direct Connect	160

Define Key Terms

Define the following key terms from this chapter and check your answers in the Glossary:

Region, Availability Zone (AZ), Local Zone, Wavelength Zone, CloudFront, Global Accelerator, Direct Connect, VPC endpoint, interface endpoint, gateway endpoint, VPC peering

Q&A

The answers to these questions appear in Appendix A. For more practice with exam format questions, use the Pearson Test Prep Software Online.

1. Why might a company host resources in different AWS Regions?

2. How does AWS decide on the location of Availability Zones inside a Region?

3. What AWS technology uses static anycast IP addresses as a starting point for optimized access to AWS resources?

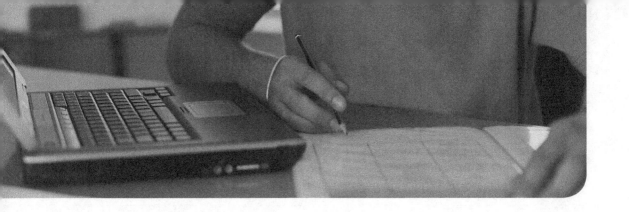

This chapter covers the following subjects:

- **EC2:** In this section of the chapter, we cover EC2, a fundamental (and early) compute service of AWS. EC is the home of virtual machines that you can spin up with ease.

- **Container Options:** In this part of the chapter, we discuss the options for managing containers in a virtualized compute environment. As you will see, AWS provides its own management service, and it also offers a public favorite: Kubernetes.

- **Serverless Compute:** Serverless compute is now all the rage in public cloud. In this part of the chapter, we talk about several of the important serverless compute options in AWS.

CHAPTER 13

AWS Compute Services

Where would cloud be without access to powerful compute options? It would be pretty boring and not nearly as heavily used. In this chapter, you will learn about the powerful services and options that AWS presents. Prepare to be impressed.

"Do I Know This Already?" Quiz

The "Do I Know This Already?" quiz allows you to assess whether you should read the entire chapter. Table 13-1 lists the major headings in this chapter and the "Do I Know This Already?" quiz questions covering the material in those sections so you can assess your knowledge of these specific areas. The answers to the "Do I Know This Already?" quiz questions appear in Appendix A, "Answers to the 'Do I Know This Already?' Quizzes and Q&A Sections."

Table 13-1 "Do I Know This Already?" Foundation Topics Section-to-Question Mapping

Foundation Topics Section	Questions
EC2	1
Container Options	2–3
Serverless Compute	4–5

CAUTION The goal of self-assessment is to gauge your mastery of the topics in this chapter. If you do not know the answer to a question or are only partially sure of the answer, you should mark that question as wrong for purposes of the self-assessment. Giving yourself credit for an answer you correctly guess skews your self-assessment results and might provide you with a false sense of security.

1. You are responsible for provisioning the EC2 compute resources for a large solution your organization is implementing in the AWS Cloud. Your cloud workloads will be unpredictable and spiky in nature, and they should not be interrupted, if possible. What pricing plan would you recommend?

   a. On-Demand Instances

   b. Savings Plans

    c. Spot Instances

    d. Reverse Plan

2. What is the AWS serverless compute solution for containers that integrates with ECS and EKS?

    a. Elastic Beanstalk

    b. Lambda

    c. EC2

    d. Fargate

3. Your organization has a Kubernetes deployment from its data center. In order to increase scalability, you would like to move this solution to the public cloud. What AWS service can make the transition simple?

    a. ECS

    b. EKS

    c. EC2

    d. Lambda

4. You are looking for an AWS service that provides a serverless alternate to EC2 and bills based on subseconds of compute usage. What service should you explore?

    a. EKS

    b. Elastic Beanstalk

    c. Lambda

    d. ECS

5. Which AWS service is often considered a PaaS offering?

    a. EC2

    b. Elastic Beanstalk

    c. Lambda

    d. EKS

Foundation Topics

EC2

Amazon *Elastic Compute Cloud (EC2)* is a web service that provides secure and resizable compute resources in the AWS Cloud. The EC2 service allows you to provision and configure capacity with minimal effort. It provides you with easy control of your compute resources.

EC2 reduces the time required to obtain and boot new servers (EC2 instances) from hours to just minutes. This efficiency allows you to scale capacity vertically (up and down, making your server resources bigger or smaller) and horizontally (out and in, adding more capacity in the form of more instances) as your computing requirements change. As you might recall from previous chapters, this property is known as *elasticity*.

The many benefits of EC2 in AWS include the following:

- EC2 allows you to control expenses as your business expands; you pay only for the resources you use as your business grows.

- EC2 provides you with the tools to build failure-resilient applications that are isolated from common failure scenarios.

- EC2 enables you to increase or decrease capacity in minutes rather than in hours or days. You can commission one, hundreds, or even thousands of server instances simultaneously.

- You have complete control of your EC2 instances. You have root access to each one, and you can interact with them as you would any traditional virtual machine.

- You can stop your EC2 instance while retaining the data on your boot partition and then subsequently restart the same instance using web service APIs. Instances can be stopped and started remotely using web service APIs.

- You can choose among multiple instance types, operating systems, and software packages. Instance types inside AWS permit the choice of emphasis on CPU, RAM, and/or networking resources. (You'll see more details later in this section.)

- EC2 integrates with most AWS services, such as Simple Storage Service (S3), Relational Database Service (RDS), and Virtual Private Cloud (VPC). This tight integration allows you to use EC2 for a wide variety of compute scenarios.

- EC2 offers a reliable environment where replacement instances can be rapidly and predictably commissioned. The service runs within Amazon's proven network infrastructure and data centers. AWS offers as much as 99.95% availability for each region.

- Amazon EC2 works in conjunction with Amazon VPC to provide security and robust networking functionality for your compute resources:

  - Your compute instances are located in a VPC with an IP address range that you specify.

  - You decide which instances are exposed to the Internet and which remain private.

  - Security groups and network access control lists (NACLs) allow you to control inbound and outbound access to and from your network interfaces.

  - You can connect your existing IT infrastructure to resources in your VPC by using industry-standard encrypted IPsec virtual private network (VPN) connections, or you can take advantage of a private AWS Direct Connect option.

- You can provision your Amazon EC2 resources as dedicated instances. Dedicated instances are Amazon EC2 instances that run on hardware dedicated to a single customer for additional isolation. Alternatively, you can provision your Amazon EC2 resources on dedicated hosts, which are physical servers with EC2 instance capacity entirely dedicated to your use. Dedicated hosts can help you address compliance requirements and reduce costs by allowing you to use your existing server-bound software licenses.

As previously mentioned, a nice feature of AWS EC2 is the wide variety of instance types you can select from to have the right hardware platform in place for your virtual machines. Instance types fall into the following categories:

- General purpose

- Compute optimized

- Memory optimized

- Accelerated computing
- Storage optimized
- HPC optimized

There are several pricing models for EC2, as shown in Figure 13-1.

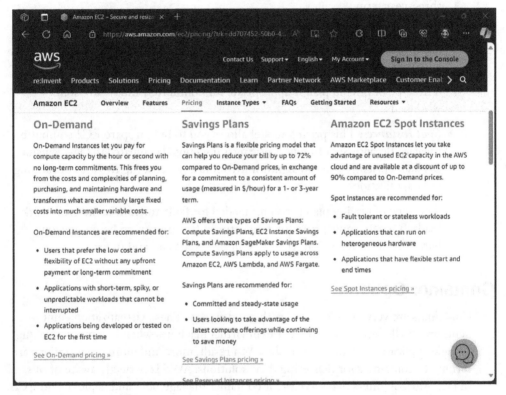

Figure 13-1 EC2 Pricing Options

These pricing options are as follows:

- ***On-Demand Instances:*** With this model, you pay for compute capacity by the hour (or even by the second with some AMIs), with no long-term commitments. You can increase or decrease your compute capacity, depending on the demands of your application, and pay the specified hourly rate only for the instances you use. The use of On-Demand Instances frees you from the costs and complexities of planning, purchasing, and maintaining hardware. As mentioned earlier in this chapter, this model also transforms what are commonly substantial fixed costs into much smaller variable costs.

This type of pricing model is appropriate when you are testing a solution for the first time, or when you are using short-term or unpredictable workloads that cannot be interrupted.

- **Savings Plans:** This model provides you with a significant discount (up to 72%) compared to On-Demand Instances pricing. In order to save that much, you must commit to a certain amount of compute resources for a one- to three-year term.

  There are three options under Savings Plans: Compute Savings Plans (which apply to usage across EC2, Lambda, and Fargate), EC2 Instance Savings Plans, and Amazon SageMaker Savings Plans.

  This type of pricing plan is appropriate for committed and steady-state workloads.

- **Spot Instances:** This pricing model allows you to bid on spare EC2 computing capacity. Because Spot Instances pricing is discounted compared to On-Demand Instances pricing, you can significantly reduce the cost (up to 90%) of running your applications.

  This type of pricing plan is recommended for fault-tolerant or stateless workloads. It is also appropriate for applications that can run on heterogeneous hardware and applications that have flexible start and end times.

Container Options

Containers are very popular—and with good reason. These virtualization components are smaller and more efficient than virtual machines when it comes to making a single application or service available. As a result, more and more organizations are turning to containers for delivering their solutions. AWS is perfectly aware of this. In fact, Amazon offers two services for container management and deployment: ECS and EKS.

Elastic Container Service (ECS)

The AWS *Elastic Container Service* (*ECS*) is a highly scalable, high-performance container management service that supports Docker containers. AWS ECS is a fully managed service, which means AWS takes care of the operational aspects, such as server provisioning, patching, and scaling. It eliminates the need for you to install, operate, and scale your own cluster management infrastructure.

Here are some other exciting benefits of AWS ECS:

- **ECS provides orchestration services:** This can help you quickly become an efficient manager of your containers at great scale.

- **ECS is similar to EC2:** ECS features automated autoscaling capabilities.

- **ECS integrates with AWS Fargate:** AWS *Fargate* is the serverless compute option for running containers.

- **ECS also supports ECS clusters:** An ECS cluster is a logical grouping of container instances, which provides another powerful scalability feature.

Elastic Kubernetes Service (EKS)

Amazon *Elastic Kubernetes Service* (*EKS*) is a fully managed Kubernetes service in the public cloud. EKS simplifies the process of deploying, managing, and scaling containerized applications using Kubernetes. With EKS, users can leverage the power of Kubernetes for container orchestration without the need to manage the underlying infrastructure.

Here are some features you should be familiar with:

- EKS integrates with the popular open-source Kubernetes platform, offering a consistent and secure way to run containerized applications.

- It allows users to create and run Kubernetes clusters in the AWS Cloud, taking advantage of AWS features such as Elastic Load Balancing (ELB) for distributing incoming traffic, AWS Identity and Access Management (IAM) for secure access control, and Amazon VPC for network isolation.

- EKS supports the seamless integration of other AWS services, making it easier for developers to build, deploy, and scale applications in a Kubernetes environment.

- EKS is designed to automatically update the Kubernetes control plane, ensuring that users have access to the latest features and security patches without manual intervention.

- Like ECS, EKS integrates seamlessly with AWS Fargate. (Remember that Fargate is the serverless compute service for running container workloads.)

Figure 13-2 shows EKS in AWS.

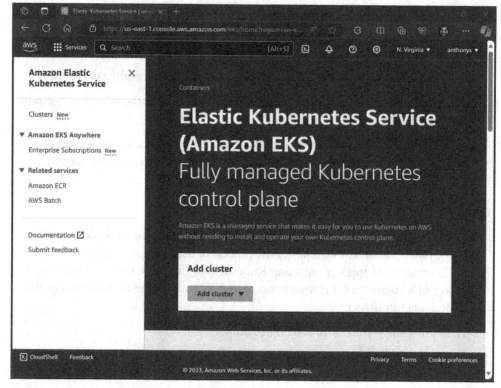

Figure 13-2 The AWS Elastic Kubernetes Service

Serverless Compute

An important revolution in public cloud technology—the invention of serverless computing—occurred years ago. Sure enough, serverless compute has remained a hugely important part of public cloud. Cloud customers no longer need to spin up virtual machines that they then must manage. Instead, serverless computing makes a pool of compute horsepower available to cloud users. With serverless compute, AWS guarantees reliability and performance, and customers can take advantage of subsecond billing for the compute resources they actually consume.

Lambda

AWS *Lambda* is an exciting alternative to EC2 instances that you must operate and maintain. Lambda provides compute resources in a fully managed (by AWS) serverless compute cloud. You send compute requirements to Lambda in a variety of different manners (such as a call from a web app), and Lambda takes care of the compute requirements for you. Subsecond metering is used for your cost calculations, so quite often Lambda is a very inexpensive way to provide the compute resources you require. It also supports many different programming languages to ease use. With Lambda, a typical workflow follows these steps:

Step 1.   You upload your code to AWS Lambda.

Step 2.   You set up your code to trigger from either other AWS services, HTTP endpoints, or in-app activity.

Step 3.   Lambda runs your code when triggered, consuming only the resources needed. (It is important to realize that like most other AWS services, Lambda provides continuous scaling, as needed.)

Step 4.   You pay for just the compute time required.

Figure 13-3 shows the creation of a Hello World function in AWS Lambda.

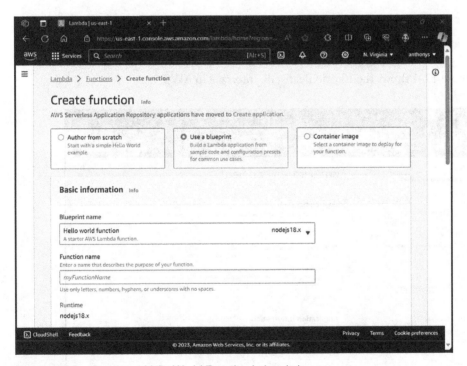

Figure 13-3   Creating a Hello World Function in Lambda

Elastic Beanstalk

Elastic Beanstalk provides a very quick and simple method for getting your applications into the AWS Cloud. It is actually a platform as a service (PaaS) offering. The infrastructure and platform are quickly built for you in the cloud, which enables quick deployment of your applications.

Elastic Beanstalk also reduces the ongoing management complexity of a deployment. Importantly, you maintain control of the platform. For example, if you want to scale your applications more aggressively, you have complete control.

Another great aspect to this service is that it supports a wide variety of languages and platforms, such as Go, Java SE, PHP, Python, and Node.js. Application upgrades are simple, as you just deploy them to Elastic Beanstalk as needed.

While it is easy to implement, Elastic Beanstalk is also robust. You supply the application code, and AWS provides components such as the following:

- Application services
- HTTP services
- Required operating systems
- Required language interpreters
- The physical hosts required

Figure 13-4 shows the Elastic Beanstalk interface in AWS.

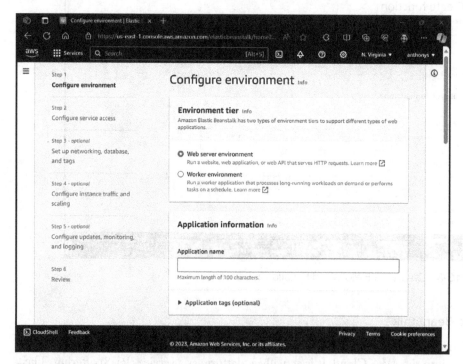

Figure 13-4   Elastic Beanstalk in AWS

Exam Preparation Tasks

As mentioned in the section "How to Use This Book" in the Introduction, you have a few choices for exam preparation: the exercises here, Chapter 22, "Final Preparation," and the exam simulation questions in the Pearson Test Prep Software Online.

Review All Key Topics

Review the most important topics in this chapter, noted with the Key Topics icon in the outer margin of the page. Table 13-2 lists these key topics and the page number on which each is found.

Table 13-2 Key Topics for Chapter 13

Key Topic Element	Description	Page Number
List	Benefits of EC2	167
List	EC2 instance types	168
List	EC2 pricing options	169
Steps	Using Lambda	173

Define Key Terms

Define the following key terms from this chapter and check your answers in the Glossary:

Elastic Compute Cloud (EC2), On-Demand Instances, Savings Plans, Spot Instances, Elastic Container Service (ECS), Fargate, Elastic Kubernetes Service (EKS), Lambda, Elastic Beanstalk

Q&A

The answers to these questions appear in Appendix A. For more practice with exam format questions, use the Pearson Test Prep Software Online.

1. Name the three pricing models for EC2.

2. What are two options for container management as a service in AWS?

3. What is the main serverless compute option in AWS?

This chapter covers the following subjects:

- **Relational Database Services:** In this section of the chapter, we discuss the "classic" relational database technologies that are supported in AWS. As you will learn, in addition to popular options (such as Microsoft SQL Server), there are now newer relational database options (such as AWS Aurora).

- **Other Databases Services:** In this part of the chapter, we examine just some of the other database technologies that are supported inside AWS.

CHAPTER 14

AWS Database Services

Databases are a major component for any IT organization. It is no surprise, therefore, that AWS provides services to support a wide variety of database technologies. In this chapter, we ensure that you are ready to describe the various database services offered by AWS.

"Do I Know This Already?" Quiz

The "Do I Know This Already?" quiz allows you to assess whether you should read the entire chapter. Table 14-1 lists the major headings in this chapter and the "Do I Know This Already?" quiz questions covering the material in those sections so you can assess your knowledge of these specific areas. The answers to the "Do I Know This Already?" quiz questions appear in Appendix A, "Answers to the 'Do I Know This Already?' Quizzes and Q&A Sections."

Table 14-1 "Do I Know This Already?" Foundation Topics Section-to-Question Mapping

Foundation Topics Section	Questions
Relational Database Services	1–3
Other Database Services	4–6

CAUTION The goal of self-assessment is to gauge your mastery of the topics in this chapter. If you do not know the answer to a question or are only partially sure of the answer, you should mark that question as wrong for purposes of the self-assessment. Giving yourself credit for an answer you correctly guess skews your self-assessment results and might provide you with a false sense of security.

1. Your supervisor has indicated that she would like you to host your company's Microsoft SQL Server environment in AWS. She wants you to maintain full control over the underlying database engine and all aspects of SQL Server management. What solution should you recommend?

   a. RDS

   b. Aurora

    c. EC2

    d. ElastiCache

2. You want to run Oracle databases in AWS, and you are interested in the lowest amount of management overhead. What option should you consider first?

    a. RDS

    b. DynamoDB

    c. ElastiCache

    d. Redshift

3. Which database engine option of AWS RDS was actually developed by AWS?

    a. Db2

    b. MariaDB

    c. PostgreSQL

    d. Aurora

4. Which AWS database is a NoSQL database solution that is often used with IoT solutions?

    a. Aurora

    b. Glacier

    c. Snowball

    d. DynamoDB

5. Which of the following is a data warehouse solution in AWS?

    a. Redshift

    b. Aurora

    c. RDS

    d. ElastiCache

6. What is the main memory-based database option in AWS?

    a. DynamoDB

    b. ElastiCache

    c. Aurora

    d. RDS

Foundation Topics

Relational Database Services

Relational databases are some of the oldest and most cherished database technologies in tech today. Is it any surprise that AWS created a service called Relational Database Service (RDS)? Amazon's marketing department definitely wanted to make it very clear: If your organization relies on relational database technologies, and you want to experience the joys of managed cloud services, AWS has an answer.

NOTE   When it comes to hosting database technologies in AWS, you are not forced into using the RDS service. Organizations that do not mind the work involved and that want full and total control over their database setup can build their database engine and technologies on virtual machines inside the EC2 service. Organizations that choose to deploy in this fashion miss out on the many management tasks that AWS experts are willing to perform for them in the managed service approach of AWS.

Relational Database Service (RDS)

The *Relational Database Service* (*RDS*) of AWS makes it easy to set up, operate, and scale a relational database in the cloud. RDS allows you to choose from seven database engines: Db2, Aurora, PostgreSQL, MySQL, MariaDB, Oracle, and Microsoft SQL Server.

Benefits of RDS include the following:

- **Fast and easy to administer:** You can use the AWS Management Console, the AWS RDS command-line interface, or simple API calls to access the capabilities of a production-ready relational database in minutes.

- **Highly scalable:** You can scale your database's compute and storage resources with only a few mouse clicks or an API call, often with no downtime.

- **Available and durable:** RDS runs on the same highly reliable infrastructure used by other AWS offerings. When you provision a multi-AZ DB instance, RDS synchronously replicates the data to a standby instance in a different Availability Zone (AZ).

- **Secure:** RDS makes it easy to control network access to your database. RDS also lets you run your database instances in a VPC, which enables you to isolate your database instances and connect to your existing IT infrastructure through an industry-standard encrypted IPsec VPN. Many RDS engine types offer encryption at rest and encryption in transit. You can also take advantage of Direct Connect.

■ **Relatively inexpensive:** You pay low rates and only for the resources you consume.

Figure 14-1 shows the AWS RDS interface in the AWS Management Console.

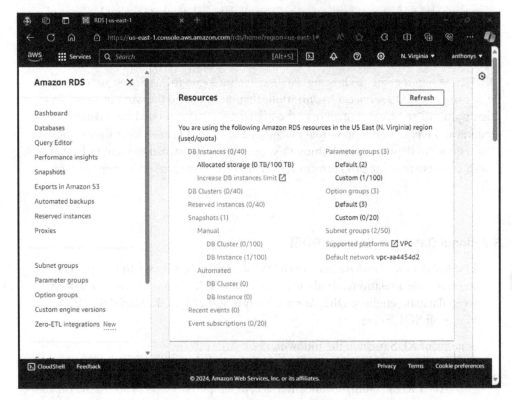

Figure 14-1   The RDS Service of AWS

Aurora

While AWS *Aurora* is one of the relational database options within the RDS service described in the preceding section, it is worth giving it some special attention in this chapter. AWS itself invented Aurora, which makes it pretty special and also makes it an option that Amazon is very excited about.

Aurora is a MySQL- and PostgreSQL-compatible relational database engine. It offers many benefits, including the following:

- **High performance:** Aurora can provide up to five times the throughput of standard MySQL or twice the throughput of standard PostgreSQL running on the same hardware.

- **Highly secure:** Aurora provides multiple levels of security for a database, including network isolation using a VPC, encryption of data at rest using keys you create and control through Key Management Service (KMS), and encryption of data in transit using SSL.

- **MySQL and PostgreSQL compatible:** The Aurora database engine is fully compatible with MySQL 5.7 and MySQL 8.0. It is also compatible with PostgreSQL 14.6.

- **Highly scalable:** You can scale your Aurora database from an instance with two vCPUs and 4 GB of memory up to an instance with 32 vCPUs and 244 GB of memory.

- **High availability and durability:** Aurora is designed to offer higher than 99.99% availability. It is also amazingly durable, ensuring that six synchronous copies of your data are running across three AZs. This is a huge advantage over standard RDS implementations.

- **Fully managed:** Aurora is a fully managed database service. Amazon handles tasks such as hardware provisioning, software patching, setup, configuration, monitoring, and backups.

Other Database Services

As time has passed, more and more specialized database types have been developed. This is partly due to the fact that relational database structures and designs do not work well for storing the data of newer and different technologies. In this section, we examine some of the various non-relational database services of AWS.

DynamoDB

Amazon *DynamoDB* is a fast and flexible NoSQL database service for all applications that need consistent, single-digit millisecond latency at any scale. It is a great fit for mobile, web, gaming, ad tech, Internet of Things (IoT), and many other applications. Figure 14-2 shows the DynamoDB service in the AWS Management Console.

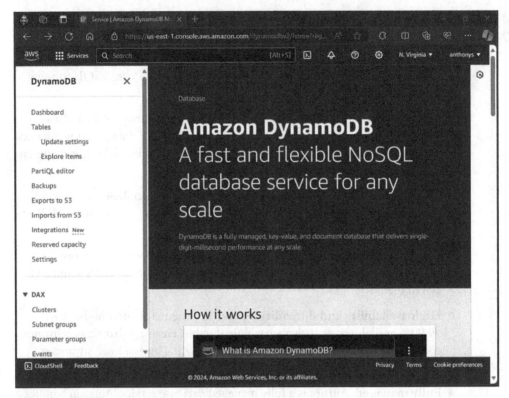

Figure 14-2 The DynamoDB Service of AWS

Benefits of DynamoDB include the following:

- **Fast, consistent performance:** DynamoDB delivers consistent, fast performance at any scale for all applications.

- **Highly scalable:** When you create a table, you specify how much request
  capacity you require. If your throughput requirements change, you update
  your table's request capacity by using the AWS Management Console or the
  DynamoDB APIs. DynamoDB manages all the scaling behind the scenes, and
  you are still able to achieve your previous throughput levels while scaling is
  underway. Instant scaling and autoscaling capabilities now exist that even assist
  you if you are unsure about the initial capacity you require.

- **Fully managed:** DynamoDB is a fully managed cloud NoSQL database
  service. You create a database table, optionally set your throughput or allow
  autoscaling, and let the service handle the rest.

- **Event-driven programming:** DynamoDB integrates with Lambda to provide triggers that enable you to architect applications that automatically react to data changes.

- **Fine-grained access control:** DynamoDB integrates with IAM for fine-grained access control.

- **Flexible:** DynamoDB supports both document and key/value data structures, giving you the flexibility to design the data architecture that is optimal for your application.

ElastiCache

ElastiCache is a web service that makes it easy to deploy, operate, and scale an in-memory cache in the cloud. The service improves the performance of web applications by allowing you to retrieve information from fast, managed, in-memory caches instead of relying entirely on slower disk-based databases. Figure 14-3 shows the ElastiCache service in the AWS Management Console.

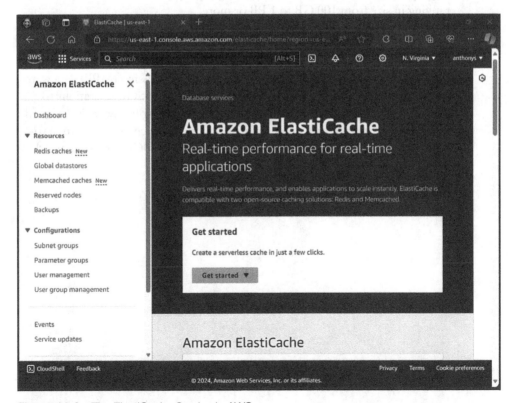

Figure 14-3   The ElastiCache Service in AWS

ElastiCache supports two open-source in-memory caching engines:

- **Redis:** Redis is a fast, open-source in-memory data store and cache. Elasti-Cache for Redis is a Redis-compatible in-memory service that delivers the ease of use and power of Redis along with availability, reliability, and performance that are suitable for the most demanding applications.

- **Memcached:** Memcached is a widely adopted memory object caching system. ElastiCache is protocol compliant with Memcached, so tools that you use today with existing Memcached environments work seamlessly with the service.

Redshift

Redshift is a fast, fully managed, petabyte-scale data warehouse that allows you to easily and cost-effectively analyze all your data using your existing business intelligence tools. Features include the following:

- **High performance:** Redshift provides high query performance on data sets ranging in size from 100 GB to 1 PB or more.

- **High efficiency:** Redshift uses columnar storage, data compression, and zone maps to reduce the amount of I/O needed to perform queries.

- **Parallel processing:** Redshift's massively parallel processing (MPP) data warehouse architecture allows it to parallelize and distribute SQL operations to take advantage of all available resources. The underlying hardware is designed for high-performance data processing, using locally attached storage to maximize throughput between the CPUs and drives and a 10GigE mesh network to maximize throughput between nodes.

Exam Preparation Tasks

As mentioned in the section "How to Use This Book" in the Introduction, you have a few choices for exam preparation: the exercises here, Chapter 22, "Final Preparation," and the exam simulation questions in the Pearson Test Prep Software Online.

Review All Key Topics

Review the most important topics in this chapter, noted with the Key Topics icon in the outer margin of the page. Table 14-2 lists these key topics and the page number on which each is found.

Table 14-2   Key Topics for Chapter 14

Key Topic Element	Description	Page Number
Overview	Relational Database Service (RDS)	179
List	Aurora benefits	181
List	DynamoDB benefits	182
Overview	ElastiCache	183

Define Key Terms

Define the following key terms from this chapter and check your answers in the Glossary:

Relational Database Service (RDS), Aurora, DynamoDB, ElastiCache, Redshift

Q&A

The answers to these questions appear in Appendix A. For more practice with exam format questions, use the Pearson Test Prep Software Online.

1. Name at least four database engines that are supported by AWS RDS.

2. What are the two open-source in-memory caching engines that AWS ElastiCache supports?

This chapter covers the following subjects:

- **Fundamental Network Services:** Virtual Private Cloud (VPC) is the main networking component of AWS. VPC is made up of many important parts, and we examine the most important of them in this section of the chapter.

- **Other Network Services:** In this section of the chapter, we detail the important Route 53 and CloudFront services. While there are many other networking services we could cover here, we cover many of them in other chapters. (For example, we discuss security groups and NACLs in Chapter 10, "Components and Resources for Security.")

CHAPTER 15

AWS Network Services

Just as networking services are a critical part of a traditional on-premises IT organization, they are also critical in an AWS Cloud environment. Of course, how much you interact directly with the networking services depends on your actual usage of AWS. For example, if you are using AWS exclusively for AWS Lambda (serverless compute), you might not be interacting with the networking services much at all—by design. Lambda shields you from the administrative overhead of working with the network. But what if you are building your entire IT organization in the cloud? You will be working on your virtual network as intensely as you would be in an on-premises environment. Hopefully, however, the cloud will make things easier, more efficient, and less costly.

"Do I Know This Already?" Quiz

The "Do I Know This Already?" quiz allows you to assess whether you should read the entire chapter. Table 15-1 lists the major headings in this chapter and the "Do I Know This Already?" quiz questions covering the material in those sections so you can assess your knowledge of these specific areas. The answers to the "Do I Know This Already?" quiz questions appear in Appendix A, "Answers to the 'Do I Know This Already?' Quizzes and Q&A Sections."

Table 15-1 "Do I Know This Already?" Foundation Topics Section-to-Question Mapping

Foundation Topics Section	Questions
Fundamental Network Services	1–3
Other Network Services	4–6

CAUTION The goal of self-assessment is to gauge your mastery of the topics in this chapter. If you do not know the answer to a question or are only partially sure of the answer, you should mark that question as wrong for purposes of the self-assessment. Giving yourself credit for an answer you correctly guess skews your self-assessment results and might provide you with a false sense of security.

1. What service of AWS provides you with a private network when you open an AWS account?

   a. RDS

   b. VPC

   c. EBS

   d. EFS

2. What component permits easy-to-configure Internet access for public subnets you are featuring inside AWS?

   a. AWS Direct Connect

   b. Security Group

   c. Internet Gateway

   d. NACL

3. What component helps ensure that an AWS VPC is highly available?

   a. Subnet

   b. Route table

   c. Internet Gateway

   d. Availability Zone (AZ)

4. What is a content delivery network solution in AWS?

   a. CloudFront

   b. EFS

   c. RDS

   d. Lambda

5. What is the DNS service offered by AWS?

   a. Kinesis

   b. CloudFront

   c. RDS

   d. Route 53

6. What type of content does AWS CloudFront work with in your solutions?

    a. VoIP and video traffic

    b. Streaming log files

    c. Relational database traffic

    d. Static and dynamic web pages

Foundation Topics

Fundamental Network Services

It is pretty amazing when you think about just how much "networking" AWS is responsible for. If we take a recent estimate of the number of AWS customers, we are looking at about 1.5 million entities (at this writing). That number is amazing enough, but when we remember that each of these customers is apportioned at least one Virtual Private Cloud, the scale of AWS becomes mind-boggling. In this section of the chapter, you'll become very comfortable with the important concept of VPCs in AWS.

Virtual Private Cloud (VPC)

When you think about virtual networking in the public cloud of AWS, think VPCs. A VPC allows you to create private virtual networks and use the same concepts that you are already familiar with from traditional networking. With a VPC, you have complete control of your network configuration. You have the ability to isolate resources from or expose resources to the public Internet or to your private host systems inside your corporation.

With AWS VPCs, there are several layers of security controls (as you would expect). For example, security groups and network access control lists (NACLs) act as firewalls. *Security groups* control traffic into and out of your Elastic Compute Cloud (EC2) instances, whereas *NACLs* control traffic into and out of your subnets in a VPC.

When you are architecting solutions in AWS, you deploy various services and resources into a VPC in order to make up the full solution. You can be very specific with service and resource placement so you know exactly where in your virtual network the resources reside. These services also conveniently inherit the security you have built into your network. Examples of services you would deploy into a VPC include EC2, Elastic File System (EFS), Relational Database Service (RDS), and Elastic Load Balancing (ELB).

These are the main features of a VPC you should be aware of:

- *High availability*: VPCs build on the high availability built into AWS Regions and Availability Zones (AZs). Your VPCs live within a Region, and you can have multiple VPCs per account.

- *Subnets*: Just like your private network infrastructures, VPCs are made up of subnets that you can use to provide segmentation at Layer 3 (the network layer).

- *Route tables*: You can use route tables to route traffic entering and exiting your subnets. You get this familiar model without needing to worry about physical routers.

- *Internet gateways (IGWs)*: An IGW gives you easy-to-configure access to the Internet for your VPC. Figure 15-1 shows an IGW in AWS.

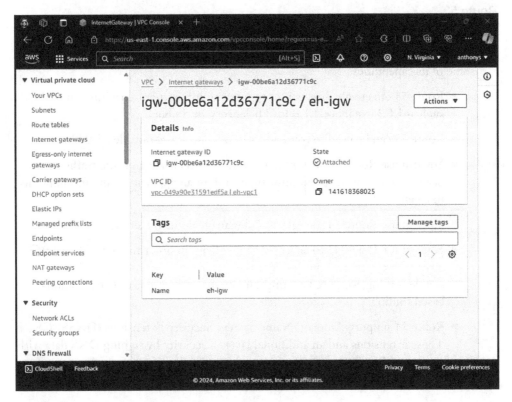

Figure 15-1 An Internet Gateway

- *NAT gateway*: A NAT gateway translates your privately addressed VPC resources to access the Internet using public IP addresses.

- *NACLs*: NACLs allow you to control access to your VPC subnets. They are stateless constructs, which means you must configure inbound and outbound rules, as there is no automatic recognition of state with traffic flows, and there are no automated access entries.

Other Network Services

While there are many other network services in AWS, two of the ones you need to be familiar with are discussed in this section: Route 53 and CloudFront. Each performs critical functions that you need to understand.

Route 53

Amazon *Route 53* is a highly available and scalable cloud Domain Name System (DNS) web service. Route 53 is capable of many valuable functions. Here are just some of its capabilities:

- Route 53 effectively directs user requests to infrastructure running in AWS, such as EC2 instances, ELB load balancers, or S3 buckets.

- Route 53 can be used to route users to infrastructure outside of AWS.

- You can use Route 53 to configure DNS health checks to route traffic to healthy endpoints or to monitor the health of an application and its endpoints independently.

- You can use Route 53 to register and manage domain names.

- You can use Route 53 to enact routing policies in order to control how traffic is distributed among your AWS resources. Options for routing policies include simple routing, weighted routing, latency-based routing, and geolocation-based routing.

- Route 53 supports Domain Name System Security Extensions (DNSSEC). These extensions add an additional layer of security by signing DNS data with cryptographic signatures.

CloudFront

AWS *CloudFront* is a global content delivery network (CDN) service for static and dynamic web content. This service accelerates delivery of your websites, APIs, video content, and other web assets. The service automatically routes requests for your content to the nearest Edge Location, so it delivers content with the best possible performance. Remember that Edge Locations, which are part of the AWS global infrastructure, are designed to help distribute content with more global coverage. Figure 15-2 shows AWS CloudFront distribution in the AWS Management Console.

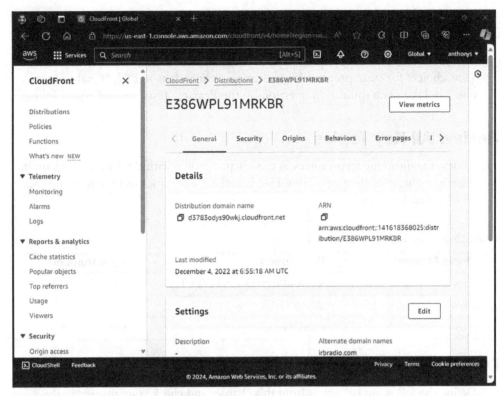

Figure 15-2   An AWS CloudFront Distribution

Other features of AWS CloudFront include the following:

■ CloudFront caches your web content at Edge Locations. This means subsequent requests for the same content can be served from the nearest Edge Location rather than from the origin server. This reduces latency and improves overall performance.

■ CloudFront supports SSL/TLS encryption to ensure secure communication between end users and the CDN. You can use your own SSL/TLS certificates or leverage AWS Certificate Manager (ACM) to obtain free certificates.

■ CloudFront can fetch content from various origin servers, including Amazon S3 buckets, EC2 instances, ELB, and custom HTTP servers. This flexibility allows you to use CloudFront with a wide range of AWS services.

■ You can control access to your content by using various authentication and authorization mechanisms, such as signed URLs or cookies, to allow only specific users or groups to access content.

Exam Preparation Tasks

As mentioned in the section "How to Use This Book" in the Introduction, you have a few choices for exam preparation: the exercises here, Chapter 22, "Final Preparation," and the exam simulation questions in the Pearson Test Prep Software Online.

Review All Key Topics

Review the most important topics in this chapter, noted with the Key Topics icon in the outer margin of the page. Table 15-2 lists these key topics and the page number on which each is found.

Table 15-2   Key Topics for Chapter 15

Key Topic Element	Description	Page Number
Overview	Virtual Private Cloud (VPC)	190
Overview	Route 53	192
Overview	CloudFront	192

Define Key Terms

Define the following key terms from this chapter and check your answers in the Glossary:

Virtual Private Cloud (VPC), NACL, security group, subnet, route table, Internet Gateway (IGW), NAT Gateway, Route 53, CloudFront , NACLs, high availability

Q&A

The answers to these questions appear in Appendix A. For more practice with exam format questions, use the Pearson Test Prep Software Online.

1. Name at least three components that are found within a VPC in AWS.

2. What is the primary AWS global infrastructure component that permits AWS CloudFront functionality?

This chapter covers the following subjects:

- **Fundamental Storage Services:** Three fundamental storage types in IT today are object-based storage, block-based storage, and file-based storage. Sure enough, AWS has fundamental services to provide these types of technologies: the object-based S3 service, the block-based EBS service, and the file-based EFS service. We will examine all three of these services in this section of the chapter.

- **Other Storage Services:** S3, EBS, and EFS are not the only AWS storage services you need to know about. In this part of the chapter, we will examine other important storage services: FSx, AWS Storage Gateway, and AWS Backup.

CHAPTER 16

AWS Storage Services

To say that cloud storage is important would be a huge understatement. AWS Simple Storage Service (S3) was the very first service ever offered by AWS. While S3 is still a frequently used fundamental storage service in AWS that we will cover in some depth in this chapter, additional storage services are also very important today.

"Do I Know This Already?" Quiz

The "Do I Know This Already?" quiz allows you to assess whether you should read the entire chapter. Table 16-1 lists the major headings in this chapter and the "Do I Know This Already?" quiz questions covering the material in those sections so you can assess your knowledge of these specific areas. The answers to the "Do I Know This Already?" quiz questions appear in Appendix A, "Answers to the 'Do I Know This Already?' Quizzes and Q&A Sections."

Table 16-1 "Do I Know This Already?" Foundation Topics Section-to-Question Mapping

Foundation Topics Section	Questions
Fundamental Storage Services	1–3
Other Storage Services	4–6

CAUTION The goal of self-assessment is to gauge your mastery of the topics in this chapter. If you do not know the answer to a question or are only partially sure of the answer, you should mark that question as wrong for purposes of the self-assessment. Giving yourself credit for an answer you correctly guess skews your self-assessment results and might provide you with a false sense of security.

1. How does S3 ensure the durability of your data?
   a. Multiple high-speed Internet connections are made to every major directory you create.
   b. Data is storage-tiered by default.

      c. Data is automatically replicated to an alternate region.

      d. Multiple copies of your data are stored in separate Availability Zones.

2. What is a common use of EBS in AWS?

      a. To receive and process streaming data for IoT

      b. To provide serverless compute resources

      c. To act as the boot volume for an EC2 server instance

      d. To makes files available to massive numbers of users and groups

3. What is the archiving/warehousing solution within S3?

      a. Glacier

      b. Snowball

      c. EFS

      d. Aurora

4. You need a solution in AWS that will help you create highly available Windows File Server shares. What service should you investigate?

      a. EBS

      b. S3

      c. EFS

      d. FSx

5. You need a cloud-backed virtual tape storage option in the cloud. What AWS service should you investigate?

      a. EFS

      b. Storage Gateway

      c. FSx

      d. EBS

6. You are looking for a backup solution in AWS that can help you protect the data stored in DynamoDB and RDS. What service should you investigate?

      a. RDS

      b. EBS

      c. EFS

      d. AWS Backup

Foundation Topics

Fundamental Storage Services

Companies today are creating massive amounts of data that needs to be stored. They are turning to block-based, file-based, and object-based storage solutions to try to keep up with their storage demands. AWS wants to be of assistance and offers many different cloud-based storage solutions covering the gamut of storage technologies. In this part of the chapter, we will examine three fundamental solutions in AWS: S3, EBS, and EFS.

Simple Storage Service (S3)

AWS *Simple Storage Service* (*S3*) is object storage with a simple web service interface to store and retrieve any amount of data from anywhere on the web. It is designed to deliver 99.999999999% durability. Figure 16-1 shows an example of storage buckets using S3.

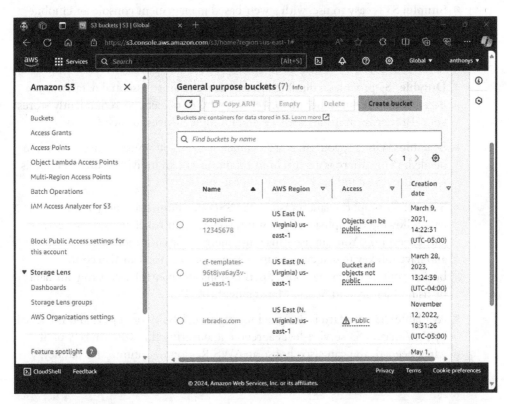

Figure 16-1   AWS S3

You can use Amazon S3 for a vast number of purposes, such as the following:

- Primary storage for cloud-native applications
- A bulk repository, or "data lake," for analytics
- A target for backup and recovery
- A target for disaster recovery purposes
- With serverless computing

You can move large volumes of data into or out of S3 with AWS's cloud data migration options. You can store data in S3 and then automatically tier the data into lower-cost, longer-term cloud storage classes like S3 Standard-Infrequent Access and Glacier for archiving. You can even use a newer storage class that reduces high availability (One Zone Infrequent Access) when you do not require high availability and want to save on storage costs. We cover the available S3 storage classes later in this section.

S3 offers many advantages, including the following:

- **Simple:** S3 is easy to use, with a web-based management console and mobile app. Amazon S3 also provides full REST APIs and SDKs for easy integration with third-party technologies. A command-line interface (CLI) is also a popular option for working with S3.

- **Durable:** S3 provides a durable infrastructure to store essential data. Amazon designed S3 for durability of 99.999999999% of objects. S3 redundantly stores your data across multiple facilities and multiple devices in each facility.

- **Scalable:** With S3, you can store as much data as you want and access it when needed. While there is a 5 TB limit on the size of an individual object, there is no limit to the number of objects you can store.

- **Secure:** S3 supports data transfer over SSL and automatic encryption of your data following the upload. If you want, you can control client-side or server-side encryption. You can use Amazon-generated or customer-generated keys and have full key management capabilities/options. You can also configure bucket policies to manage object permissions and control access to your data by using Identity and Access Management (IAM).

- **Available:** S3 Standard is designed for high availability of objects and is backed by the Amazon S3 service-level agreement, ensuring that you can rely on it when needed. You can also choose an AWS Region to optimize for latency, minimize costs, or address regulatory requirements.

- **Low cost:** S3 allows you to store large amounts of data at a small cost. Using lifecycle policies, you can configure the automatic migration of your data to different storage tiers within AWS.

- **Simple data transfer:** Amazon provides multiple options for cloud data migration and allows you to easily and cost-effectively move large volumes of data into or out of S3. You can choose from network-optimized, physical disk-based, and third-party connector methods for import to or export from S3.

- **Integrated:** S3 is deeply integrated with other AWS services to make it easier to build solutions that use a range of AWS services.

- **Easy to manage:** S3 storage management features allow you to take a data-driven approach to storage optimization, data security, and management efficiency. These enterprise-class capabilities give you data about your data so that you can manage your storage based on that personalized metadata.

While technically part of the S3 service, Amazon Glacier is a secure, durable, and extremely low-cost storage service for data archiving and long-term backup. With Glacier, you can do the following:

- Reliably store large or small amounts of data for as little as $0.004 per gigabyte per month.

- Save money compared to on-premises storage options.

- Keep costs low yet suitable for varying retrieval needs.

S3 Storage Classes

While initially S3 did not offer many different storage classes, times have changed. Today, AWS offers many different classes to permit you to save on costs while providing the required levels of durability. At this writing, the following storage classes are available in AWS S3:

- **S3 Standard:** This is the default storage class. If you do not specify a storage class, this class is assigned to your data.

- **S3 Express One Zone:** This is a high-performance, single-zone S3 storage class. Express One Zone is the lowest-latency cloud object storage class available today. Also, your data is redundantly stored on multiple devices within a single Availability Zone (AZ).

- **Reduced Redundancy:** This class is designed for noncritical, reproducible data. As the name implies, you sacrifice redundancy with this class.

- **S3 Intelligent-Tiering:** This storage class automatically moves your data to the most cost-effective storage tier associated with the Intelligent-Tiering class. This storage class uses three access tiers: Frequent Access, Infrequent Access, and Archive Instant Access. In addition to using these three tiers, you can also choose to archive data from this class into two different archive tiers: Archive Access and Deep Archive Access.

- **S3 Standard-IA:** With this storage class, object data is stored across multiple AZs.

- **S3 One Zone-IA:** With this storage class, object data is stored in only one AZ.

- **S3 Glacier Instant Retrieval:** This class archives your data in such a way that it is available within milliseconds, as needed.

- **S3 Glacier Flexible Retrieval:** This class archives your data in such a way that portions of the data can be retrieved in minutes. Data stored in the S3 Glacier Flexible Retrieval storage class has a minimum storage duration period of 90 days and can be accessed in as little as 1 to 5 minutes by using an expedited retrieval.

S3 Lifecycles

To assist you in saving storage costs, AWS S3 makes the configuration of storage lifecycles very simple. A lifecycle is a set of rules that define actions that S3 will take automatically for you with your data. S3 can use two types of automated actions with your data: transition actions and expiration actions. AWS uses transition actions to automatically move your data between S3 storage classes, and it uses expiration actions to automatically delete your data.

S3 lifecycles can be of tremendous benefit to you and your organization. Consider a company that is planning on uploading (and sharing) documents via an S3 bucket. Within the first 60 days, these documents might be accessed frequently by several employees. After 60 days, the access might switch to infrequent. After 120 days, it might be appropriate to archive the documents. Thanks to S3 lifecycles, you can easily construct rules to automate these transitions within your storage classes. Figure 16-2 shows the configuration of S3 lifecycles in the AWS Management Console.

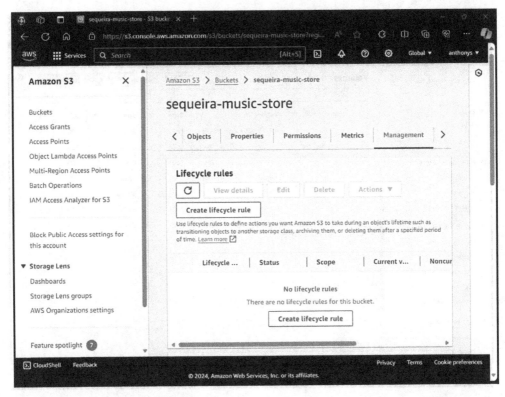

Figure 16-2   Lifecycles in AWS S3

Elastic Block Store (EBS)

When you spin up a virtual machine in the EC2 service of AWS, that machine is going to need a boot volume in order to function. AWS *Elastic Block Store* (*EBS*) provides persistent block storage volumes for use with EC2 instances in the AWS Cloud. Each Amazon EBS volume is automatically replicated within its Availability Zone to protect you from component failure, offering high availability and durability.

EBS volumes offer the consistent and low-latency performance needed to run your workloads. With Amazon EBS, you can scale your usage up or down within minutes—all while paying a low price for only what you provision. Figure 16-3 shows the EBS volumes in AWS on the EC2 dashboard.

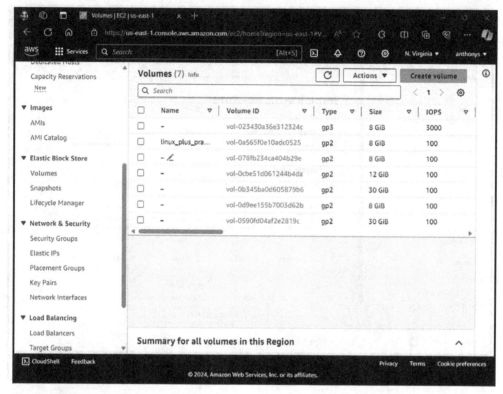

Figure 16-3   EBS Volumes in AWS

Features of EBS include the following:

- **High-performance volumes:** You can choose between solid-state disk (SSD)-backed and hard disk drive (HDD)-backed volumes that can deliver the performance you need for your most demanding applications.

- **Availability:** Each Amazon EBS volume is designed for 99.999% availability and automatically replicates within its Availability Zone to protect your applications from component failure.

- **Encryption:** Amazon EBS encryption provides seamless support for data at rest and data in transit between EC2 instances and EBS volumes.

- **Access management:** Amazon's flexible access control policies allow you to specify who can access which EBS volumes, ensuring secure access to your data.

- **Snapshots:** You can protect your data by creating point-in-time snapshots of EBS volumes, which are backed up to Amazon S3 for long-term durability.

Elastic File System (EFS)

AWS *Elastic File System* (*EFS*) provides simple, scalable file storage for use with EC2 instances in the AWS Cloud, and it can also be used by on-premises servers in your organization. EFS is a fully managed AWS service that is easy to use. EFS offers a simple interface that allows you to create and configure file systems quickly and easily. Features of AWS EFS include the following:

- **Shared file storage:** EFS permits multiple AWS EC2 instances to access the same EFS file system simultaneously.

- **Support for NFSv4:** EFS offers robust support for Network File System version 4. This makes AWS EFS compatible with many systems that rely on NFS, including most Linux systems.

- **Data lifecycle management:** Like AWS S3, EFS provides lifecycle management features that permit cost optimization through the automated movement of data between storage tiers.

- **File system access points:** EFS supports access points, allowing you to create and manage application-specific access to your file systems. Access points provide a way to securely access a file system, and you can create multiple access points for different applications or user groups.

Other Storage Services

While the AWS services S3, EBS, and EFS can be considered the foundation of storage in the AWS Cloud, there are plenty of other storage services that might be critical for your organization. In this section, we will examine three of them: FSx, AWS Storage Gateway, and AWS Backup.

FSx

AWS *FSx* is a service that helps you easily set up and manage shared file storage in the cloud. It's like having a virtual drive in the cloud, where you can store and access your files. One of its key features is simplicity: It takes care of technical details, so you can focus on using your files rather than worrying about how to store them.

With AWS FSx, you can choose between two types of file systems: one for Windows and another for Lustre. The Windows file system is great if you're using applications that are familiar with Windows file-sharing, and the Lustre file system is optimized for high-performance computing and big data workloads.

Setting up AWS FSx is quick and easy. You can scale your file system to fit your needs, making it bigger or smaller as your storage requirements change. In addition, FSx integrates with other AWS services, providing a seamless experience for your applications. Whether you're running a business application, processing big data, or using high-performance computing, AWS FSx simplifies the process of managing file storage in the cloud.

Storage Gateway

AWS *Storage Gateway* is a powerful service that connects your on-premises environment with AWS Cloud storage. Think of it as a bridge between your local data center and the cloud. This service makes it easy for you to extend your storage into the AWS Cloud seamlessly.

There are four types of storage gateway configurations to choose from, based on your needs:

- **S3 File Gateway:** This is like having a cloud-backed file share. It allows you to store and retrieve files in Amazon S3 while still using familiar protocols like NFS or SMB.

- **FSx File Gateway:** This is similar to S3 File Gateway, but it works in conjunction with your FSx file shares. Remember that these shares are created for the Windows and Lustre file systems.

- **Volume Gateway:** This is like having a virtual hard drive in the cloud. It lets you use your existing applications to store data in the cloud, as either blocks of data or snapshots.

- **Tape Gateway:** This is like having a virtual tape library in the cloud. It's useful for businesses that still need to manage tape backups but want to do so more efficiently in the AWS Cloud.

Setting up AWS Storage Gateway is simple. You download and install a virtual appliance on your on-premises hardware, and it connects to your AWS storage resources. Once this is set up, your applications can use the gateway to store and retrieve data, just as they would with local storage. AWS Storage Gateway helps you make the most of the cloud without having to completely overhaul your existing infrastructure, providing a flexible and scalable solution for your storage needs. Figure 16-4 shows the configuration of a storage gateway in AWS.

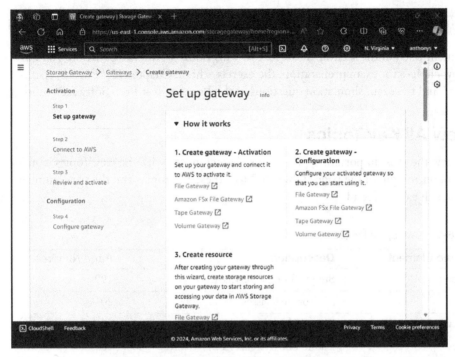

Figure 16-4   Configuring a Storage Gateway in AWS

AWS Backup

AWS Backup is a service that helps you safeguard your important data stored in the AWS Cloud. AWS Backup simplifies the process of backing up and recovering your information, so you don't have to worry about losing files, databases, or other data.

With AWS Backup, you can centrally manage backups across various AWS services. This means you don't have to use different tools for each service; AWS Backup brings them all together in one place. It supports popular AWS services like EBS, RDS, and DynamoDB. This centralized management makes it easier to set up and monitor your backups and ensures that your data is protected.

Setting up backups with AWS Backup is straightforward. You can create backup plans to schedule when and how often your data is backed up. Plus, you have the flexibility to choose the storage destination for your backups, such as Amazon S3. AWS Backup also allows you to define retention policies, which determine how long you want to keep your backups, so you're in control of your data lifecycle.

If something goes wrong and you need to recover your data, AWS Backup simplifies that process, too. You can easily restore your information from the backups you've created. AWS Backup gives you peace of mind, knowing that your data is securely backed up in the AWS Cloud and ready for recovery if the need arises.

Exam Preparation Tasks

As mentioned in the section "How to Use This Book" in the Introduction, you have a few choices for exam preparation: the exercises here, Chapter 22, "Final Preparation," and the exam simulation questions in the Pearson Test Prep Software Online.

Review All Key Topics

Review the most important topics in this chapter, noted with the Key Topics icon in the outer margin of the page. Table 16-2 lists these key topics and the page number on which each is found.

Table 16-2 Key Topics for Chapter 16

Key Topic Element	Description	Page Number
Overview	Simple Storage Service (S3)	199
List	S3 Storage Classes	201
Overview	Elastic Block Store (EBS)	203
Overview	Elastic File System (EFS)	205
List	Four types of AWS storage gateways	206

Define Key Terms

Define the following key terms from this chapter and check your answers in the Glossary:

Simple Storage Service (S3), Elastic Block Store (EBS), Elastic File System (EFS), FSx, Storage Gateway, AWS Backup

Q&A

The answers to these questions appear in Appendix A. For more practice with exam format questions, use the Pearson Test Prep Software Online.

1. Name at least two of the storage classes available in AWS S3.

2. Name at least two of the feature options available in AWS Storage Gateway.

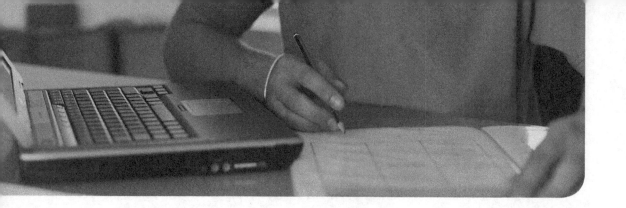

This chapter covers the following subjects:

- **Artificial Intelligence/Machine Learning Services:** Artificial intelligence (AI)/machine learning (ML) is one of the most popular areas of IT today. This section of the chapter details some of the most popular AI and ML services available today in AWS.

- **Data Analytics Services:** Another hugely popular area of IT is data analytics. Sure enough, AWS provides many services in this area, and we'll look at some of the most popular of them in this section.

CHAPTER 17

AWS Artificial Intelligence and Data Analytics Services

In this chapter, we'll delve into the exciting realm of artificial intelligence (AI)/machine learning (ML) services in AWS. In addition, we will explore some amazing data analytics services offered by AWS. This is an important chapter as it addresses some of the most popular and hyped up topics in IT today.

AWS, as you would expect, does a fantastic job of making what might be very complex technologies quite simple to implement. This chapter covers the AWS services available in these areas.

"Do I Know This Already?" Quiz

The "Do I Know This Already?" quiz allows you to assess whether you should read the entire chapter. Table 17-1 lists the major headings in this chapter and the "Do I Know This Already?" quiz questions covering the material in those sections so you can assess your knowledge of these specific areas. The answers to the "Do I Know This Already?" quiz questions appear in Appendix A, "Answers to the 'Do I Know This Already?' Quizzes and Q&A Sections."

Table 17-1 "Do I Know This Already?" Foundation Topics Section-to-Question Mapping

Foundation Topics Section	Questions
Artificial Intelligence/Machine Learning Services	1–3
Data Analytics Services	4–6

CAUTION The goal of self-assessment is to gauge your mastery of the topics in this chapter. If you do not know the answer to a question or are only partially sure of the answer, you should mark that question as wrong for purposes of the self-assessment. Giving yourself credit for an answer you correctly guess skews your self-assessment results and might provide you with a false sense of security.

1. You have been tasked with training a machine-learning model for a project in your organization. What AWS service can assist you with this?

   a. Kendra

   b. Athena

   c. SageMaker

   d. Lex

2. What AWS service helps you offer intelligent natural language searching in your solutions?

   a. Lex

   b. Kendra

   c. SageMaker

   d. QuickSight

3. You are interested in adding AI to your customer service chat. What AWS service should you investigate?

   a. Kendra

   b. SageMaker

   c. Athena

   d. Lex

4. What AWS service permits SQL queries against data stored in S3 buckets?

   a. Athena

   b. QuickSight

   c. Kinesis

   d. Glue

5. What is an option for ETL data services in AWS?

   a. Glue

   b. Athena

   c. SageMaker

   d. Neptune

6. What service of AWS can assist you in creating powerful data visualizations such as charts and graphs?

   a. Athena

   b. QuickSight

   c. Glue

   d. Kinesis

Artificial Intelligence/Machine Learning Services

I don't want to take anything for granted in this section, so let's begin by defining AI and ML. Artificial intelligence (AI) refers to computer systems or machines that are designed to perform tasks that typically require human intelligence, such as learning, reasoning, problem-solving, and decision-making. A subset of this exciting discipline is machine learning (ML), which involves the algorithms and models that enable computers to learn patterns from data and make predictions or decisions without explicit programming.

AI and ML are lofty disciplines that typically require the latest and greatest technologies and lots of available resources (like CPU, memory, and storage). AWS is perfectly positioned to help companies take advantage of these cutting-edge technologies.

SageMaker

AWS *SageMaker* is a smart assistant that you can use to build and train machine learning models without needing to be a coding expert. It provides easy-to-use tools to help you gather and prepare data, pick the right algorithm, and then train and deploy your model, all in one convenient place on the AWS Cloud platform. Figure 17-1 shows AWS SageMaker in the AWS Management Console.

AWS SageMaker offers several features that simplify the ML lifecycle. Here are just some of them:

- **Built-in algorithms:** SageMaker comes with a variety of prebuilt algorithms for common ML tasks—such as classification, regression, and clustering—which means you don't need to create models from scratch.

- **Notebook instances:** SageMaker provides Jupyter notebook instances, which allow you to create and share documents that contain live code, equations, visualizations, and narrative text.

- **Training jobs:** You can use SageMaker to easily train your ML models at scale, distributing the training process across multiple instances.

- **Model hosting:** Once your model is trained, SageMaker makes it simple to deploy, host, and integrate it with your applications.

- **Managed endpoints:** SageMaker provides managed endpoints for deploying models, making it easy to handle real-time predictions and batch processing.

- **Autopilot:** SageMaker enables you to automate the end-to-end process of building, training, and deploying ML models with minimal effort, making it suitable for users with limited ML expertise.

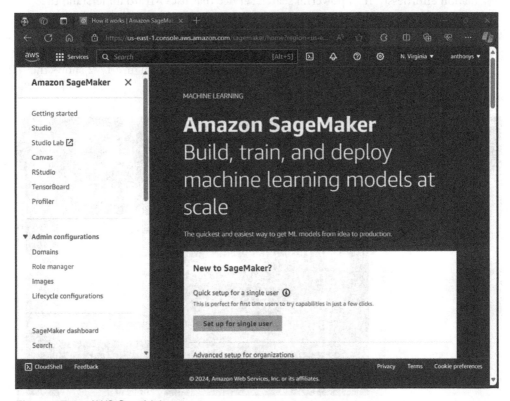

Figure 17-1   AWS SageMaker

Lex

AWS *Lex* makes it easy to create virtual assistants for your applications. It's a service that helps you build chatbots and conversational interfaces using natural language understanding. Think of it as the brain behind a chatbot. Lex understands user inputs, extracts key information, and can respond in a way that makes sense.

This service is handy for creating interactive experiences in your applications, whether for answering customer queries, handling reservations, or guiding users through processes. You can integrate Lex into various platforms, such as mobile apps or websites, to make it easier for users to interact with your applications using just their words. Plus, Lex is powered by the same technology as Amazon Alexa, so it's got some serious language smarts under the hood.

Kendra

AWS *Kendra* is a super-smart search engine that is designed to help you find information effortlessly. It's a powerful search service that uses ML to understand the context and meaning behind your queries. Instead of just matching keywords, Kendra comprehends natural language, making it feel like you're having a conversation with your search engine. It's great for handling complex searches across vast amounts of data in documents, FAQs, or other sources. Figure 17-2 shows the Kendra service in the AWS Management Console.

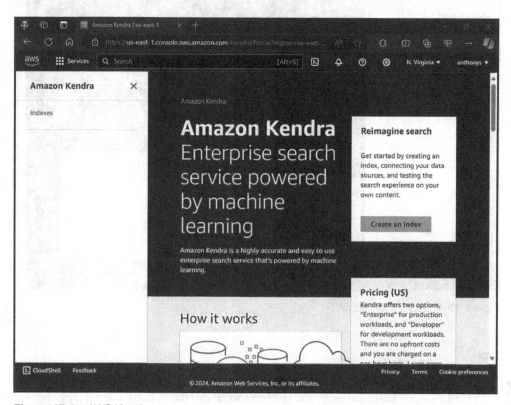

Figure 17-2   AWS Kendra

AWS Kendra includes the following features:

- **Semantic search:** Kendra uses machine learning algorithms to understand the semantics of the content and improve the accuracy of search results by recognizing nuances of and relationships between words.

- **Relevance tuning:** Kendra allows you to fine-tune search results to prioritize certain documents or sources based on your preferences. It enables you to ensure that the most important information is surfaced first.

- **Rich document support:** Kendra can handle a variety of document types, including PDFs, Word documents, HTML, and more, making it versatile for different types of content.

- **Query suggestions:** Kendra provides query suggestions to guide users and help them refine their search queries for better results.

- **Natural language query enhancement:** Kendra assists users in constructing more effective queries by suggesting natural language improvements, making the search process more intuitive.

Data Analytics Services

AWS offers a suite of data analytics services that can help a small startup or a large enterprise make informed decisions by extracting meaningful patterns from data. AWS provides scalable and flexible solutions to analyze data efficiently. With services like AWS Athena, and AWS Glue, you can turn raw data into actionable intelligence. The AWS Cloud makes data analytics accessible, allowing you to focus on uncovering valuable insights without the hassle of managing complex infrastructure.

Athena

When I first tried the AWS *Athena* service, I thought it was pure magic. Athena is a serverless, interactive query service that makes it possible to analyze data residing in AWS S3 buckets using standard SQL expressions. With Athena, you don't need complex data transformation or loading processes. You dump the data into S3, and you are ready to directly query the data in its raw, native format.

Athena uses Trino and Presto, which are open-source distributed SQL query engines that enable you to execute SQL queries across your data stored in S3. Athena supports various data formats, including Avro, Parquet, ORC, JSON, and CSV, ensuring compatibility with a wide range of data structures. In addition, Athena integrates with the AWS Glue Data Catalog (discussed next) to streamline the metadata management process and enhance query efficiency.

Glue

The AWS *Glue* service provides ETL (extract, transform, and load) services for your data analytics. An ETL system in data analytics is like an automated data organizer that collects information from different places, cleans it up, and arranges it neatly so that your analysts can easily make sense of it. It's basically the behind-the-scenes work that ensures your data is ready and polished for analysis.

The Glue Data Catalog acts as a central repository for metadata about your data sources, transformations, and targets. AWS Glue crawlers automatically scan and catalog data in various formats across different storage systems, creating a searchable and organized metadata store.

The ETL process is handled by Glue Jobs, which allows you to define and execute Python or Scala code for data transformation. Glue provides a serverless execution environment and allows you to scale your ETL jobs based on demand without managing the underlying infrastructure.

Glue features tight integration with other AWS services and supports a variety of potential data sources and destinations, including S3, Redshift, and RDS.

QuickSight

AWS *QuickSight* is a business intelligence service that makes it easy to visualize and explore your data. It allows you to create interactive dashboards and reports, providing insights from various data sources with just a few clicks.

QuickSight is designed to be user friendly, enabling both technical and nontechnical users to derive meaningful insights from their data through intuitive and customizable visualizations.

AWS QuickSight offers several key features that make it a powerful and user-friendly business intelligence service:

- **Easy data integration:** QuickSight seamlessly connects to various data sources, including AWS services, databases, and third-party applications, making it convenient to analyze data from different platforms.

- **Intuitive visualizations:** QuickSight provides a wide range of customizable and interactive visualizations, such as charts, graphs, and maps, to allow users to represent data in ways that best communicate insights.

- **Insights:** QuickSight's Auto Insights feature uses machine learning to automatically discover hidden trends, patterns, and anomalies in data, saving users time in the analysis process.

- **Smart recommendations:** QuickSight offers intelligent recommendations for the most suitable visualizations based on the type of data and the analysis performed, enhancing the user experience and aiding in data exploration.

- **SPICE:** QuickSight uses the Super-fast, Parallel, In-memory Calculation Engine (SPICE), which provides high-performance data processing for quick and responsive analytics, even with large datasets.

■ **Ad hoc analysis:** Users can perform ad hoc analysis by dragging and dropping fields to create new visualizations on the fly, enabling quick exploration and understanding of data.

■ **Dashboard storytelling:** QuickSight supports the creation of interactive dashboards and stories that allow users to present and share insights in a narrative format and enhance the communication of data-driven stories.

Kinesis

AWS *Kinesis* is a fully managed platform designed for real-time processing of streaming data at scale. It enables an organization to ingest, process, and analyze large volumes of real-time data from diverse sources, such as Internet of Things (IoT) devices, applications, and logs. Figure 17-3 shows AWS Kinesis in the AWS Management Console.

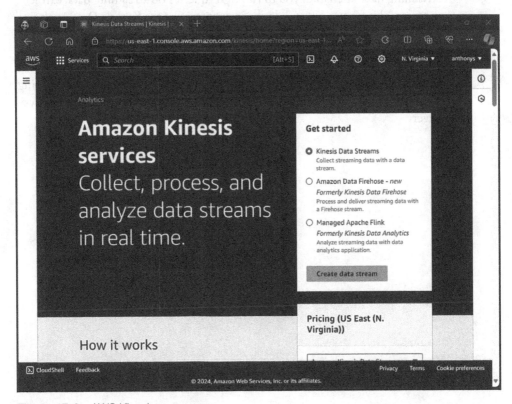

Figure 17-3 AWS Kinesis

Kinesis offers a suite of services that cater to specific aspects of streaming data workflows:

- **Kinesis Data Streams:** This service allows you to collect and process real-time data streams. It enables you to scale the number of streaming data shards based on the volume of data, ensuring efficient handling of varying workloads. With Data Streams, developers can build applications that rapidly respond to changing data and extract valuable insights in real time.

- **Kinesis Data Firehose:** This service simplifies the process of loading streaming data into other AWS services or external destinations and eliminates the need for manual intervention. It automates data delivery, transformation, and compression, streamlining the data pipeline and reducing management overhead.

- **Kinesis Data Analytics:** This service facilitates the real-time analysis of streaming data. It enables you to run SQL queries on streaming data, extract meaningful information, and derive insights on the fly. Kinesis Data Analytics enables an organization to gain actionable intelligence from its streaming data in order to make informed decisions and drive innovation.

As you can see, AWS Kinesis is a comprehensive and scalable solution for managing the entire lifecycle of your streaming data, from ingestion and processing to analysis and delivery.

Exam Preparation Tasks

As mentioned in the section "How to Use This Book" in the Introduction, you have a few choices for exam preparation: the exercises here, Chapter 22, "Final Preparation," and the exam simulation questions in the Pearson Test Prep Software Online.

Review All Key Topics

Review the most important topics in this chapter, noted with the Key Topics icon in the outer margin of the page. Table 17-2 lists these key topics and the page number on which each is found.

Table 17-2 Key Topics for Chapter 17

Key Topic Element	Description	Page Number
List	SageMaker features	214
Overview	Lex	215
Overview	Athena	217
Overview	Kinesis	219

Define Key Terms

Define the following key terms from this chapter and check your answers in the Glossary:

SageMaker, Lex, Kendra, Athena, Glue, QuickSight, Kinesis

Q&A

The answers to these questions appear in Appendix A. For more practice with exam format questions, use the Pearson Test Prep Software Online.

1. Name and briefly describe the AWS AI/ML service that is powered by the same technology as Amazon Alexa.

2. Name and briefly describe the AWS technology that aims to manage your data streaming lifecycle from ingestion to analysis.

This chapter covers the following subjects:

- **Business Application Services:** This section of the chapter describes several services that provide key business needs, like email and customer service. It also covers AWS tools that foster integration between services.

- **Customer Engagement Services:** In this section of the chapter, you will learn about several different services that aim to improve the AWS customer experience.

- **Developer Services:** AWS has many tools and services designed to thrill your developers. In this section of the chapter, you will learn about many important developer services.

- **End-User Compute Services:** In this section of the chapter, you will learn about methods of making applications and even entire desktops available via remote access.

- **IoT Services:** IoT is a growing trend in modern compute. In this section of the chapter, you'll learn about two fundamental IoT services of AWS.

CHAPTER 18

Other AWS Services

This chapter should really drive home the idea that if you have an IT need, AWS most likely has a way to help. In this chapter, we'll peruse a number of different categories of IT and services in each category.

"Do I Know This Already?" Quiz

The "Do I Know This Already?" quiz allows you to assess whether you should read the entire chapter. Table 18-1 lists the major headings in this chapter and the "Do I Know This Already?" quiz questions covering the material in those sections so you can assess your knowledge of these specific areas. The answers to the "Do I Know This Already?" quiz questions appear in Appendix A, "Answers to the 'Do I Know This Already?' Quizzes and Q&A Sections."

Table 18-1 "Do I Know This Already?" Foundation Topics Section-to-Question Mapping

Foundation Topics Section	Questions
Business Application Services	1–2
Customer Engagement Services	3–4
Developer Services	5–6
End-User Compute Services	7–8
IoT Services	9–10

CAUTION The goal of self-assessment is to gauge your mastery of the topics in this chapter. If you do not know the answer to a question or are only partially sure of the answer, you should mark that question as wrong for purposes of the self-assessment. Giving yourself credit for an answer you correctly guess skews your self-assessment results and might provide you with a false sense of security.

1. You are interested in having emails sent to a select list of your employees when your business application has a certain event occur. What AWS service should you consider?

   a. SQS

   b. SNS

   c. EventBridge

   d. SES

2. You need a service that can help with messaging between parts of your application running across various AWS services. What service should you consider?

   a. SQS

   b. EventBridge

   c. Lex

   d. SES

3. Your supervisor has tasked you with locating specific freelance assistance with various aspects of your ongoing and planned AWS projects. What tool in AWS should you consider?

   a. Activate for Startups

   b. SageMaker

   c. AWS Managed Services

   d. AWS IQ

4. What program offers credits to businesses getting started in the AWS Cloud?

   a. AWS IQ

   b. AWS Connect

   c. Activate for Startups

   d. AWS Managed Services

5. Your supervisor wonders if there is an integrated development environment (IDE) inside the AWS Cloud for your developers to take advantage of. What service should you recommend?

   a. CodeDeploy

   b. CodeBuild

   c. AppConfig

   d. Cloud9

6. As you become more and more familiar with the AWS command-line syntax, you are finding that using the CLI is much faster than using a GUI such as the AWS Management Console. What AWS feature brings the AWS CLI to the Management Console?

   a. Cloud9

   b. CloudShell

   c. CodeDeploy

   d. CodeStar

7. You would like to provide persistent Windows desktops to a group of your users who are working with Chromebooks in the field. What service of AWS should you investigate?

   a. Kinesis

   b. IoT Greengrass

   c. AppStream 2.0

   d. WorkSpaces

8. What AWS service helps you make possible secure access to internal websites, using nothing more than a web browser?

   a. WorkSpaces

   b. WorkSpaces Web

   c. AppStream 2.0

   d. IoT Core

9. What IoT service of AWS helps you connect the many devices that make up your IoT deployment?

   a. IoT Greengrass

   b. IoT Core

   c. AppStream 2.0

   d. WorkSpaces Web

10. What AWS IoT service helps you build IoT applications on your various edge devices?

   a. WorkSpaces

   b. AppStream 2.0

   c. IoT Core

   d. IoT Greengrass

Foundation Topics

Business Application Services

Do you need help with customer service or perhaps with email services for your new business? In this section, we will look at services that help you with these tasks, and we will also examine services that enable integration between your AWS business applications and AWS services.

Amazon Connect

Amazon *Connect* is a customer service solution that helps your business set up and manage its customer support systems. Amazon Connect allows your company to create a reliable and efficient contact center in the cloud.

With Connect, your business can easily handle customer calls and chats, and it can even automate responses. Connect provides tools for managing customer interactions, analyzing data, and improving the overall customer experience. Also, Connect is user friendly and allows your business to scale its customer service operations based on its needs. Figure 18-1 shows Amazon Connect in the AWS Management Console.

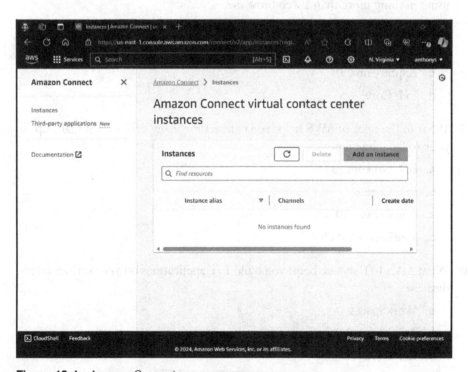

Figure 18-1 Amazon Connect

Simple Email Service (SES)

The AWS *Simple Email Service* (*SES*) makes it easy for your business to send emails. It's a reliable and cost-effective way to manage your email communications.

With AWS SES, you can send marketing emails, transactional messages, or any other type of email without the hassle of managing your email infrastructure. It provides a simple and straightforward way to integrate email sending capabilities into your applications or websites, ensuring that your messages reach your customers effectively.

AWS SES also includes features such as bounce and complaint tracking to help you maintain a good sender reputation and ensure that your emails land in your recipients' inboxes. It's a handy tool for businesses looking for a straightforward solution to handle their email needs.

EventBridge

You can think of AWS *EventBridge* as a smart hub for your applications' events and data. It allows different parts of your software systems to communicate easily by sharing events. It is a central place where your applications can send and receive information without direct connections.

With EventBridge, you can effortlessly connect various services within—and even outside—AWS. It simplifies the process of building and managing event-driven architectures, making it easier for your applications to work together seamlessly. Whether it's reacting to changes in your system, triggering workflows, or coordinating different processes, AWS EventBridge streamlines the flow of information, making your applications more agile and responsive.

Simple Notification Service (SNS)

The AWS *Simple Notification Service* (*SNS*) allows you to easily configure notifications for events that occur in AWS and your AWS solutions. It helps you send notifications to a bunch of different devices or distributed systems, making sure the right information reaches the right place. SNS supports various message formats, including SMS, email, and even push notifications for mobile apps.

SNS is a handy tool for keeping your users informed about important updates or events. With SNS, you can easily set up communication channels to ensure that when something important happens in your application, the news is promptly delivered to all the interested parties, whether they're using a smartphone, email, or another connected device. It's like having a reliable and flexible messenger service in the cloud for your applications' communication needs.

Simple Queue Service (SQS)

The AWS *Simple Queue Service* (*SQS*) is like a virtual waiting line for messages in the cloud. It helps different parts of an application communicate by allowing them to send and receive messages without being directly connected. If an application has tasks that need to be done in the background, SQS helps manage these tasks efficiently.

When one component of your system has a message (a task), the component puts the message in the queue, and another component picks it up when it's ready to process. This ensures that tasks are handled in a reliable and orderly manner, without one part of the application overwhelming another. AWS SQS provides a straightforward way to enhance the flexibility and reliability of communication between different components of your system, making your applications more scalable and responsive.

Customer Engagement Services

AWS has services that help you get started and ensure that you are operating efficiently inside the AWS Cloud. We'll examine several of its remarkable offerings in this category in this section.

Activate for Startups

AWS *Activate for Startups* is a program that provides valuable resources and credits to help startups get off the ground. It's like a kickstart package for new businesses looking to leverage the power of the cloud.

As part of this program, startups receive AWS credits, which act as a virtual currency that can be used to access various AWS services, including computing power, storage, databases, and more. Activate for Startups allows startups to build and scale their applications without worrying about hefty up-front costs.

AWS Activate for Startups also offers technical support, training, and other business benefits. Startups gain access to a community of like-minded entrepreneurs, networking opportunities, and expert advice to help navigate the complexities of building and growing a business.

AWS Activate for Startups is designed to empower startups, providing them with the tools and support they need to innovate, iterate, and succeed in today's competitive business landscape. It's a valuable resource for fledgling companies, offering a helping hand as a new organization embarks on a journey toward success in the digital world.

AWS IQ

AWS *IQ* is a service that simplifies the process of finding and hiring freelance experts for your cloud projects. It's like having a curated marketplace of skilled professionals ready to assist you with your specific AWS-related needs. Whether you're looking for help with architecture, development, or troubleshooting, AWS IQ connects you with freelancers who have the expertise to get the job done.

To use AWS IQ, you can post your project requirements on the platform, detailing what you need assistance with and your budget. Freelancers then apply to work on your project, and you can review their profiles, skills, and proposals to find the right fit. Once you select a freelancer, you can collaborate with them directly through the platform to get your project completed efficiently.

AWS IQ provides a secure and transparent way to access specialized skills on demand, making it easier for businesses to find the right expertise without the hassle of a lengthy hiring process. Whether you're a small startup or a large enterprise, AWS IQ offers a flexible and convenient solution for sourcing external talent to support your AWS-related initiatives.

AWS Managed Services

The AWS *Managed Services* (AMS) tool allows you to use the expertise of AWS internal engineers to help manage and operate your AWS infrastructure. It's a fully managed service that takes care of day-to-day operational tasks, allowing you to focus more on your business goals and less on the nitty-gritty details of managing a cloud environment. With AMS, AWS handles routine activities like patching, monitoring, and backups, ensuring that your AWS environment is secure, up-to-date, and running smoothly.

AMS provides a set of best practices and automation to streamline operations, making it easier for your business to scale its operations in the cloud. It simplifies the management of AWS resources, improves efficiency, and helps maintain a secure and compliant environment. The service is designed to cater to a wide range of organizations, from startups to enterprises, providing them with a hassle-free way to leverage the full potential of AWS without the burden of extensive operational management.

AWS Managed Services helps take the complexity out of AWS management, allowing businesses to enjoy the benefits of a well-managed and optimized cloud infrastructure without the need for extensive in-house expertise. It's a valuable solution for those looking to offload operational tasks, reduce risks, and focus on driving innovation in their business.

Developer Services

Your developers certainly do not want to be left out of the great things the AWS Cloud can bring. Fortunately for them, AWS provides a very large number of services and tools targeted directly at developer teams.

> **NOTE**   Because there are many AWS tools available for developers, and a lot of them have similar names, you might consider using flash cards to help memorize the functions of these different services.

AppConfig

AWS *AppConfig* is a feature that is made available in the AWS Systems Manager service. AppConfig is a handy tool that helps you manage configurations for your applications in the cloud. It allows you to easily control and change settings in your apps without having to redeploy the entire application.

With AppConfig, you can adjust features or settings, and you can even roll out new changes gradually to minimize disruptions. It ensures that your applications are always up to date with the latest configurations, making it simpler for developers to maintain and update software settings without causing downtime. AppConfig streamlines the process of managing configurations for your applications in a flexible and efficient way.

Cloud9

AWS *Cloud9* provides you with your own virtual coding playground in the cloud. It's an integrated development environment (IDE) that allows you to write, run, and debug code without needing to set up your own development environment. Cloud9 enables collaboration with teammates in real time and makes it easy to work on coding projects together.

Cloud9 provides a web-based interface that makes it easy to access your coding environment from anywhere, as long as you have an Internet connection. Whether you're building web applications, running serverless functions, or working on other coding projects, AWS Cloud9 simplifies the development process by providing a flexible and collaborative space for coding in the cloud.

CloudShell

What developer does not love a good command-line interface (CLI)? AWS *Cloud-Shell* provides your developers and system operators with a virtual command line in their AWS Cloud. It gives your staff a convenient way to access and manage their AWS resources directly from the AWS Management Console.

CloudShell provides a preconfigured, secure environment with popular command-line tools, eliminating the need for users to set up their own local development environments. With CloudShell, you can run commands, write scripts, and manage AWS resources using the command line, all within your web browser. Figure 18-2 shows the CloudShell interface in the AWS Management Console.

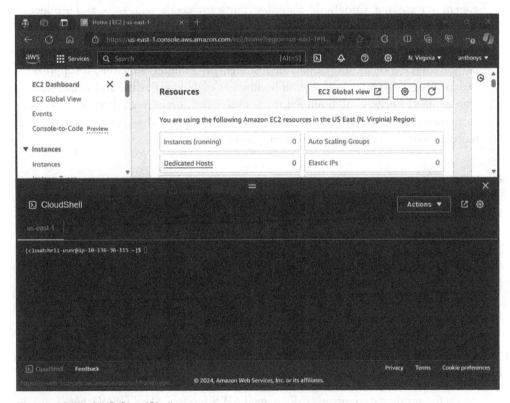

Figure 18-2 AWS CloudShell

CodeArtifact

Another cloud-based tool that your developers might just love is AWS *CodeArtifact*. This tool serves as a digital warehouse for your developer's software packages. CodeArtifact is a secure and fully managed service that helps developers store, manage, and share software artifacts such as packages, dependencies, and libraries. With CodeArtifact, they can create their own repositories to organize and control access to your packages.

CodeArtifact acts as a reliable and scalable hub for software artifacts, making it easier for developers to fetch and share code components across different projects. CodeArtifact aims to simplify the package management process, ensuring that your software development workflow is smooth, efficient, and well organized.

CodeBuild

As its name suggests, AWS *CodeBuild* is a service that enables an automated build system in the cloud. CodeBuild compiles your source code, runs tests, and produces deployable artifacts—all without requiring you to manage the infrastructure.

With CodeBuild, you can easily set up build projects for your applications, specifying the source code location, build environment, and build commands. It supports various programming languages and build tools, making it flexible and adaptable to your project's needs. CodeBuild helps streamline the development process, ensuring that your code is built and tested consistently, allowing you developer teams to focus more on writing code than on managing build servers.

CodeCommit

AWS *CodeCommit* is a secure and scalable home for developers' source code in the AWS Cloud. CodeCommit provides a fully managed version control service, allowing your developers to store, manage, and collaborate on their code securely.

CodeCommit supports Git, a popular version control system that makes it easy for teams to track changes, collaborate on projects, and maintain a history of their codebase. CodeCommit lets you create a central repository for your code, and it integrates seamlessly with other AWS services, offering a reliable solution for version control and freeing you from needing to manage your own infrastructure.

CodeDeploy

Ready for another straightforwardly named AWS service? AWS *CodeDeploy* automates the process of releasing new features or other code updates, making it easier to ensure a smooth deployment without downtime. CodeDeploy allows you to define deployment steps and handles the heavy lifting, such as installing the latest version of your application, managing rollback procedures, and monitoring the deployment progress.

CodeDeploy supports a variety of deployment strategies, letting you control how updates are rolled out—whether across all servers at once or gradually—to reduce potential issues. With AWS CodeDeploy, you can streamline your deployment process, making it more efficient and reliable, while also minimizing the risk of disruptions for your users.

CodePipeline

Developers often use a pipeline during the creation of software—a sort of digital assembly line for software that guides code changes through the different stages of the release process. *CodePipeline* is an AWS Cloud service that automates the steps from source code to deployment, allowing your developers to create a continuous delivery pipeline with ease.

With CodePipeline, you define the stages and actions for your pipeline, such as source code retrieval, building, testing, and deployment. Once set up, it monitors your code changes and automatically moves them through each stage, providing a visual representation of your delivery process. CodePipeline integrates seamlessly with other AWS services and third-party tools, offering a straightforward way to organize and automate your software release workflow.

CodeStar

AWS *CodeStar* is designed to have your developers up and running, developing in the AWS Cloud as quickly as possible. Think of it as a one-stop shop for building, managing, and deploying applications on AWS.

NOTE   This text covers AWS CodeStar because the information for the latest Cloud Practitioner exam makes it clear that this technology may be covered on your exam. However, AWS has announced that it will be discontinuing support for this tool on July 31, 2024. Please keep this in mind as you are planning your AWS strategies and adoptions.

CodeStar is a user-friendly tool that simplifies the entire software development process. With CodeStar, you can easily set up a project, choose your preferred programming language, and collaborate with team members using integrated tools. It streamlines the workflow by automating the creation of necessary resources, such as code repositories, build pipelines, and deployment configurations. CodeStar supports various application types, making it suitable for a wide range of projects, from web applications to backend services.

AWS X-Ray

When you visit the doctor, an X-ray might be needed to further investigate an issue you are experiencing. AWS *X-Ray* performs a similar function, helping you figure out what is occurring behind the scenes with your applications.

X-Ray allows your developers to trace and analyze the requests your applications make as they run. With X-Ray, developers can see how different parts of their application are connected and identify any bottlenecks or issues. It provides a visual representation of your application's architecture, making it easier to understand and optimize performance. X-Ray helps developers and operators troubleshoot problems, improve efficiency, and ensure that applications are running as smoothly as possible in the AWS Cloud.

AWS Amplify

Like so many other companies today, your organization might be tasked with creating many web and mobile applications. The AWS *Amplify* service can turbo-boost this process.

Amplify is a development platform that simplifies the process of creating scalable and secure applications. With Amplify, you can easily set up your backend, add authentication, and integrate features like storage and APIs without getting bogged down by complex configurations. Amplify supports various front-end frameworks, making it adaptable to your preferred development environment. Amplify also provides a set of tools to streamline the deployment and hosting of your applications, ensuring that they are both robust and performant.

AppSync

What about applications your company might be developing that require synchronization to data? AWS *AppSync* to the rescue. AppSync is a fully managed service that simplifies the development of scalable and secure applications by enabling real-time data synchronization. With AppSync, your developers can effortlessly connect their apps to various data sources, such as databases, application programming interfaces (APIs), or even AWS DynamoDB.

AppSync supports offline capabilities, which means your app can still function even when not connected to the Internet, and changes get synced up when it's reconnected. AppSync handles the heavy lifting of data management, making it easier for developers to focus on building engaging and responsive user experiences. Whether you're creating a web or mobile app, AWS AppSync helps you seamlessly integrate and synchronize data, fostering a smoother and more dynamic user experience.

End-User Compute Services

Because the AWS Cloud has basically unlimited resources inside it, it is an amazing place to run your applications and solutions. But what about clients that might lack the necessary resources to run such solutions? One approach in IT today is to permit remote access to these applications (and even full desktops). AWS has a variety of remote desktop-like solutions for you to explore. Let's look at some of them.

AppStream 2.0

AppStream 2.0 is another perfectly named AWS service that does just what its name suggests: It provides a streaming service for your applications in AWS. AppStream 2.0 allows you to run desktop applications in the cloud and stream them directly to users' devices. With AppStream, you don't need to worry about installing or updating software on individual devices; everything happens in the AWS Cloud.

AppStream 2.0 is particularly useful for resource-intensive applications that may not run smoothly on every device. AppStream provides a responsive and secure environment that enables users to access and use applications seamlessly, regardless of their device capabilities. Whether you're running complex design software or data analysis tools, AWS AppStream ensures a consistent and efficient experience for your users, without the hassle of local installations.

AWS WorkSpaces

AppStream 2.0 is an amazing technology, but it won't help you if you want to make an entire Windows or Linux desktop available to a user anytime, anywhere, and on any device they might have. However, AWS offers a solution for this: *WorkSpaces*.

WorkSpaces is a managed desktop computing service that lets you provide a secure and flexible working environment for your users. With WorkSpaces, your team can access a fully functional desktop from any device, whether it's a computer, a tablet, or even a mobile phone. WorkSpaces eliminates the need for everyone to have their own physical computer setup, as everything happens in the cloud.

AWS WorkSpaces offers a range of configurations, allowing you to customize computing power and resources based on your specific needs. It's a convenient solution for remote work, providing a consistent and secure desktop experience without the need for complex hardware setups. Figure 18-3 shows the AWS WorkSpaces console in AWS.

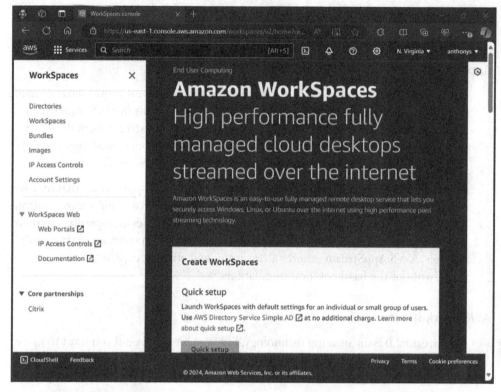

Figure 18-3   AWS WorkSpaces

WorkSpaces Web

So you have AppStream 2.0 for making applications available from the cloud, and you have WorkSpaces for making persistent desktops available from the cloud. But what if you want to make internal websites or applications available via nothing more than a web browser? That is the job of AWS *WorkSpaces Web*.

Thanks to this AWS service, you do not have to worry about setting up special client software on your users' machines. You also do not have to worry about provisioning a virtual private network (VPN) in order to secure the access. Your users just need what they surely already have: a web browser capable of standard Internet security mechanisms.

IoT Services

As I write this chapter, the buzz in IT is all about AI. Before this trend, the buzz was all about the Internet of Things (IoT)—the network of everyday objects, like appliances, devices, and sensors. Once these devices are networked, they can potentially share data and communicate with each other over the network and/or the Internet. For example, perhaps you have a smart fridge that can detect when you are running low on eggs and automatically order more for you. The potential for such technology is nearly limitless, and AWS wants to help. In this section of the chapter, we will examine just a couple of the IoT technologies available in the AWS Cloud.

IoT Core

At the core of the AWS approach to IoT is a service aptly named ***IoT Core***. This service is all about connectivity. It is like a digital conductor that helps devices communicate smoothly with the AWS Cloud.

IoT Core enables connected devices, like sensors or gadgets, to securely send and receive data. IoT Core manages this flow of information, making it easy for devices to interact with cloud applications and other connected devices. With AWS IoT Core, you can collect, process, and act on data generated by your IoT devices to create powerful and responsive IoT applications, without the complexity of managing the underlying infrastructure. Figure 18-4 shows IoT Core in the AWS Management Console.

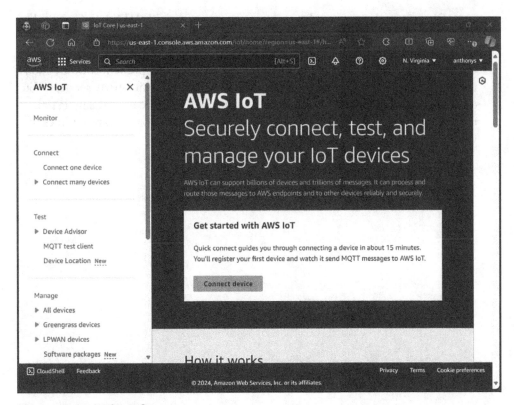

Figure 18-4 AWS IoT Core

IoT Greengrass

While the AWS IoT Core service is all about connectivity, the AWS *IoT Greengrass* service is all about implementing your IoT applications. IoT Greengrass is an open-source IoT edge runtime and cloud service that helps you build, deploy, and manage IoT applications on your devices.

Thanks to IoT Greengrass, you can accomplish these features:

- Build software that enables your devices to act locally on the data they generate
- Allow IoT devices to make predictions based on machine learning models
- Permit IoT devices to filter and aggregate device data
- Enable IoT devices to collect and analyze data closer to where that data is generated
- Allow IoT devices to react autonomously to local events
- Permit IoT devices to communicate securely with other devices on the local network
- Greengrass devices can also communicate securely with AWS IoT Core and export IoT data to the AWS Cloud

You can use IoT Greengrass to build edge applications using prebuilt software modules that can connect your edge devices to AWS services or third-party services. You can also use IoT Greengrass to package and run your software using Lambda functions, Docker containers, native operating system processes, or custom runtimes of your choice.

Exam Preparation Tasks

As mentioned in the section "How to Use This Book" in the Introduction, you have a few choices for exam preparation: the exercises here, Chapter 22, "Final Preparation," and the exam simulation questions in the Pearson Test Prep Software Online.

Review All Key Topics

Review the most important topics in this chapter, noted with the Key Topics icon in the outer margin of the page. Table 18-2 lists these key topics and the page number on which each is found.

Table 18-2   Key Topics for Chapter 18

Key Topic Element	Description	Page Number
Overview	Simple Notification Service (SNS)	227
Overview	Simple Queue Service (SQS)	228
Overview	AWS IQ	229
Overview	CodeArtifact	231
Overview	AWS WorkSpaces	235
Overview	IoT Core	237

Define Key Terms

Define the following key terms from this chapter and check your answers in the Glossary:

Connect, Simple Email Service (SES), EventBridge, Simple Notification Service (SNS), Simple Queue Service (SQS), Activate for Startups, IQ, Managed Services, AppConfig, Cloud9, CloudShell, CodeArtifact, CodeBuild, Code Commit, CodeDeploy, CodePipeline, CodeStar, X-Ray, Amplify, AppSync, AppStream 2.0, WorkSpaces, WorkSpaces Web, IoT Core, IoT Greengrass

Q&A

The answers to these questions appear in Appendix A. For more practice with exam format questions, use the Pearson Test Prep Software Online.

1. Describe the AWS Connect service of AWS.

2. What service of AWS helps developers store, manage, and share software components like packages, dependencies, and libraries?

3. What IoT service of AWS seeks to extend AWS Cloud capabilities to local devices?

This chapter covers the following subjects:

- **General AWS Pricing Practices:** This part of the chapter provides general guidance on pricing in AWS across several different areas that could potentially save you on costs.

- **Fundamentals of Compute Pricing:** This section of the chapter ensures that you are familiar with the various compute purchase options that are available with AWS. (Hint: There are probably more options than you think!)

CHAPTER 19

AWS Pricing Models Compared

In addition to the many other advantages AWS provides, this public cloud offering can save you money. However, you can most effectively save money only if you understand the pricing model in general as well as the various factors that go into charges for the main services of AWS. This chapter ensures that you have this knowledge. Although this chapter doesn't cover every service, it discusses the factors involved in the charges for the main AWS services and provides some examples to help you understand how you may be charged for other services.

"Do I Know This Already?" Quiz

The "Do I Know This Already?" quiz allows you to assess whether you should read the entire chapter. Table 19-1 lists the major headings in this chapter and the "Do I Know This Already?" quiz questions covering the material in those sections so you can assess your knowledge of these specific areas. The answers to the "Do I Know This Already?" quiz questions appear in Appendix A, "Answers to the 'Do I Know This Already?' Quizzes and Q&A Sections."

Table 19-1 "Do I Know This Already?" Foundation Topics Section-to-Question Mapping

Foundation Topics Section	Questions
General AWS Pricing Practices	1–3
Fundamentals of Compute Pricing	4–6

CAUTION The goal of self-assessment is to gauge your mastery of the topics in this chapter. If you do not know the answer to a question or are only partially sure of the answer, you should mark that question as wrong for purposes of the self-assessment. Giving yourself credit for an answer you correctly guess skews your self-assessment results and might provide you with a false sense of security.

1. You are concerned about charges for data transfers when you are working with your AWS resources. Which of these statements is true?

   a. In general, there are no charges for data transfers into or out of AWS storage services.

   b. In general, there are no charges for data transfers out of AWS.

   c. In general, there are no charges for data transfers into AWS.

   d. In general, there are no charges for data transfers into or out of AWS network services.

2. Which AWS service remains free for usage even after the expiration of your Free Tier account?

   a. EC2

   b. VPC

   c. EFS

   d. RDS

3. Which parameter can influence the cost of your AWS S3 storage implementation?

   a. Storage class

   b. Data transfer in

   c. Volume type

   d. Snapshots

4. What is the default pricing model for EC2 instances in AWS?

   a. Savings Plan

   b. Spot Instance

   c. Reserved Instance

   d. On-Demand Instance

5. What does AWS recommend for your choice of pricing plan when you want to prepurchase compute resources to save money and take advantage of AWS resource pooling?

   a. On-Demand Instance

   b. Savings Plan

   c. Spot Instance

   d. Dedicated Host pricing

6. What pricing model of AWS allows you to bid on unused compute capacity in a select region in order to save money over standard On-Demand Instance pricing?

   a. Spot Instance

   b. Savings Plan

   c. Dedicated Instance

   d. On-Demand Instance

General AWS Pricing Practices

Remember that the general concept of pricing in AWS follows the utility company model. Furthermore, AWS pricing is based on these general concepts:

- **Pay as you go:** AWS allows you to pay as you go, without excessive long-term commitments. This ensures adaptability and helps eliminate CapEx costs for IT.

- **Pay less when you reserve:** You can use reserved EC2 instances or Savings Plan instances to save as much as 72% over On-Demand Instances. These pricing models for EC2 are covered in the next section.

- **Pay even less per unit by using more:** Services like S3 and EC2 offer volume discounts as your AWS infrastructure grows.

- **Pay even less as AWS grows:** AWS is constantly learning how to host the cloud more efficiently; as it saves costs, AWS passes its savings on to you.

If yours is a very large enterprise, realize that AWS can also offer custom pricing models. This might be required if you have a very large-volume project and the standard pricing model would appear to be cost-prohibitive.

Also, remember that you can start with the Free Tier of service. Keep in mind that some services of AWS, including these, can remain free (given certain service levels):

- VPC

- CloudFormation

- IAM

- Auto Scaling

It is important to understand the general cost categories of AWS:

- Compute

- Storage

- Data transfers out (aggregated across services)

In general, there are no charges for the following:

- Data transfers in

- Data transfers between AWS services

A number of variables go into the pricing of the different fundamental services. Here are some to give you a feel for your ability to control costs:

- **EC2:** Total clock hours of usage, amount and distribution of load balancing, machine configuration, detailed monitoring, machine purchase type, software/OS, elastic IP addresses, number of instances (including those created by Auto Scaling), and cross-AZ data transfer

- **S3:** Storage type, storage class, requests, and data transfer out

- **EBS:** Volume type, IOPS, and snapshots

- **RDS:** Total clock hours of usage, additional storage, database configuration, purchase type, deployment type, number of databases, data transfer out, and provisioned storage

- **CloudFormation:** Traffic distribution location, requests and data transfer out

Fundamentals of Compute Pricing

For some organizations, compute makes up a vast amount of the total expenditure when it comes to AWS costs. It is little surprise, therefore, that over the decades of its operation, AWS has added more and more flexible pricing models when it comes to compute costs. In this section, we cover the various models.

On-Demand Instance Pricing

The default pricing model when you use AWS EC2 to spin up virtual machine resources is the *On-Demand Instance pricing* model. This is a hugely popular option, and it is not just because it is the default. With this model, you are not committed to any baseline amount of usage. You can launch a virtual machine for seven minutes, and you are billed for just seven minutes of usage. AWS recommends this model for these users:

- Users who do not need discounts for long-term commitments and want the flexibility of a pay-as-you-go model

- Users who are working with applications that have short-term, spiky, or unpredictable workloads

- Users who are working with brand-new applications that they need to test in AWS, possibly over a very short term

Reserved Instance Pricing

Reserved Instance pricing is no longer recommended as often as it once was because AWS has created the Saving Plan pricing model (covered later). Because the Reserved Instance pricing model is still offered (and still tested on certification exams), we need to cover it here.

When you use Reserved Instance pricing, you can save up to 72% off of the On-Demand Instance pricing model. AWS provides this discount because you are committing to a certain amount of computing horsepower over time.

You can choose between three payment options when using the Reserved Instance pricing model:

- **All Upfront:** You pay for the entire reserved instance term with one up-front payment. This option provides you with the largest discount compared to On-Demand Instance pricing.

- **Partial Upfront:** You make a low up-front payment and are then charged a discounted hourly rate for the instance for the duration of the reserved instance term.

- **No Upfront:** You do not need to make any up-front payment, and you get a discounted hourly rate for the duration of the term.

Who would benefit from choosing the Reserved Instance pricing model? This is what AWS says:

- Users who have stable and consistent workloads and can predict their computing needs over longer time frames

- Users who want to save costs in exchange for longer-term commitments to AWS

- Users who are under strict budgets and need predictability when it comes to AWS compute costs

Savings Plan Pricing

Just like Reserved Instance pricing, the AWS *Saving Plans pricing* option saves you money (up to 72%) over the default On-Demand Instance pricing model by having you commit to purchasing compute resources over a certain time frame. In fact, AWS recommends the use of Savings Plans over Reserved Instances. Savings

Plan pricing offers you the flexibility to change your usage as your needs evolve. For example, with a compute savings plan, lower prices will automatically apply when you change from C4 to C6g instances, shift a workload from EU (Ireland) to EU (London), or move a workload from EC2 to Fargate or Lambda.

Currently, AWS offers three types of Saving Plan pricing models: the compute savings plan, the EC2 instance savings plan, and the AWS SageMaker savings plan.

AWS recommends the Saving Plan pricing option for the following users:

- Users who have steady-state usage requirements and have committed resource needs from AWS

- Users who want to take advantage of the very latest compute options from AWS while still saving money over the default On-Demand Instance pricing model

NOTE An advantage to the Reserved Instance and Savings Plan models is that the compute resources are guaranteed to be available in the region you are working with. I have tried to spin up large on-demand EC2 resources in specific regions, only to have AWS inform me that the resources are not presently available.

Spot Instance Pricing

One of the most interesting pricing plans for AWS compute resources is the *Spot Instance pricing* plan. With this pricing plan, users can bid on unused compute capacity available with AWS. Since the compute resources are unused, AWS offers them at a remarkable discount of up to 90% when compared to the default On-Demand Instance pricing model. Figure 19-1 shows the Spot Instance pricing option from the EC2 area of the AWS Management Console.

Spot Instance pricing is recommended for the following AWS users:

- Users who are working with fault-tolerant or stateless workloads

- Users who are running applications on heterogeneous hardware

- Users who are running applications that have flexible start and end times

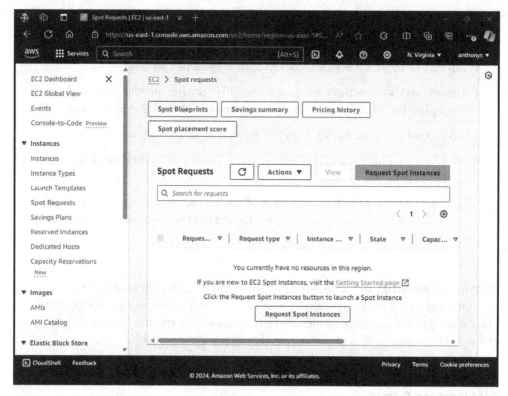

Figure 19-1 The EC2 Spot Request Interface

Dedicated Host Pricing

With the ***Dedicated Host pricing*** model, you purchase a dedicated EC2 server from AWS. Notice how unique this is. Normally, you are assigned compute resources from a large pool, and you are typically on hardware that is shared between different AWS customers. The Dedicated Host option is more costly than the previously mentioned cost models.

Even though this option is more expensive compared to the On-Demand Instance pricing model, you might be able to save costs when it comes to licensing. The Dedicated Host pricing model might allow you to use your existing server-bound software licenses, including Windows Server, SQL Server, and SUSE Linux Enterprise Server.

To make the Dedicated Host pricing model more flexible, AWS offers Dedicated Host pricing in On-Demand Instance and Savings Plan variations. Figure 19-2 shows the Dedicated Host request process from the EC2 area of the AWS Management Console.

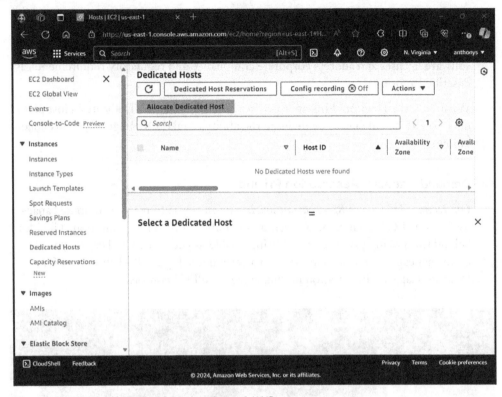

Figure 19-2 The Dedicated Host Interface of AWS

The Dedicated Host pricing model is recommended for the following users:

- Users who need to save money on licensing costs

- Users who have workloads that need to run on dedicated physical servers

- Users who want to offload host maintenance to the experts at AWS while at the same time controlling the maintenance windows to support their business objectives

- Users who need to meet the security policy of their organization or compliance body

Dedicated Instance Pricing

Dedicated Instance pricing is very similar to the Dedicated Host pricing model. You can use both the Dedicated Host and Dedicated Instance pricing options to launch EC2 instances on physical servers that are dedicated to your use. The big difference between the two models is that the Dedicated Host model gives you additional visibility and control over how instances are placed on a physical server. Specifically, you can consistently deploy your instances to the same physical server over time. As a result, the Dedicated Host model enables you to use your existing server-bound software licenses and address corporate compliance and regulatory requirements, as described above.

What does the Dedicated Instance pricing plan offer that the Dedicated Host plan does not? It is really just a single item: the ability to take advantage of per-instance billing.

On-Demand Capacity Reservation Pricing

On-Demand Capacity Reservation pricing permits you to reserve compute capacity for your EC2 instances in a specific Availability Zone for any duration. The idea behind this pricing plan is to avoid being unable to get on-demand capacity in the event that capacity constraints occur in a certain AZ. Figure 19-3 shows the On-Demand Capacity Reservation pricing area of the EC2 console.

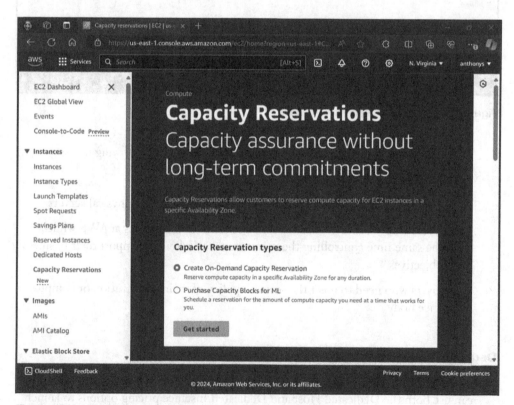

Figure 19-3 The On-Demand Capacity Reservation Interface

AWS recommends On-Demand Capacity Reservation pricing for these users:

- Users who have business-critical events or workloads that require capacity assurance

- Users who have workloads that need to meet regulatory requirements for high availability

- Users who are provisioning compute resources to meet disaster recovery plans

NOTE   Related to this pricing model is the AWS EC2 Capacity Blocks for ML pricing plan. As the name makes clear, this model is designed for the reservation of GPU instances needed for machine learning workloads (which are often significant).

Exam Preparation Tasks

As mentioned in the section "How to Use This Book" in the Introduction, you have a few choices for exam preparation: the exercises here, Chapter 22, "Final Preparation," and the exam simulation questions in the Pearson Test Prep Software Online.

Review All Key Topics

Review the most important topics in this chapter, noted with the Key Topics icon in the outer margin of the page. Table 19-2 lists these key topics and the page number on which each is found.

Table 19-2   Key Topics for Chapter 19

Key Topic Element	Description	Page Number
Overview	On-Demand Instance pricing	245
Overview	Reserved Instance pricing	246
Overview	Savings Plan pricing	246
Overview	Spot Instance pricing	247
Overview	Dedicated Host pricing	248

Define Key Terms

Define the following key terms from this chapter and check your answers in the Glossary:

On-Demand Instance pricing, Reserved Instance pricing, Savings Plan pricing, Spot Instance pricing, Dedicated Host pricing, Dedicated Instance pricing, On-Demand Capacity Reservation pricing

Q&A

The answers to these questions appear in Appendix A. For more practice with exam format questions, use the Pearson Test Prep Software Online.

1. List two cases in which you are not typically charged for data transfers associated with AWS.

2. What AWS pricing model permits you to accommodate your existing server-bound licensing requirements?

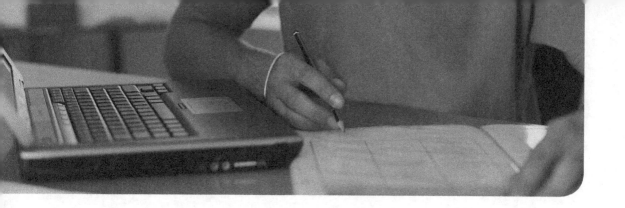

This chapter covers the following subjects:

- **AWS Billing and Cost Management:** This part of the chapter discusses the AWS Billing and Cost Management console and the many powerful tools that are available there for understanding and controlling your AWS costs.

- **AWS Organizations:** This section of the chapter covers the AWS Organizations tool, which can be extremely valuable for companies that have many different AWS accounts and want control over the cloud environment that directly impacts billing and costs.

CHAPTER 20

Resources for Billing, Budgets, and Cost Management

AWS is not going to be well received in your enterprise if you cannot afford it or if it does not provide the cost savings that were expected. This chapter helps you achieve the cost controls you want with AWS. It describes tools and best practices you should consider using in the areas of costs and billing.

"Do I Know This Already?" Quiz

The "Do I Know This Already?" quiz allows you to assess whether you should read the entire chapter. Table 20-1 lists the major headings in this chapter and the "Do I Know This Already?" quiz questions covering the material in those sections so you can assess your knowledge of these specific areas. The answers to the "Do I Know This Already?" quiz questions appear in Appendix A, "Answers to the 'Do I Know This Already?' Quizzes and Q&A Sections."

Table 20-1 "Do I Know This Already?" Foundation Topics Section-to-Question Mapping

Foundation Topics Section	Questions
AWS Billing and Cost Management	1–3
AWS Organizations	4–5

CAUTION The goal of self-assessment is to gauge your mastery of the topics in this chapter. If you do not know the answer to a question or are only partially sure of the answer, you should mark that question as wrong for purposes of the self-assessment. Giving yourself credit for an answer you correctly guess skews your self-assessment results and might provide you with a false sense of security.

1. The AWS Budgets tool can provide you with visualizations of costs. What tool does Budgets use to present this information?

   a. Billing Conductor

   b. Pricing Calculator

   c. Cost Explorer

   d. SNS

2. Your boss is excited to move to AWS, but he is very concerned about the anticipated costs. Based on these fears, what tool should you show your boss?

   a. Cost and Usage Reports

   b. Cost Explorer

   c. Billing Conductor

   d. Pricing Calculator

3. What AWS cost management tool allows you to segment your accounts into logical billing groups?

   a. Billing Conductor

   b. Cost Explorer

   c. Pricing Calculator

   d. Cost and Usage Reports

4. What AWS tool permits you to manage multiple AWS accounts in a single interface?

   a. Cognito

   b. Organizations

   c. Kinesis

   d. Athena

5. What are the logical containers you can use in AWS Organizations to group member accounts?

   a. IAMs

   b. Service control policies (SCPs)

   c. Organizational units (OUs)

   d. Tag groups

Foundation Topics

AWS Billing and Cost Management

AWS Billing and Cost Management is the service you use to pay your AWS bill, monitor your usage, and budget your current and future costs. AWS automatically charges the credit card you provided when you signed up for a new account with AWS. Charges appear on your credit card bill monthly.

You can view or update credit card information and designate a different credit card for AWS to charge on the Payment Methods page in the Billing and Cost Management console. Figure 20-1 shows the AWS Billing and Cost Management console.

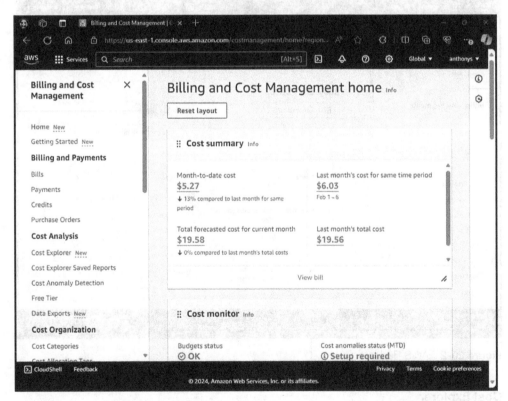

Figure 20-1 AWS Billing and Cost Management

The Billing and Cost Management service provides features you can use to estimate and plan your AWS costs, receive alerts if your costs exceed a threshold that you set, assess your biggest investments in AWS resources, and, if you work with multiple AWS accounts, simplify your accounting.

Budgets

You can use Budgets to track your AWS usage and costs. *Budgets* uses the cost visualization provided by Cost Explorer to show the status of your budgets and provide forecasts of your estimated costs. You can also use Budgets to track your AWS usage, including your Free Tier usage. Finally, you can use Budgets to create AWS SNS notifications that alert you when you go over your budgeted amounts or when your estimated costs exceed your budgets. Figure 20-2 shows the Budgets interface in the AWS Management Console. Notice that this is just one of the many excellent tools available in the AWS Billing and Cost Management console.

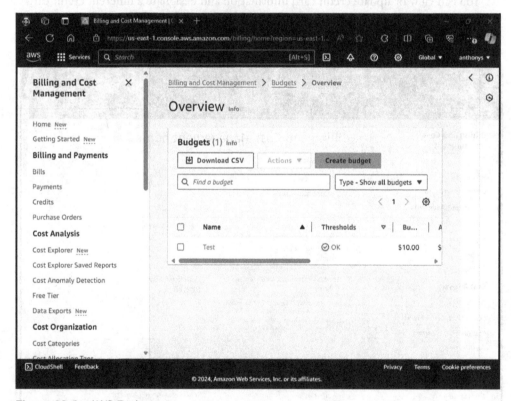

Figure 20-2   AWS Budgets

Cost Explorer

The AWS Billing and Cost Management console includes the valuable *Cost Explorer* tool for viewing your AWS cost data as a graph. With Cost Explorer, which is provided free of charge, you can filter graphs by values such as API operation, Availability Zone, AWS service, custom cost allocation tag, Amazon EC2 instance type, purchase option, region, usage type, and usage type group. If you use consolidated billing, you can also filter by member account. In addition, you can see a forecast of future costs based on your historical cost data.

Billing Conductor

A relatively new tool in the Billing and Cost Management section of AWS is the *Billing Conductor*. This handy service allows you to customize your bill computation and display your billing data in a meaningful way.

The Billing Conductor segments your accounts into logical billing groups. You might base these groups on your customers or your business units. For each of your logical billing groups, you will have an applied pricing plan, which allows you to apply a percentage-based markup or discount on top of AWS On-Demand rates to all usage accrued by the billing group's associated accounts. Your custom configurations are used to compute cost and usage data that is visible on the Bills page and available by the Cost & Usage Report. The billing group's associated accounts can also view their respective pro forma costs in the AWS Cost Explorer.

Pricing Calculator

The AWS *Pricing Calculator* is a handy tool that lets you estimate how much your AWS usage will cost before you actually start using it. You can pick and choose the services you need and adjust the settings to match your usage, and the calculator gives you a price tag. It allows you to budget for your cloud adventures, helping you plan and avoid surprises when the bill comes. Whether you're launching a new project or tweaking your existing setup, the Pricing Calculator is your go-to helper for understanding and predicting your AWS expenses.

Cost and Usage Reports

The *Cost and Usage Reports* tool allows you to have AWS publish billing reports to an Amazon S3 bucket that you own. You can receive reports that break down your costs by the hour or month, by product or product resource, or by tags that you define yourself. AWS updates the report in your bucket once a day, in comma-separated values (CSV) format. You can view the reports using spreadsheet software such as Microsoft Excel or access them from an application by using the Amazon S3 API.

NOTE While the current Certified Cloud Practitioner exam requires you to have knowledge of the AWS Cost and Usage Reports feature of AWS, you shouldn't fall too deeply in love with this feature. AWS has announced that this tool will be deprecated on June 1, 2024, and it is replacing it with the Data Exports tool.

Cost Allocation Tags

You can think of AWS *Cost Allocation Tags* as a tool that provides sticky notes for your cloud resources to help you organize and track your spending. You can use this tool to label different resources based on projects, departments, or any other category that makes sense for your business. This way, when you get your AWS bill, it's not just a big list of costs; you can see exactly where your money is going.

You might want to separate expenses for different teams or keep tabs on specific projects; whatever the case may be, these tags help tremendously. In short, Cost Allocation Tags makes it easier to understand and manage your AWS spending by adding a helpful layer of organization to your cloud resources.

AWS Organizations

AWS *Organizations* is a service that enables the creation of a hierarchical structure for managing multiple AWS accounts within an organization. Figure 20-3 shows the AWS Organizations dashboard in the AWS Management Console.

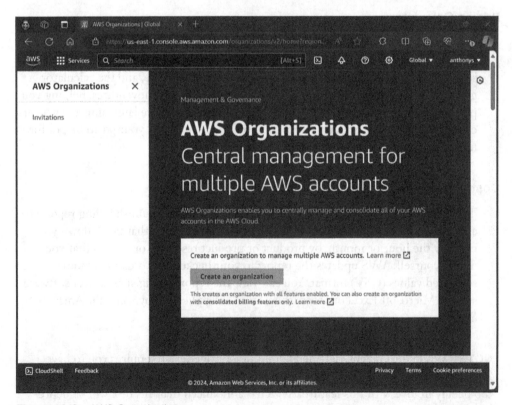

Figure 20-3   AWS Organizations

Organizations provides centralized management and governance, allowing an administrator to define and enforce policies across the entire organization. These are the main features of this tool:

- **Management and member account structure:** In Organizations, the management account is the top-level AWS account in the organizational hierarchy. It has administrative control over all member accounts. Member accounts are individual AWS accounts associated with the organization, each serving specific purposes or workloads.

- **Organizational units (OUs):** OUs are logical containers for grouping member accounts to reflect the organizational structure, making it easier to apply policies and manage resources.

- **Service control policies (SCPs):** SCPs are applied at the root or to OUs or accounts to define permissions and control access to AWS services. SCPs help enforce security and compliance standards.

- **Consolidated billing:** For many AWS administrators, this feature alone makes Organizations a beloved tool. The centralized billing feature makes it possible to aggregate charges from all member accounts and provide a unified view of costs and usage across the organization.

- **Policy-based management:** This powerful feature enables the application of IAM policies, SCPs, and other policies at the organization, OU, or account levels to govern access and resource usage.

- **Organizational view:** The organizational view is a graphical representation of the organizational structure that helps visualize relationships between accounts and OUs.

- **Tag policies:** Tag policies allow organizations to define and enforce tagging standards, ensuring consistent tagging practices across accounts for better resource tracking and cost management.

- **Cross-account resource access:** AWS facilitates secure access to resources across accounts, enabling organizations to share resources while maintaining control over permissions.

Exam Preparation Tasks

As mentioned in the section "How to Use This Book" in the Introduction, you have a few choices for exam preparation: the exercises here, Chapter 22, "Final Preparation," and the exam simulation questions in the Pearson Test Prep Software Online.

Review All Key Topics

Review the most important topics in this chapter, noted with the Key Topics icon in the outer margin of the page. Table 20-2 lists these key topics and the page number on which each is found.

Table 20-2   Key Topics for Chapter 20

Key Topic Element	Description	Page Number
Overview	Cost Explorer	258
Overview	Pricing Calculator	259
List	AWS Organizations features	261

Define Key Terms

Define the following key terms from this chapter and check your answers in the Glossary:

Budgets, Cost Explorer, Billing Conductor, Pricing Calculator, Cost and Usage Reports, Cost Allocation Tags, Organizations

Q&A

The answers to these questions appear in Appendix A. For more practice with exam format questions, use the Pearson Test Prep Software Online.

1. Explain the purpose of Cost Allocation Tags in AWS.

2. Describe the AWS Organizations service.

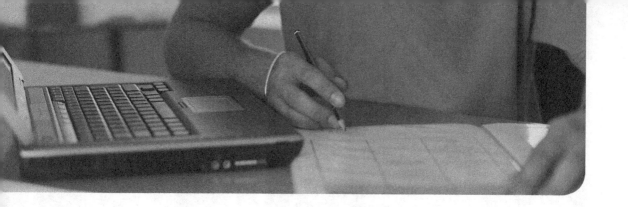

This chapter covers the following subjects:

- **AWS Technical Resources:** A wealth of technical resources can assist you throughout your work with AWS. This section of the chapter details many of these resources for you.

- **AWS Support Options:** There are many different support options when it comes to AWS, from a free basic plan to a pricey enterprise plan. In this section of the chapter, you'll learn about the different options.

CHAPTER 21

AWS Technical Resources and AWS Support Options

This chapter begins presenting superb resources you can take advantage of completely free of charge. In fact, to access AWS documentation, you don't even need an account with AWS. Some of the free tools that are covered in this chapter include the AWS Whitepapers and Blogs. This chapter also provides information about numerous other tools that can assist you technically with your AWS work and resources.

Even if you have been working with AWS for a long time, at some point you might require support assistance from an Amazon employee. This chapter provides you with an overview of how support works in AWS. It also provides a detailed breakdown of the different support options so you can begin thinking about the best plan for your AWS implementation.

"Do I Know This Already?" Quiz

The "Do I Know This Already?" quiz allows you to assess whether you should read the entire chapter. Table 21-1 lists the major headings in this chapter and the "Do I Know This Already?" quiz questions covering the material in those sections so you can assess your knowledge of these specific areas. The answers to the "Do I Know This Already?" quiz questions appear in Appendix A, "Answers to the 'Do I Know This Already?' Quizzes and Q&A Sections."

Table 21-1 "Do I Know This Already?" Foundation Topics Section-to-Question Mapping

Foundation Topics Section	Questions
AWS Technical Resources	1–3
AWS Support Options	4–6

> **CAUTION**   The goal of self-assessment is to gauge your mastery of the topics in this chapter. If you do not know the answer to a question or are only partially sure of the answer, you should mark that question as wrong for purposes of the self-assessment. Giving yourself credit for an answer you correctly guess skews your self-assessment results and might provide you with a false sense of security.

1. Which of the following resources is often a source for exam questions and topics?

   a. FAQs

   b. IEEE standards docs

   c. Wikipedia.org

   d. NIST standards

2. Which statement regarding the AWS documentation is false?

   a. The AWS documentation is carefully categorized to assist your usage.

   b. The documentation consists of user guides and references, broken down by topic.

   c. You cannot access the documentation of AWS without at least a Free Tier account.

   d. The documentation is accessed online.

3. You have discovered that a group of cybercriminals are using AWS resources to carry out their abuse. What team in AWS should you report this activity to?

   a. AWS Trust and Safety

   b. Trusted Advisor

   c. TAM

   d. Concierge

4. What minimal level of support gives you access to a TAM?

   a. Developer

   b. Enterprise On-Ramp

   c. Business

   d. Basic

5. What service in AWS allows core checks to be performed by any customer, regardless of their support plan level?

    a. CloudFront

    b. CloudFormation

    c. CloudTrail

    d. Trusted Advisor

6. What level of support in AWS offers a response time of less than 15 minutes?

    a. Developer

    b. Enterprise On-Ramp

    c. Enterprise

    d. Business

Foundation Topics

AWS Technical Resources

Let's begin this chapter with a tour of the many technical resources that are available for you when it comes to AWS. As mentioned earlier, many of these incredible resources are available completely free of charge.

Documentation, Whitepapers, and Blogs

The AWS documentation is very good. It is an excellent mix of theory and practical step-by-step guides. You can find the AWS documentation at https://docs.aws.amazon.com. Figure 21-1 shows the AWS documentation home page.

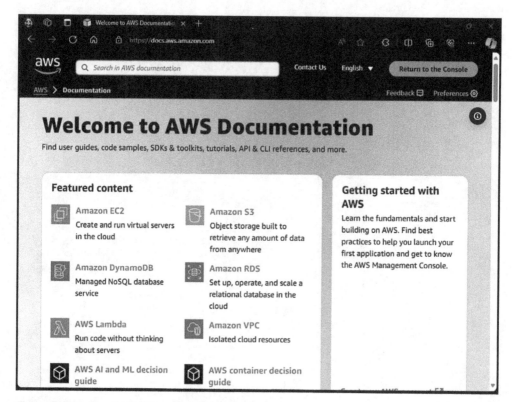

Figure 21-1 The AWS Online Documentation

To say that the body of documentation is massive would be an understatement. Keep in mind that there are typically many different sections under each category and topic in the documentation. For example, if you select Amazon EC2 under the Featured Content area, you reach the Amazon Elastic Compute Cloud Documentation home page shown in Figure 21-2.

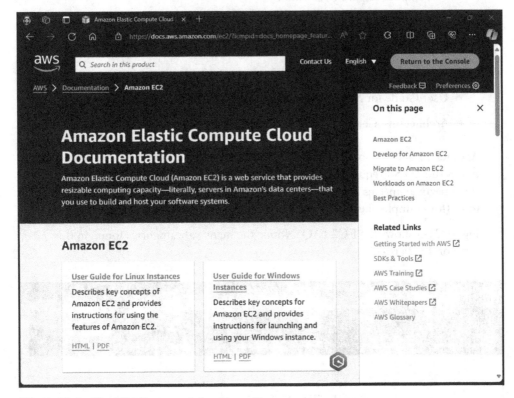

Figure 21-2 The EC2 Documentation Home Page

This page leads you to the breakdown of the EC2 documentation, which currently (at this writing) consists of the following:

- User Guide for Linux Instances
- User Guide for Windows Instances
- Amazon EC2 Instance Types
- User Guide for AWS Nitro Enclaves
- API Reference
- EC2 Section for the AWS CLI Reference
- EC2 Instance Connect API Reference
- EC2 Auto Scaling User Guide

- Amazon EC2 Auto Scaling Section of the AWS CLI Reference
- EC2 Auto Scaling API Reference
- VM Import/Export User Guide
- Amazon Linux 2 User Guide
- Amazon Linux 2 Release Notes
- Amazon Linux 2023
- User Guide for Microsoft SQL Server on Amazon EC2
- Architecture Center: Compute and HPC Best Practices

Another excellent resource that Amazon makes available as part of its documentation is the AWS Frequently Asked Questions (FAQs), located at https:// aws.amazon.com/faqs. These documents are also categorized and broken down by topic (for example, the EC2 FAQ).

Figure 21-3 shows the EC2 FAQ. Notice the many subcategories found in this Amazon EC2 area.

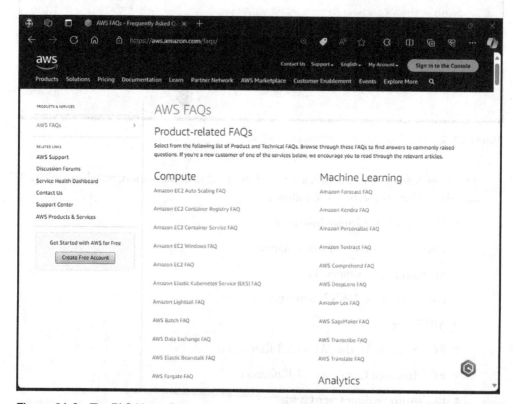

Figure 21-3   The FAQ Home Page

Reading FAQs is a fun way to learn very relevant aspects of the technologies and how they operate. In addition, AWS certification exam authors love to draw question material from the AWS FAQs.

Figure 21-4 shows another excellent free resource: the AWS Whitepapers & Guides documentation.

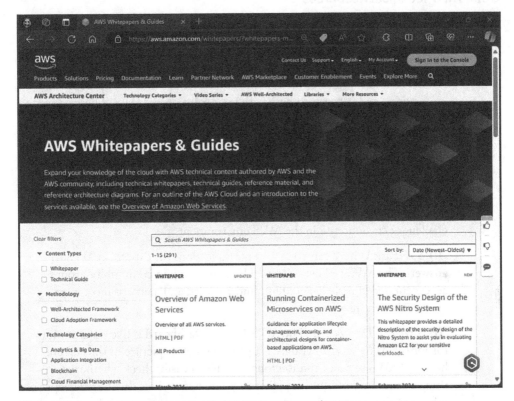

Figure 21-4   The AWS Whitepapers & Guides Documentation

This resource is a comprehensive collection of documents that offer in-depth insights, best practices, and detailed information on various aspects of cloud computing. These resources cover a wide range of topics, including architecture, security, compliance, and implementation strategies. Aimed at developers, architects, and IT professionals, the whitepapers and guides serve as valuable references to help users understand AWS services, optimize their infrastructure, and navigate complex technical challenges.

Finally, there is also a feature called AWS Blogs. This is a dynamic platform that delivers a constant stream of articles, updates, and insights related to cloud computing, covering a diverse range of topics, including new service announcements, best practices, case studies, and in-depth technical content.

Other AWS Technical Resources

While the preceding resources are nothing short of amazing, there are plenty of other technical resources that you might want to avail yourself of. Here are some of the biggest that you should know:

- *AWS Prescriptive Guidance*: This AWS website provides best practice strategies, guides, and patterns to help with your solutions in AWS. These resources were developed by AWS technology experts and the global community of AWS partners.

- *AWS Knowledge Center*: This AWS website helps you find information, troubleshoot issues, and get support for your AWS services. It includes a collection of articles, documentation, FAQs, and forums where you can seek answers to your questions, learn about best practices, and explore solutions to common challenges encountered in the AWS environment.

- *AWS re:Post*: Where can you go to post questions for experts in AWS to answer? The AWS re:Post website. Here you can join community groups, access curated knowledge content, find answers, and, perhaps most importantly, ask your questions.

- *AWS Health Dashboard*: The AWS Health Dashboard is like a status monitor for the AWS services you use. It provides a clear picture of the current health of AWS services and Regions so you can easily check whether everything is running smoothly or if there are any issues. This dashboard keeps you informed about planned maintenance, service interruptions, and any other events that might affect your use of AWS.

- *AWS Health API*: Instead of checking the AWS Health Dashboard manually, you can use the AWS Health API to automatically retrieve and integrate real-time updates about the health of your AWS resources into your applications or systems.

- *AWS Trust and Safety*: The AWS Trust and Safety team reviews any AWS abuse reports you submit. This is how you can effectively notify AWS if you discover users leveraging the cloud services for inappropriate/illegal behavior.

- *AWS Partner Training and Certification*: The AWS Partner Training and Certification program offers training and certification opportunities for partners, allowing them to enhance their knowledge and expertise in AWS technologies. By completing the training and certification opportunities, partners gain recognition for their skills and can better support customers in their AWS journey.

- *AWS Partner Events*: The AWS Partner Events program brings together businesses and experts interested in AWS. It serves as a space for learning, networking, and collaboration. In these events, participants can gain insights into the latest AWS technologies, share experiences, and connect with other partners and professionals in the field.

- *AWS Partner Volume Discounts*: The AWS Partner Volume discounts program offers partners the opportunity to access discounted pricing as they increase their usage of AWS services. The more AWS resources the partners use, the more they save. This program aims to reward partners for their growing commitment to AWS, providing a cost-effective way to scale up cloud resources.

- *AWS Marketplace*: The AWS Marketplace is a convenient hub for discovering and deploying applications for tasks like data analytics, security, and machine learning. The AWS Marketplace applications are provided by vendors (and partners) that create AWS solutions.

- *AWS Professional Services*: The AWS Professional Services program allows access to experienced professionals who can help you plan, implement, and optimize your cloud solutions. Whether you're just starting with AWS or looking to enhance your existing setup, the AWS Professional Services team offers support and expertise tailored to your specific needs.

AWS Support Options

Amazon provides a rich set of AWS resources as well as human resources to assist you in AWS. There are different plans you can invest in to try to match your needs and your budget with a plan that makes sense for your organization. Figure 21-5 shows the AWS Support home page.

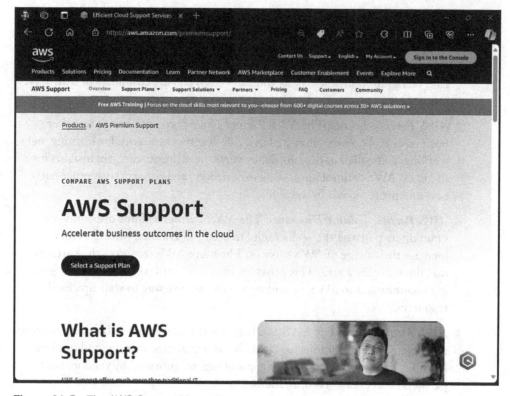

Figure 21-5 The AWS Support Home Page

AWS Support centers around these goals:

- **Proactive guidance:** Your support plan might include access to a Technical Account Manager (TAM). The TAM is your primary point of contact and provides guidance, architectural review, and ongoing communication to keep you informed and well prepared as you plan, deploy, and proactively optimize your solutions. The TAM offers the following:

  - A dedicated voice within AWS to serve as your technical point of contact and advocate

  - Proactive guidance and best practices to help optimize your AWS environment

  - Orchestration and access to the breadth and depth of technical expertise across the full range of AWS

- **Best practices:** One of the valuable support resources is AWS Trusted Advisor. This online resource helps you provision your resources following best practices to help reduce cost, increase performance and fault tolerance, and improve security by optimizing your AWS environment. As you'll learn in the next part of this chapter, four core checks are available to all AWS customers. The full power of AWS Trusted Advisor is available with Business and Enterprise support plans. Trusted Advisor offers the following:

- Guidance on getting the optimal performance and availability based on your requirements

- Opportunities to reduce your monthly spend and retain or increase productivity

- Best practices to help increase security

- **Account assistance:** Included as part of the Enterprise support plan, the Concierge team is composed of AWS billing and account experts who specialize in working with enterprise accounts. This Concierge team will quickly and efficiently assist you with your billing and account inquiries, and work with you to implement billing and account best practices. Concierge support includes the following:

  - 24/7 access to AWS billing and account inquiries

  - Guidance and best practices for billing allocation, reporting, consolidation of accounts, and root-level account security

  - Access to Enterprise account specialists for payment inquiries, training on specific cost reporting, assistance with service limits, and facilitation of bulk purchases

- **Launch support:** For planned events, including advertising and product launches, promotions, and infrastructure migrations where a significant increase in demand for your resources is expected, Infrastructure Event Management (IEM) delivers highly focused engagement to provide architectural and scaling guidance. This tool aligns real-time operational resources to support the success of your event. IEM is included with Enterprise support and is available for an additional fee with Business support plans. It includes the following:

  - Event planning and preparation based on your use case and objectives

  - Resource recommendations and deployment guidance based on anticipated capacity needs

  - Dedicated attention from your AWS support team during your event

  - Guidance and support as you scale resources to normal operating levels, post-event

Comparing the Plans

The current support plans available from AWS are as follows:

- **Basic:** The *Basic support plan* is free of charge and begins when you sign up for your Free Tier account. This plan continues past Free Tier expiration should you not elect for one of the paid plans.

- **Developer:** The *Developer support plan* is the recommended plan if you are experimenting with or testing AWS.

- **Business:** The *Business support plan* is the minimum recommended tier if you are currently running production workloads in AWS.

- **Enterprise On-Ramp:** The *Enterprise On-Ramp support plan* tier is recommended if you have business-critical workloads in AWS.

- **Enterprise:** The *Enterprise support plan* tier is recommended if you have mission-critical workloads in AWS.

Clearly, you should match your expected support needs with the paid plan that makes the most sense for you. In order to do that, you should use Table 21-2 carefully in order to make the correct choice. Please keep in mind that this table reflects the details at the time of this writing and does not include the free Basic support plan. To see the most complete information (if needed), be sure to visit https://aws.amazon.com/premiumsupport/plans/.

Table 21-2 The Various Support Plans of AWS

	Developer	Business	Enterprise On-Ramp	Enterprise
Cost	$29/month	$100/month	$5,500/month	$15,000/month
Fastest Response Time	< 12 hours	< 1 hour	< 30 minutes	< 15 minutes
Technical Account Manager	—	—	Pool of TAMs available	Dedicated TAM
Trusted Advisor	Service quota and security checks	Full set of checks	Full set of checks	All checks and recommendations
Billing Support	—	—	Concierge service	Proactive support

Exam Preparation Tasks

As mentioned in the section "How to Use This Book" in the Introduction, you have a few choices for exam preparation: the exercises here, Chapter 22, "Final Preparation," and the exam simulation questions in the Pearson Test Prep Software Online.

Review All Key Topics

Review the most important topics in this chapter, noted with the Key Topics icon in the outer margin of the page. Table 21-3 lists these key topics and the page number on which each is found.

Table 21-3   Key Topics for Chapter 21

Key Topic Element	Description	Page Number
List	Other AWS technical resources	272
Table 21-2	The various support plans of AWS	276

Define Key Terms

Define the following key terms from this chapter and check your answers in the Glossary:

AWS Prescriptive Guidance, AWS Knowledge Center, AWS re:Post, AWS Health Dashboard, AWS Health API, AWS Trust and Safety, AWS Partner Training and Certification, AWS Partner Events, AWS Partner Volume Discounts, AWS Marketplace, AWS Professional Services, Basic support plan, Developer support plan, Business support plan, Enterprise On-Ramp support plan

Q&A

The answers to these questions appear in Appendix A. For more practice with exam format questions, use the Pearson Test Prep Software Online.

1. What are the purposes for the AWS Health Dashboard and Health API?

2. What are the four paid support plans of AWS?

CHAPTER 22

Final Preparation

Are you excited for your exam after reading this book? I sure hope so. In this chapter, we'll take a more detailed look at the certification exam and how you can be sure to ace it. And if you read this book simply to understand AWS and were not really considering certification, maybe this chapter will convince you to give it a try!

The first 21 chapters of this book cover the technologies, protocols, design concepts, and considerations required to be prepared to pass the AWS Certified Cloud Practitioner (CLF-C02) exam. Although these chapters supply detailed information, most people need a bit more preparation. This chapter details a set of tools and a study plan to help you complete your preparation for the exam.

This chapter has three main sections. The first section lists the AWS Certified Cloud Practitioner exam information and breakdown. The second section shares some important tips to keep in mind to ensure that you are ready for this exam. The final section of this chapter provides a suggested study plan you can use now that you have completed all the earlier chapters in this book.

Exam Information

Here are details you should be aware of regarding the exam that maps to this text:

Question Types: Multiple choice and multiple choice with multiple correct answers (there are no "Choose all that apply" types of questions)

Number of Questions: 65

Time Limit: 130 minutes

Required Passing Score: 700 out of 1,000 (15 questions are not graded)

Available Languages: English, Japanese, Simplified Chinese, Korean

Exam Fee: $100 USD

Exam ID Code: CLF-C02

This exam seeks to validate a candidate's ability to do the following:

- Explain the value of the AWS Cloud.

- Understand and explain the AWS shared responsibility model.

- Understand security best practices.

- Understand AWS Cloud costs, economics, and billing practices.

- Describe and position the core AWS services, including compute, network, database, and storage services.

- Identify AWS services for common use cases.

AWS certification exam authors recommend the following skills and experience for candidates wanting to pass this exam:

- Have at least 6 months of experience with the AWS Cloud in any role, including technical, managerial, sales, purchasing, or financial.

- Have a basic understanding of IT services and their uses in the AWS Cloud platform.

The exam is broken up into four different domains. Here are those domains and the percentage of the exam dedicated to each of them:

- **Cloud Concepts:** 24%

- **Security and Compliance:** 30%

- **Cloud Technology and Services:** 34%

- **Billing, Pricing, and Support:** 12%

Here are the task statements for these four domains:

Domain 1: Cloud Concepts

1.1 Define the benefits of the AWS Cloud.

1.2 Identify design principles of the AWS Cloud.

1.3 Understand the benefits of and strategies for migration to the AWS Cloud.

1.4 Understand concepts of cloud economics.

Domain 2: Security and Compliance

2.1 Understand the AWS shared responsibility model.

2.2 Understand AWS Cloud security, governance, and compliance concepts.

2.3 Identify AWS access management capabilities.

2.4 Identify components and resources for security.

Domain 3: Cloud Technology and Services

3.1 Define methods of deploying and operating in the AWS Cloud.

3.2 Define the AWS global infrastructure.

3.3 Identify AWS compute services.

3.4 Identify AWS database services.

3.5 Identify AWS network services.

3.6 Identify AWS storage services.

3.7 Identify AWS artificial intelligence and machine learning (AI/ML) services and analytics services.

3.8 Identify services from other in-scope AWS service categories.

Domain 4: Billing, Pricing, and Support

4.1 Compare AWS pricing models.

4.2 Understand resources for billing, budget, and cost management.

4.3 Identify AWS technical resources and AWS Support options.

Getting Ready

Here are some important tips to keep in mind to ensure that you are ready to take and pass the exam:

- **Build and use a study tracker:** Consider using the exam objectives shown in this chapter to build a study tracker for yourself. Such a tracker can help ensure that you have not missed anything and that you are confident for your exam. As a matter of fact, this book offers a sample study planner as a website supplement.

- **Think about your time budget for questions on the exam:** When you do the math, you will see that, on average, you have one minute per question. While this does not sound like a lot of time, keep in mind that many of the questions will be very straightforward, and you will take 15 to 30 seconds on those. This leaves you extra time for other questions on the exam.

- **Watch the clock:** Check in on the time remaining periodically as you are taking the exam. You might even find that you can slow down pretty dramatically if you have built up a nice block of extra time.

- **Get some earplugs:** The testing center might provide earplugs but get some just in case and bring them along. There might be other test takers in the center with you, and you do not want to be distracted by their screams. I personally have no issue blocking out the sounds around me, so I never worry about this, but I know it is an issue for some.

- **Plan your travel time:** Give yourself extra time to find the center and get checked in. Be sure to arrive early. As you test more at a particular center, you can certainly start cutting it closer time-wise.

- **Bring in valuables but get ready to lock them up:** The testing center will take your phone, your smartwatch, your wallet, and other such items and will provide a secure place for them.

- **Testing at home:** Pearson offers home testing now. Be sure to follow all the instructions carefully if you are using this option, including testing your system prior to the exam and ensuring that your testing environment matches the requirements. You will be monitored during the whole exam, and it is important to follow instructions explicitly.

- **Get rest:** Most students report that getting plenty of rest the night before the exam boosts their success. All-night cram sessions are not typically successful.

- **Take notes:** You will be given note-taking implements and should not be afraid to use them. I always jot down any questions I struggle with on the exam. I then memorize them at the end of the test by reading my notes over and over again. I always make sure I have a pen and paper in the car, and I write down the issues in my car just after the exam. When I get home—with a pass or fail—I research those items!

- **Use the FAQs in your study:** The Amazon test authors have told me they love to pull questions from the FAQs they publish at the AWS site. The FAQs are a really fun and valuable read anyway, so go through them for the various services that are key for this exam.

- **Use the practice exam questions to prepare:** The chapters in this book provide many practice exam questions. Be sure to go through them thoroughly. Don't blindly memorize answers; let the questions really demonstrate where you are weak in your knowledge and then study up on those areas.

Suggested Plan for Final Review/Study

This section lists a suggested study plan from the point at which you finish reading through Chapter 21 until you take the AWS Certified Cloud Practitioner exam. You can ignore this plan, use it as is, or just take suggestions from it.

The plan involves three steps:

Step 1. **Review key topics and "Do I Know This Already?" questions:** You can use the table that lists the key topics in each chapter or just flip the pages looking for key topics. Also, reviewing the "DIKTA?" questions from the beginning of the chapter can be helpful for review.

Step 2. **Review "Q&A" sections:** Go through the Q&A questions at the end of each chapter to identify areas where you need more study.

Step 3. **Use the Pearson Test Prep practice test software to practice:** You can use the Pearson Test Prep app to study using a bank of unique exam-realistic questions available only with this book.

Summary

The tools and suggestions listed in this chapter have been designed with one goal in mind: to help you develop the skills required to pass the AWS Certified Cloud Practitioner exam. This book has been developed from the beginning to give you facts and also help you learn how to apply the facts. No matter what your experience level leading up to taking the exam, it is our hope that the broad range of preparation tools, and even the structure of the book, will help you pass the exam with ease. We hope you do well on the exam.

Glossary of Key Terms

A

Activate for Startups   A program that provides credits, technical support, training, and other resources to help early-stage startups build and scale their businesses on the AWS Cloud platform.

Agility   The ability of AWS to foster innovation in organizations.

Amazon GuardDuty   A managed threat detection service that uses machine learning and threat intelligence to continuously monitor network and account activities, providing real-time alerts and insights to help users detect and respond to potential security threats within their AWS environment.

Amazon Inspector   A security assessment service that automates the identification of vulnerabilities and security issues in EC2 instances and applications, providing users with actionable insights to enhance overall security.

Amplify   A set of tools and services that simplifies the process of building scalable and secure web and mobile applications by providing a streamlined development workflow, built-in CI/CD, and features like authentication and API management.

Application Programing Interface (API)   An interface provides programmatic access to resources in AWS. API stands for application programming interface.

API Gateway   A fully managed service that allows an organization to create and publish secure APIs to scale in AWS.

AppConfig   A service that enables the deployment, updating, and monitoring of application configurations in a controlled and validated manner, ensuring consistent and secure management of application settings across distributed environments.

AppStream 2.0   A fully managed application streaming service that enables users to securely access desktop applications from a web browser, allowing for flexible and scalable delivery of software to a variety of devices.

AppSync   A fully managed service that simplifies the development of scalable and secure serverless applications by providing a flexible and real-time data synchronization infrastructure for web and mobile applications.

Artifact   A central resource for compliance-related information.

Athena   A service that allows an organization to analyze data stored in AWS S3 using standard SQL queries, making it easy to discover insights from data without the need for complex data transformations or managing a database.

Aurora   A MySQL- and PostgreSQL-compatible relational database engine that is available in AWS RDS.

Auto Scaling   A service for automatic addition and subtraction of resources based on various factors, such as the demand for resources.

Automation   The automatic generation and/or performance of required IT tasks.

Availability   The quality of being able to be used or obtained.

Availability Zone (AZ)   A division of geographic locations within regions; each Availability Zone contains at least one separate and distinct data center.

AWS Audit Manager   A compliance management service that automates the assessment and management of the compliance of AWS resources against industry standards and regulations, streamlining audit preparations, risk assessments, and reporting to help organizations maintain a secure and compliant environment.

AWS Auditor Learning Path   A learning path for AWS that focuses on those in auditor, compliance, and legal roles.

AWS Backup   A fully managed backup service that centralizes and automates the backup of data across AWS services, enabling efficient and consistent data protection for applications and resources in the AWS Cloud.

AWS Config   A service that provides a detailed inventory and configuration history of AWS resources, enabling users to assess, audit, and track changes over time to ensure compliance, troubleshoot issues, and gain insights into resource relationships within their AWS environment.

AWS Global Infrastructure   The AWS distributed network of data centers strategically located worldwide, providing scalable and reliable cloud computing services to users around the world.

AWS IAM Identity Center   An AWS service that connects customers' on-premises directory services with the AWS Cloud. This service was once called the AWS Single Sign-On Service.

AWS Knowledge Center   A centralized resource that provides customers with access to a wide range of documentation, articles, and solutions to help them effectively navigate and troubleshoot issues related to AWS.

AWS Marketplace   An online store that enables AWS customers to discover, purchase, and deploy a wide variety of software and services from third-party vendors that is seamlessly integrated with their AWS accounts.

AWS Partner Network   The AWS global partner program that seeks to help partners build successful AWS solutions.

AWS Professional Services   A program that allows access to a global team of experts who can help plan and implement AWS solutions.

AWS Secrets Manager   An AWS service that enables secure storage, retrieval, and automatic rotation of sensitive information such as API keys and database passwords used by applications.

AWS Security Blog   A platform that publishes articles and updates to keep users informed about the latest security best practices, features, and insights, helping them effectively manage and enhance the security of their AWS environments.

AWS Security Center   A comprehensive hub that offers resources, best practices, and tools to assist users in enhancing the security of their AWS environments by providing insights, recommendations, and actionable information on security-related topics.

AWS Security Hub   A centralized security service that aggregates and prioritizes security alerts and compliance findings from various AWS services and third-party tools, offering a comprehensive view to manage and respond to potential threats across multiple AWS accounts.

AWS Shared Responsibility Model   The overall security model followed by AWS, which divides the client responsibilities from those of Amazon.

AWS Shield   A managed distributed denial-of-service (DDoS) protection service that safeguards applications and websites by automatically detecting and mitigating DDoS attacks, ensuring the availability and resilience of AWS resources against malicious traffic.

AWS Systems Manager   An AWS service that automates operational tasks, facilitates configuration management, and provides a unified interface for monitoring and controlling resources across an AWS environment.

AWS Well-Architected Framework   A framework that provides best practices to help architects design and build secure, high-performing, resilient, and efficient infrastructures for their applications on the AWS Cloud.

B

Basic Support Plan   The AWS support plan that is included free of charge for every account.

Billing Conductor   A service that supports an organization's billing and reporting workflows by customizing the billing rates, credits and fees, and shared overhead costs at the organization's discretion. This tool makes it possible to get a view of costs that align with an organization's business logic.

Budgets   A tool that helps in setting cost and usage limits for AWS resources so an organization can track expenses and receive alerts if it is approaching or exceeding its predefined budget.

Business Support Plan   A support plan that features a response time of 1 hour.

C

Cloud Adoption Framework (CAF)   A comprehensive set of guidelines, best practices, and tools designed to help organizations successfully plan, implement, and govern their cloud adoption journey on the AWS platform.

CapEx   Fixed costs that often represent the cost model used when purchasing on-premise IT resources. CapEx stands for capital expenditures.

Cloud Financial Management (CFM)   Strategic planning, monitoring, and optimization of cloud resources to effectively manage costs and maximize the value of cloud investments.

Cloud9   A cloud-based integrated development environment (IDE) that allows developers to write, run, and debug code using a web browser, providing a collaborative and flexible coding environment.

CloudFormation   A service that gives developers and systems administrators an easy way to create and manage a collection of related AWS resources, provisioning and updating them in an orderly and predictable fashion.

CloudFront   A global content delivery network (CDN) service that accelerates delivery of websites, APIs, video content, or other web assets.

CloudShell   A browser-based shell provided by AWS that offers a command-line interface (CLI) with preinstalled tools for managing and automating AWS resources directly from the AWS Management Console.

CloudTrail   A web service that records AWS API calls for an account and delivers log files to an organization.

CloudWatch   A monitoring service for AWS Cloud resources and the applications an organization runs on AWS.

CodeArtifact   A fully managed artifact repository service that helps organizations securely store, manage, and share software packages used in their development processes.

CodeBuild   A fully managed continuous integration service that compiles source code, runs tests, and produces software packages, automating the build and release processes in a scalable and customizable environment.

CodeCommit   A fully managed source control service that enables secure and scalable hosting of private Git repositories for version control of code and collaborative software development.

CodeDeploy   A fully managed code deployment service that helps an organization deploy software to things like EC2 instances.

CodePipeline   A fully managed continuous integration and continuous delivery (CI/CD) service that automates the build, test, and deployment phases of the release process, allowing developers to deliver software updates more reliably and rapidly.

CodeStar   A fully managed service that enables developers to quickly develop, build, and deploy applications on AWS by providing a unified and collaborative environment with preconfigured project templates and built-in CI/CD pipelines.

Community Cloud   A cloud provisioned for use by a select group of companies or organizations.

Compliance   Conformity in fulfilling specific requirements.

Confidentiality   The process of keeping data secure (often through encryption).

Connect   A cloud-based contact center service that enables businesses to set up and manage customer interactions through various communication channels.

Cost Allocation Tags   A tool that enables an organization to assign labels to resources in its cloud environment in order to categorize and track expenses more granularly so it can understand and manage costs based on specific attributes or projects within the AWS infrastructure.

Cost and Usage Reports   A tool that provides detailed insights into AWS spending by generating comprehensive reports, helping an organization analyze usage patterns, identify cost drivers, and make informed decisions to manage and optimize its cloud expenses.

Cost Explorer   A service that provides a user-friendly interface for visualizing and understanding an organization's AWS spending patterns, helping it analyze costs, identify trends, and make informed decisions to optimize its cloud expenses.

Cost Optimization   A pillar of the AWS Well-Architected Framework that focuses on minimizing expenses by optimizing resource usage and selecting the most cost-effective services and architectures.

D

Dedicated Host Pricing   A pricing model for compute in AWS that allows an organization to have its own dedicated host server in the AWS Cloud. This pricing model permits an organization to use its own server-bound licensing agreements.

Dedicated Instance Pricing   A pricing model for compute in AWS that allows an organization to have its EC2 instances on dedicated hardware. This model offers per-instance pricing options.

Developer Support Plan   The first level of support plan that provides an organization with access to tech support.

Direct Connect   An alternative to a shared Internet connection to AWS; it is a completely private connection from an organization's on-premises network to the AWS facilities.

Database Migration Service (DMS)   A fully managed service that enables seamless and efficient migration of databases to AWS, supporting a variety of source and target database engines, while minimizing downtime and ensuring data integrity during the migration process.

DynamoDB   A fast and flexible NoSQL database service for all applications that need consistent, single-digit-millisecond latency at any scale.

E

Elastic Block Store (EBS)   A service that offers persistent block storage volumes for use with EC2 instances.

Elastic Compute Cloud (EC2)   A service that makes virtual machines available in AWS and provides a managed environment for Docker containers.

Economies of Scale   The cost advantages that a business gains as it increases its production output, leading to lower average costs per unit produced.

Elastic Container Service (ECS)   A fully managed container orchestration service for deploying, managing, and scaling Docker containers on AWS.

Edge Locations   Locations that deliver cached CloudFront content.

Elastic File System (EFS)   A service that provides simple, scalable file storage for use with Amazon EC2 instances in the AWS Cloud.

Elastic Kubernetes Service (EKS)   A fully managed service that simplifies the deployment, management, and scaling of containerized applications using Kubernetes on AWS.

Elastic Beanstalk   A service that permits an organization to upload code and have it hosted automatically by AWS.

Elastic Load Balancing   The AWS tool for distributing requests for a resource among various resources.

ElastiCache   A web service that makes it easy to deploy, operate, and scale an in-memory cache in the cloud.

Elasticity   The ability of the cloud to grow or shrink resources dynamically based on demand or other factors.

Enterprise Support Plan   The premier level of support available in AWS, which features a response time of just 15 minutes.

EventBridge   A serverless event bus service that makes it easy to connect and automate workflows across various AWS services and third-party applications.

F

Fargate   A serverless compute engine for containers that enables an organization to run Docker containers without managing the underlying infrastructure.

Federation   The process of permitting an account to use its access with another trusted service in order to access AWS.

Free Tier   A trial account for AWS that is completely free, given certain constraints.

FSx   A fully managed, highly performant file storage service that provides native compatibility with popular file systems like Windows File Server and Lustre, simplifying the deployment and operation of scalable and reliable file storage in the AWS Cloud.

Fault Tolerance (FT)   The property that enables a system to continue operating properly in the event of the failure of some of its components.

G

Gateway Endpoint   An AWS global infrastructure component that targets specific IP routes in a virtual private cloud routing table used for private traffic destined for the DynamoDB or S3 service.

Glacier   A secure, durable, and extremely low-cost storage service for data archiving and long-term backup. Glacier is actually a storage class of the popular AWS S3 storage service.

Global Accelerator   An AWS networking service that provides anycast static IP addresses to help optimize inbound traffic flows destined for AWS resources.

Glue   A service that simplifies and automates the process of extracting, transforming, and loading data (ETL), making it easier to prepare and move data between data stores for analysis or other purposes.

Groups   A collection of user accounts in the AWS Identity and Access Management system; permissions are assigned to groups.

H

High Availability (HA)   The ability of a system or service to remain operational and accessible for users, typically achieved through redundancy and failover mechanisms to minimize downtime.

Health API   An API that provides AWS service health information. You can use this Health API to create your own custom AWS health dashboards in your own management applications.

Health Dashboard   An AWS website that displays status information for the various services of AWS and can alert an organization to AWS maintenance windows.

Hybrid Cloud   A mixed environment in which some cloud technologies are hosted privately and public cloud resources are used for other technologies.

I

Infrastructure as a Service (IaaS)   A cloud computing model in which customers can create virtualized computing resources like servers, storage, and networking from a provider on a pay-as-you-go basis.

Infrastructure as Code (IaC)   The practice of managing and provisioning computing infrastructure through machine-readable definition files, enabling automated deployment and scaling of resources.

Identity and Access Management (IAM)   A service that enables an organization to securely control access to AWS services and resources for its users.

Integrity   Assurance that data is not manipulated at rest or in transit.

Interface Endpoint   An AWS global infrastructure component that provides a private connection option for a service or AWS resource.

Internet Gateway   A horizontally scaled, redundant, and highly available virtual component that allows communication between instances in a virtual private cloud and the Internet, facilitating inbound and outbound traffic.

IoT Core   A managed cloud service that facilitates secure and scalable communication between Internet of Things (IoT) devices and the AWS Cloud, enabling the development of IoT applications with efficient device management and data processing capabilities.

IoT Greengrass   A service that extends AWS Cloud capabilities to local devices, allowing them to run AWS Lambda functions, keep device data in sync, and communicate with the AWS Cloud even when offline.

IQ   A platform that connects customers with certified AWS experts for on-demand assistance, consulting, and project work to help businesses effectively leverage AWS.

K–L

Kendra   A service that facilitates a powerful and efficient search within an organization's data by using natural language processing to understand and retrieve information from various sources, such as documents and FAQs.

Kinesis   A service that makes it simple to collect, process, and analyze real-time streaming data, allowing an organization to gain insights and react quickly to changing conditions in its applications or business.

Knowledge Center   An AWS website that helps an organization find information, troubleshoot issues, and get support for its AWS solutions.

Lambda   The main serverless compute service of AWS.

Lex   A service that allows an organization to build conversational interfaces (chatbots) using natural language understanding and processing, enabling interactions with users through voice and text in applications.

Local Zone   An AWS global infrastructure component that can be used to locate compute, storage, and other services closer to major population and industry centers.

M–N

Managed Services   A fully managed offering that provides operational support for AWS infrastructure, automates common maintenance tasks, and helps businesses focus on their applications by offloading the day-to-day management of their AWS environment.

Mechanical Sympathy   A concept that refers to understanding and leveraging low-level hardware characteristics to optimize software performance and efficiency.

Multifactor Authentication (MFA)   A multi-step login process that requires users to enter more than just a password.

NAT Gateway   A managed service that enables instances within a private subnet of a virtual private cloud to initiate outbound Internet traffic while providing a scalable and highly available solution for Network Address Translation without the need for user-managed infrastructure.

Network Access Control List (NACL)   An optional layer of security for a virtual private cloud (VPC) that acts as a firewall for controlling traffic moving between subnets in the VPC.

Networking and Content Delivery   A service category that features low-latency delivery of cached content to specific geographic locations.

O

On-Demand Capacity Reservation Pricing   A pricing model for compute in AWS that permits an organization to reserve compute capacity for its EC2 instances in a specific Availability Zone for any duration. This plan helps avoid the risk of hitting capacity constraints in select Availability Zones in AWS.

On-Demand Instances   EC2 instances that are launched at a current price of compute time.

On-Demand Pricing   The default pricing model for AWS compute resources that does not require any commitment from the user and is extremely flexible.

Operational Excellence   A pillar of the AWS Well-Architected Framework that focuses on ensuring efficient operations by continuously improving processes and procedures.

OpEx   An expense that an organization incurs through its normal business operations. AWS permits organizations to use this model for most of the IT expenditures. OpEx stands for operational expenditures.

OpsWorks   A configuration management service that uses Chef or Puppet; an automation platform that treats server configurations as code.

Orchestration   The scheduling and coordination of automated tasks for an entire process or workflow.

Organizations   A service that helps an organization centrally manage and govern multiple AWS accounts by creating a hierarchical structure, making it easier to apply policies and control access across the organization.

P

Platform as a Service (PaaS)   A cloud computing model that allows customers to develop, run, and manage applications without the complexity of building and maintaining the underlying infrastructure. PaaS stands for platform as a service.

Partner Events   A program at AWS that seeks to bring together (in person and virtually) all partners from around the world.

Partner Training and Certification   A training and certification program aimed at AWS Partners. Achieving these certifications permits the partners to easily demonstrate their AWS skill levels.

Partner Volume Discounts   A program that allows partners to receive deeper and deeper discounts on AWS pricing as they consume more AWS resources.

Performance Efficiency   A pillar of the AWS Well-Architected Framework that aims to optimize resource utilization and maximize system performance to meet varying workload demands.

Prescriptive Guidance   An AWS website that provides best practice strategies, guides, and patterns to help with an organization's AWS solutions.

Pricing Calculator   A tool that allows users to estimate the cost of using various AWS services based on their specific usage requirements, helping them plan and budget for their cloud expenses.

Private Cloud   Cloud technology that is kept "in-house" and fully managed by a private organization.

Public Cloud   Computing services offered by third-party providers over the public Internet.

Q–R

QuickSight   A service that enables users to easily create interactive and visual dashboards, as well as perform ad hoc analysis on their data stored in various AWS and external sources.

Relational Database Services (RDS)   A service that makes it easy to set up, operate, and scale a relational database in the cloud.

re:Post   An AWS forum website that allows users to join AWS communities and ask questions of seasoned AWS users.

Redshift   A fast, fully managed, petabyte-scale data warehouse that makes it simple and cost-effective for an organization to analyze all its data by using its existing business intelligence tools.

Region   A physical, geographic location in the world where AWS creates multiple Availability Zones.

Reliability   A pillar of the AWS Well-Architected Framework which emphasizes building systems that can recover from failures and meet business requirements consistently.

Reserved Instances Pricing   A pricing model for compute resources in AWS that offers savings over On-Demand Instances pricing based on the fact that an organization commits to the purchase of compute horsepower in advance.

Reserved Instances Pricing   Instances at a fixed price that an organization has contractually reserved for its purposes.

Role   A security concept that is similar to a user account but with no credentials; used to provide access from one AWS service to another.

Route 53   A highly available and scalable cloud Domain Name System (DNS) web service.

Route Table   A virtual networking component that contains a set of rules, known as routes, that define the paths for network traffic within a virtual private cloud and determine how traffic is directed between subnets and to external destinations.

Simple Storage Service (S3)   A flexible, object-based storage service for a wide variety of purposes. S3 stands for Simple Storage Service.

S

Software as a Service (SaaS)   A software distribution model in which applications are hosted by a third-party cloud provider and made available to customers over the Internet.

SageMaker   A service that helps an organization build, train, and deploy machine learning models easily without requiring deep expertise in machine learning infrastructure.

Savings Plans Pricing   A pricing model for AWS compute resources that can save as much as 72% over On-Demand Instances pricing. This model requires the user to commit to the purchase of a specific amount of compute resources over a given time period. It tends to offer more flexibility than the similar Reserved Instances pricing plan.

Savings Plans Pricing   A pricing option for EC2 that permits great discounts in exchange for 1- to 3-year commitments from customers.

Security   A pillar of the AWS Well-Architected Framework that emphasizes implementing robust security measures to protect data, systems, and assets in the cloud environment.

Security Group   A built-in firewall that is associated with EC2 instances and provides security at the protocol and port levels.

Security in the Cloud   In the AWS shared responsibility model, the security tasks that are the responsibility of the AWS customer.

Security of the Cloud   In the AWS shared responsibility model, the security tasks that are the responsibility of AWS.

Service Catalog   A service that allows an organization to create and maintain a catalog of IT resources approved for use with AWS.

Simple Email Service (SES)   A scalable and cost-effective email sending service that allows businesses to send and receive emails securely and efficiently.

Simple Monthly Calculator   A free AWS tool that allows an organization to calculate its monthly AWS costs for various services.

Snowball   A service that provides a secure and efficient way to transfer large amounts of data into and out of the AWS Cloud by using physical storage devices, known as Snowball devices, which are shipped to customers and then returned to AWS for data transfer.

Simple Notification Service (SNS)   A fully managed messaging service that enables the delivery of messages, notifications, and alerts to a distributed set of recipients via multiple communication protocols.

Spot Instances Pricing   A pricing model for AWS compute resources that allows an organization to bid on unused compute capacity in the AWS Cloud. This plan can offer up to 90% savings over the default On-Demand Instances pricing model.

Simple Queue Service (SQS)   A fully managed message queuing service that allows decoupling and asynchronous communication between distributed software components, enabling scalable and reliable application architectures.

Storage Gateway   A hybrid cloud storage service that seamlessly integrates on-premises environments with scalable and secure cloud storage, providing a bridge between on-premises applications and AWS storage services.

Subnet   A TCP/IP subnetwork within a virtual private cloud of AWS.

Sustainability   A pillar of the AWS Well-Architected Framework that encourages the use of environmentally friendly practices and technologies to reduce the environmental impact of cloud infrastructure operations.

Systems Manager   A tool for grouping resources for ease of monitoring and configuration changes.

T–X

Trust and Safety   A team at AWS that handles abuse reports from AWS users. Examples of abuse include using email services for spam or launching cybersecurity attacks from AWS virtual private clouds.

Wavelength Zone   An AWS global infrastructure component that places compute and storage services at the edge of 5G networks to reduce latency for mobile customers.

Web Application Firewall (WAF)   A security service that helps protect web applications from common web exploits and vulnerabilities by allowing administrators to configure rules that control access to the web content.

WorkSpaces   A fully managed, secure desktop as a service (DaaS) solution that allows users to access their desktop environments from anywhere, providing a flexible and scalable approach to virtualized computing.

WorkSpaces Web   An AWS service that permits access to internal websites or applications for clients that are using just a web browser.

X-ray   A distributed tracing service that helps developers analyze and understand the behavior of microservices-based applications by providing insights into requests, latency, and dependencies across the entire application architecture.

Answers to the "Do I Know This Already?" Quizzes and Q&A Sections

Answers to the "Do I Know This Already?" Quizzes

Chapter 1

1. **d.** Dedicated hardware
2. **c.** Elasticity
3. **b.** SaaS
4. **b.** EC2
5. **a.** S3
6. **d.** VPC

Chapter 2

1. **d.** OpEx
2. **b.** Pay as you go
3. **b.** Availability Zones
4. **c.** Edge Locations
5. **b.** AWS Auto Scaling
6. **d.** Virtual Load Balancer

Chapter 3

1. **a.** Simplicity
2. **c.** Perform operations as code
3. **d.** Frequent, small, and reversible
4. **b.** Assure full traceability in all operations
5. **a.** In all layers of the architecture
6. **a.** Manage changes through automation

7. **c.** Reliability

8. **d.** Democratize advanced technologies

9. **b.** You have matched business goals to the appropriate technologies.

10. **c.** Adopt a consumption model

11. **d.** Cloud Financial Management

12. **a.** Anticipate and adopt new and more efficient technology solutions

13. **b.** Sustainability

Chapter 4

1. **d.** Product transformation

2. **b.** Governance

3. **c.** Platform

4. **c.** DMS

5. **b.** Snowball

Chapter 5

1. **a.** Limited flexibility in adjusting to changing business requirements

2. **b.** No financial stresses of large up-front capital expenditures

3. **c.** Physical security costs

4. **c.** Increased collaboration between development and operations teams through DevOps practices

5. **d.** Improved disaster recovery mechanisms, including automated backups

Chapter 6

1. **b.** 1 year

2. **c.** EC2

3. **a.** The AMI is noted as "Free Tier Eligible."

4. **c.** Key pair

Chapter 7

1. **a.** The AWS customer

   d. Amazon AWS

2. **c.** Which AWS services the customer chooses to use

3. **b.** Deferred

4. **d.** IAM policies

5. **c.** Virtualization software on the host

6. **d.** AWS

Chapter 8

1. **c.** Encryption

2. **b.** IAM

3. **b.** independent

   c. third-party

4. **d.** Physical host security playbooks

5. **b.** Audit Manager

Chapter 9

1. **d.** Federation

2. **b.** Role

3. **a.** To follow the concept of least privilege

4. **c.** Use MFA with these accounts

5. **d.** IAM Identity Center

6. **b.** Secrets Manager

Chapter 10

1. **c.** Your virtual network interface card

2. **a.** Your subnet

3. **b.** Security Blog

4. **a.** Security Center

5. **a.** Trusted Advisor

6. **d.** Not all checks are available with a Free Tier account.

Chapter 11

1. **d.** Because all actions can be implemented through API calls

2. **a.** Reduction in required security measures

3. **d.** CloudFormation

4. **b.** Elimination of the need for experimentation

5. **d.** Monitoring and logging

6. **b.** OpsWorks

7. **c.** Hybrid

8. **a.** AWS VPN

Chapter 12

1. **a.** At least two

2. **d.** CloudFront

3. **a.** Regions in North America rely on the presence of the other North American Regions.

4. **a.** At least one

5. **c.** As an independent failure domain

6. **a.** Via different grids from independent utilities

7. **b.** Direct Connect

8. **b.** VPC peering

9. **a.** Local Zone

Chapter 13

1. **a.** On-Demand Instances

2. **d.** Fargate

3. **b.** EKS

4. **c.** Lambda

5. **b.** Elastic Beanstalk

Chapter 14

1. **c.** EC2

2. **a.** RDS

3. **d.** Aurora

4. **d.** DynamoDB

5. **a.** Redshift

6. **b.** ElastiCache

Chapter 15

1. **b.** VPC

2. **c.** Internet Gateway

3. **d.** Availability Zone (AZ)

4. **a.** CloudFront

5. **d.** Route 53

6. **d.** Static and dynamic web pages

Chapter 16

1. **d.** Multiple copies of your data are stored in separate Availability Zones.

2. **c.** To act as the boot volume for an EC2 server instance

3. **a.** Glacier

4. **d.** FSx

5. **b.** Storage Gateway

6. **d.** AWS Backup

Chapter 17

1. **c.** SageMaker

2. **b.** Kendra

3. **d.** Lex

4. **a.** Athena

5. **a.** Glue

6. **b.** QuickSight

Chapter 18

1. **b.** SNS
2. **a.** SQS
3. **d.** AWS IQ
4. **c.** Activate for Startups
5. **d.** Cloud9
6. **b.** CloudShell
7. **d.** WorkSpaces
8. **b.** WorkSpaces Web
9. **b.** IoT Core
10. **d.** IoT Greengrass

Chapter 19

1. **c.** In general, there are no charges for data transfers into AWS.
2. **b.** VPC
3. **a.** Storage class
4. **d.** On-Demand Instance
5. **b.** Savings Plan
6. **a.** Spot Instance

Chapter 20

1. **c.** Cost Explorer
2. **d.** Pricing Calculator
3. **a.** Billing Conductor
4. **b.** Organizations
5. **c.** Organizational units (OUs)

Chapter 21

1. **a.** FAQs
2. **c.** You cannot access the documentation of AWS without at least a Free Tier account.
3. **a.** AWS Trust and Safety
4. **b.** Enterprise On-Ramp
5. **d.** Trusted Advisor
6. **c.** Enterprise

Answers to the Q&A

Chapter 1

1. On-demand self-service

   Broad network access

   Resource pooling

   Rapid elasticity

   Measured service

2. Private

   Public

   Hybrid

   Community

Chapter 2

1. Elasticity in AWS refers to the ability to dynamically scale computing resources up or down (or in and out) based on demand, allowing for cost optimization and efficient use of resources.

2. AWS Regions are geographically dispersed locations that provide users with options for deploying resources closer to end users while ensuring high availability and fault tolerance.

AWS Availability Zones are isolated data centers within AWS Regions that are designed to provide redundancy, fault tolerance, and low-latency connectivity, enabling high availability and resilience for hosted applications and services.

AWS edge locations are points of presence located in various cities around the world, serving as endpoints for content delivery and providing low-latency access to AWS services.

Chapter 3

1. Perform operations as code

   Make frequent small and reversible changes to the architecture to improve it

   Refine your operational procedures frequently to improve them

   Anticipate failures and have recovery plans in place

   Learn from any operational failures in your architecture

2. Use strong identity practices in your architecture

   Ensure full traceability in all operations

   Implement security in absolutely all layers of your architecture

   Make a concerted effort to automate as many of the security best practices as possible

   Secure information at rest as well as in transit

   As much as possible, keep people away from data

   Prepare as much as possible for the inevitable security events in your architecture and cloud

   Manage changes through automation

Chapter 4

1. Business

   People

   Governance

   Platform

   Security

   Operations

2. AWS Database Migration Service (DMS)

Chapter 5

1. Advantages include:

   Increased flexibility

   Little to no up-front commitments

   Increased elasticity

   Increased cost transparency

2. Costs can include:

   Hardware

   Building/facilities

   Maintenance

   Personnel

   Scalability

   Power and energy

   Redundancy

   Software licensing

   Physical security

   Insurance

3. Benefits include:

   Cost savings

   Elasticity

   Fast deployment

   Increased reliability

   Increased security

   Lifecycle management

   DevOps practices

   IT focus

Chapter 6

1. Possible answers include:

   CloudFormation

   SQS

   CloudWatch

   Lambda

   Key Management Service

2. In order to remain within the Free Tier limits

Chapter 7

1. The physical and environmental security controls used by Amazon

2. Customer data

   Platform, applications, Identity and Access Management (IAM) policies

   Guest operating systems

   Network and firewall configurations

   Client-side data encryption

   Server-side encryption (file system and/or data)

   Networking traffic protection (encryption, integrity, and identity)

3. Cloud software, including compute, storage, networking, and database software

   Hardware

   AWS global infrastructure, including Regions, Availability Zones, and Edge Locations

Chapter 8

1. AWS Marketplace offers many affordable (and free) security solutions, including anti-malware, IPS, and policy management tools.

2. Services include:

   Inspector

   Security Hub

   GuardDuty

   Shield

Chapter 9

1. Roles

2. The root account

Chapter 10

1. AWS Marketplace is an online store that allows customers to discover, purchase, and deploy a wide variety of third-party software and services on the AWS cloud platform.

2. A network access control list (NACL) in AWS is a simple firewall feature that you can apply to subnet(s) inside a Virtual Private Cloud (VPC).

Chapter 11

1. Automation is often used with:

   Backup generation and retention

   Security compliance

   Code deployments

   AWS infrastructure changes

2. Management access options include:

   The AWS Management Console

   The AWS CLI

   SDKs and APIs

Chapter 12

1. A company might choose to host resources in different Regions for a number of reasons. For example, a company might choose a Region that is close to a large number of its customers in order to speed up applications used by those customers. A company might also host resources in different Regions to improve the disaster recovery (DR) capabilities of the organization.

2. Amazon ensures that the Availability Zones are as far apart as possible to promote fault tolerance and disaster recovery. Separate flood plains are targeted.

3. The AWS Global Accelerator service features the use of static anycast IP addresses as it attempts to improve the speed of routing inbound traffic to the desired resources in AWS.

Chapter 13

1. The three pricing models available for EC2 are On-Demand Instances, Savings Plans, and Spot Instances.

2. The two main options for container management in AWS are ECS and EKS.

3. Lambda is the main serverless compute option in AWS.

Chapter 14

1. AWS RDS fully supports Aurora, Db2, MariaDB, Microsoft SQL Server, MySQL, Oracle, and PostgreSQL.

2. AWS ElastiCache supports the open-source in-memory caching engines Redis and Memcached.

Chapter 15

1. Options include subnets, route tables, Internet gateways, security groups, network access control lists, and NAT gateways.

2. AWS CloudFront is powered by AWS Edge Locations.

Chapter 16

1. AWS storage classes include S3 Standard, S3 Express One Zone, Reduced Redundancy, S3 Intelligent-Tiering, S3 Standard-IA, S3 One Zone-IA, S3 Glacier Instant Retrieval, S3 Glacier Flexible Retrieval, and S3 Glacier Deep Archive.

2. There are currently four different options available in AWS Storage Gateway: S3 File Gateway, Tape Gateway, FSx File Gateway, and Volume Gateway.

Chapter 17

1. The AWS Lex service uses the same technology as Amazon Alexa. This service is designed to help you bring AI chatbots and virtual assistants into your applications.

2. The AWS Kinesis suite of services aims to help you ingest and analyze streaming data.

Chapter 18

1. AWS Connect is a customer service solution that helps a business set up and manage its customer support systems. Connect enables a company to create a reliable and efficient contact center in the cloud.

2. The AWS CodeArtifact service is a secure and fully managed service that helps developers store, manage, and share software artifacts like packages, dependencies, and libraries. With CodeArtifact, developers can create their own repositories to organize and control access to your packages.

3. The IoT Greengrass service extends AWS Cloud capabilities to local devices, allowing them to run AWS Lambda functions, keep device data in sync, and communicate with the AWS Cloud even when offline.

Chapter 19

1. You are not typically charged in AWS for your data transfers into the cloud and for your data transfers between AWS services.

2. The Dedicated Host pricing model can accommodate your existing server-bound licensing requirements.

Chapter 20

1. The purpose of Cost Allocation Tags in AWS is to enable users to categorize and track expenses by attaching metadata labels to resources in order to provide a more detailed and granular understanding of cost distribution across different projects, departments, or attributes in the cloud infrastructure.

2. AWS Organizations is a management service that simplifies the administration of multiple AWS accounts by creating a hierarchical structure that allows for centralized control, policy application, and consolidated billing for improved organization-wide governance.

Chapter 21

1. The AWS Health Dashboard and Health API are tools to help users monitor the health and status of the services of AWS itself. The AWS Health Dashboard offers a centralized view of service health, providing real-time information about service disruptions, planned maintenance, and other events that may impact AWS customers.

2. The four paid support options are Developer, Business, Enterprise On-Ramp, and Enterprise.

AWS Certified Cloud Practitioner CLF-C02 Cert Guide Exam Updates

Over time, reader feedback allows Pearson to gauge which topics give our readers the most problems when taking the exams. To assist readers with those topics, the authors create new materials clarifying and expanding on those troublesome exam topics. As mentioned in the Introduction, the additional content about the exam is contained in a PDF on this book's companion website, at http://www.pearsonitcertification.com/title/9780138285999.

This appendix is intended to provide you with updated information if AWS makes minor modifications to the exam upon which this book is based. When AWS releases an entirely new exam, the changes are usually too extensive to provide in a simple update appendix. In those cases, you might need to consult the new edition of the book for the updated content. This appendix attempts to fill the void that occurs with any print book. In particular, this appendix does the following:

- Mentions technical items that might not have been mentioned elsewhere in the book

- Covers new topics if AWS adds new content to the exam over time

- Provides a way to get up-to-the-minute information about content for the exam

Always Get the Latest at the Book's Product Page

You are reading the version of this appendix that was available when your book was printed. However, given that the main purpose of this appendix is to be a living, changing document, it is important that you look for the latest version online at the book's companion website. To do so, follow these steps:

Step 1. Browse to www.ciscopress.com/title/9780138285990.

Step 2. Click the **Updates** tab.

Step 3. If there is a new Appendix B document on the page, download the latest Appendix B document.

> **NOTE**   The downloaded document has a version number. Comparing the version of the print Appendix B (version 1.0) with the latest online version of this appendix, you should do the following:
>
> - **Same version:** Ignore the PDF that you downloaded from the companion website.
>
> - **Website has a later version:** Ignore this Appendix B in your book and read only the latest version that you downloaded from the companion website.

Technical Content

The current version (1.0) of this appendix does not contain additional technical coverage.

Index